Utopia on T

Revised edition

One of the great post-war visions was of the ideal housing environment. The reality is squalor and social breakdown.

What went wrong? Utopia on Trial presents the evidence to establish links between social malaise – from litter and vandalism to children in care – and the design and layout of modern estates.

Using the results of the author's detailed study of houses and blocks of flats covering over 100,000 dwellings, Utopia on Trial also shows why so many housing improvement schemes have proved to be ineffectual and a huge waste of public – and private – money.

Utopia on Trial proposes *effective* practical measures to put right past mistakes and to avoid them in the future.

The findings of Utopia on Trial are of vital concern to all those involved in housing, youth work, social welfare and local government – from architects and town planners to doctors, the police, social workers and schoolteachers.

Alice Coleman is Professor of Geography at King's College, London, where she is also Director of the Land Use Research Unit.

Utopia on Trial

Vision and Reality in Planned Housing

Alice Coleman

*with the Design Disadvantagement Team
of the Land Use Research Unit
King's College London*

Sarah Brown

Lise Cottle

Pauline Marshall

Celia Redknap

Rachel Sex

Hilary Shipman
London

Hilary Shipman Limited
19 Framfield Road
Highbury
London N5 1UU

First edition published 1985, reprinted 1985, 1986
Second edition published 1990, reprinted 1994

British Library Cataloguing in Publication Data
Coleman, Alice
  Utopia on trial: vision and reality in
  planned housing.
  1. Housing—Great Britain
  I. Title   II. Kings College London. *Design
  Disadvantagement Team*
  307'.336   HD7333.A

ISBN 0-948096-25-X

Cover design by David Bennett Books

Typeset by Infotype Ltd, Eynsham, Oxford
and Florencetype Ltd, Kewstoke, Avon
Printed and bound in Great Britain by
Biddles Ltd, Guildford and King's Lynn

Contents

Tables

Figures

Preface

Utopia on Trial reports the findings of a large and intensive research investigation entitled *Design Disadvantagement in Housing*. It has involved a team of up to six people over a period of five years and would not have been possible without the generous financial support of the Joseph Rowntree Memorial Trust. We are greatly indebted to the Trustees and also to the Trust's Director, Robin Guthrie, for his constructive interest.

The work was carried out by the Land Use Research Unit at King's College, London, and directed by Alice Coleman. The other main participants were Lise Cottle (1979-84), Rachel Sex (1979-83), Sarah Brown (1980-84), and Pauline Marshall (1981-83). Celia Redknap worked in the Unit on an independent study of *The Effect of Entrance Designs in Blocks of Flats*, sponsored by the Nuffield Small Grants Scheme, and joined the Design Disadvantagement Team in 1983. Her role as Chairman of a Tenants' Association in Southwark afforded valuable insights from within the housing system. Smaller, but valued, contributions were made by Peter Rhodes, Kevin Gowans, Bob Eade and Nicholas Fyfe, while Inga Feaver gave stalwart administrative assistance from 1979-82.

The team has been greatly assisted by information and comment from many people. Oscar Newman was the original inspiration for the project and also gave valuable advice. Frances Reynolds kept us in touch with her sociological work on the Omega Estate, and Anne Power explored with us the parallel roles of design and management. David Adams of the Greater London Council Housing Department gave many kinds of help over a long period, and Councillor Mrs Pat Kirwan and Ken Hackney, both of Westminster, took the constructive step of commissioning our first contract for a design-disadvantagement survey, which led to the first decision to implement our findings.

Councillors, officers and tenants of many local authorities were helpful in many ways and we are grateful for the information and insights imparted by various medical and social service organisations. British Telecom provided data on vandalism in telephone kiosks and we received welcome cooperation from the police in many quarters.

We appreciate the academic support given by John Freeman, criminologist, and David Herbert, crime geographer and the parts played

vii

by Ray Moxley of the Westminster Architects' Consortium and W.A. Stevenson of Bellway Homes. We also thank Roma Beaumont and Gordon Reynell who drew the graphs, Dawn Jarvis who typed the complex tables in the appendices, and the patient staff of the King's College Computer Centre.

We have found the research stimulating and rewarding. Our hope now is that it will serve to improve the living environments of Britain.

Alice Coleman

Preface to second edition

Since the first appearance of this book in 1985, the design disadvantagement research has continued with an increasingly practical
flavour. Some 3,000 more blocks and 10,000 more houses have been
surveyed in Britain and abroad and, despite cultural differences, the
effect of faulty design appears to be similar. Some of the fruits of this
research are incorporated into the final chapter.

There have been many reports of the successful application of one
or more of the improvement methods advocated in Chapter VIII and
these have paved the way for a five-year programme of systematic
trials: the DICE Project. DICE (Design Improvement Controlled
Experiment) is based at King's College in London, and sponsored by
the Department of the Environment with £50 million of subsidy for
selected estates. This is such a positive step forward that the fourth
printing of *Utopia on Trial* seems to be an appropriate time for a
second edition.

Alice Coleman

Mutiple determinants of problems
solved not by one house, no
matter how bold.

I The Problem of Modern Housing

What is wrong with modern housing estates? Everyone agrees that many of them are in serious trouble but there is no consensus as to the cause. Blame is cast in all directions – on planners, architects, housing authorities, developers, residents, children, cleaners, caretakers, the police, and other scapegoats – but these cross-currents can flourish only because there has been no real factual evidence to sift out the true from the false. Without a firm foundation of truth it is all too possible that policies for improvement may be wrong, and that expensive rehabilitation schemes may prove ineffective and a waste of money.

This is a challenge that has been taken up by the Land Use Research Unit at King's College in the University of London. This unit has a long tradition of establishing previously unknown facts about the British environment and showing that many of its problems are directly attributable to mistaken policies. In the beginning, nothing was further from its purpose than a criticism of policy. Its first venture, launched in 1960, was the Second Land Utilisation Survey of Britain, intended as a national record of a boom period to contrast with Professor Sir L. Dudley Stamp's original survey during the Great Depression of the 1930s. Stamp, at the London School of Economics, inspired a great army of geographical volunteers in colleges and schools, to map the use made of every plot of the nation's land, and the second survey recruited no fewer than 3,000 trained people, mainly geography teachers, to carry out a self-funded follow-up in greater detail. It was assumed, correctly, that agriculture would present a more prosperous and efficient face and it was also assumed, incorrectly, that the introduction of planning in 1948 would have solved the two great urban problems: decay in the city's core and sprawl at its edges. Unfortunately, both of these seemed to be worse than 30 years earlier, in spite of official control of the use of land.

Since then the Land Use Research Unit has probed one form of problem land use after another: dereliction and disuse, farmland loss, afforestation potential, recreational use, the supply of building land and so on. It has always worked on the principle that, where land use is concerned, a large comprehensive survey will yield more accurate and reliable information than small samples, and its vegetation survey, for example, covered all 33,000 square kilometres of moorland and marsh, woodland and waste, heath and common in the whole of England and Wales. The resulting Wildscape Atlas, which is in preparation, has twice received the Nature Conservancy Council's accolade of approval, and extensive use has been made of it by many individuals and organisations.

Consequently, when the Land Use Research Unit turned to the theme of problem housing, it naturally thought in terms of detailed mapping on a scale that would generally be considered daunting — so much so that many people have difficulty in believing what they hear. When a Parliamentary Committee was told that the research covered over 4,000 blocks of flats, one member queried whether this was a slip for 4,000 individual flats. It was no slip. The 4,099 blocks contain 106,520 dwellings, which accommodate perhaps a quarter of a million people, and 4,172 houses were thrown in for good measure. The study area includes the whole of the two London boroughs that contain more council flats than any other (Southwark and Tower Hamlets), and also, for comparison, an out-of-town estate on the south-east side of Oxford (Blackbird Leys). Outside these study areas, members of the research team have also looked at houses and flats in a wide range of areas from the City of Westminster and the London boroughs of Bromley, Camden, Croydon, Lambeth and Newham to Birmingham, Coventry, Chester, Runcorn, Liverpool, Birkenhead, St. Helen's, Manchester, High Wycombe, Toronto, Puerto Rico and Hong Kong. This breadth of scope is intended as an antidote to the claims of people who feel justified in pointing to a single block of flats as sufficient 'proof' of their own opinions.

What has been studied on this enormous scale is the most glaring difference between modern problem estates and the ordinary unplanned housing of the past: design and layout. These features have been mapped in detail and rigorously tested to see which of them are associated with various lapses in civilised behaviour: litter-dropping, graffiti-scrawling, vandalism, pollution by excrement, and family breakdown leading to children being placed in care.

Of the various design features that have been mapped, 15 have emerged as commonly deleterious in blocks of flats. One of them is the well-publicised high-rise design, which has already attracted so much revulsion that the pressure of public opinion has largely brought about its cessation. However, building height is not the only detrimental feature, or even the worst one. There are 14 others of which we need to beware.

A few of them may sometimes occur in estates of houses and if they do they are usually detrimental there as well.

Informed opinion, such as that of the police or local housing officers, suggests that the forms of social malaise tested are far from being the only things that plague residents of problem estates. There are many other kinds of stress and trauma, including crime, fear, anxiety, marital breakdown, and physical and mental disorders that would largely be avoidable in more socially stabilising environments. Designs which have this disadvantaging effect are an iniquitous imposition upon people who cannot cope with them, especially as there is every reason to believe that most of them could cope perfectly well with life in more traditional houses.

Where have the disadvantaging designs sprung from, and why does planning control, with its emphasis on better housing, fail to protect people against them? The alarming answer is that they are the creation of officialdom. The bureaucratic hand of the Department of the Environment (DoE) and its predecessors — the Ministries of Town and Country Planning, and Housing and Local Government — has issued numerous design guidelines which local housing authorities have felt constrained to follow. The best-known example is the trend towards high-rise flats, which was backed up by subsidies in proportion to the number of storeys built. Another unpopular doctrine is discouragement of party fences, which has led to disasters such as Clover Hall in Rochdale. Clover Hall was a successful estate of houses until it was subjected to 'design improvement', which, among other things, eliminated the fences; subsequently it became an area of social problems. Official recommendations such as these not only initiated and multiplied detrimental features but also precluded the exercise of individual taste which used to provide checks and balances in housing evolution. Yet the DoE continued to act as the fountainhead of design wisdom and shrugged off all criticism.

Because of the DoE's reluctance to take design problems seriously, this book has been written as an analogy with a trial. What is put on trial is the ideal environment, Utopia, which design control was intended to create and which has been retrospectively described by a noted American architect, Philip Johnson, as follows:

> 'We really believed, in a quasi-religious sense, in the perfectibility of human nature, in the role of architecture as a weapon of social reform . . . the coming Utopia when everyone would live in cheap prefabricated flat-roofed multiple dwellings — heaven on earth.'

Individual taste creates healthy evolution

The trial opens in Chapter II with an outline of the salient events leading up to it. This is followed by a discussion of the nature of the evidence in Chapter III and an account of the 15 design suspects in Chapter IV. Chapter V is the major part of the case for the prosecution and, after that, dissenters have a chance to cross-examine and present alternative views of their own in Chapter VI.

At this point it will seem clear that a verdict of guilty is fully justified, and Chapters VII and VIII go on to consider preventive measures and corrective measures respectively. Prevention would seem to lie in a decision to build no more flats and concentrate on houses instead, but the question arises as to what sort of houses. The various test measures show that inter-war houses consistently perform better than those of either the pre-1914 or post-1945 vintage. Modern house design seems to have deteriorated over the decades as the DoE recommended increasingly undesirable designs, for example, faceless facades and the abandonment of the traditional streetscape.

Corrective measures involve the rehabilitation of the blocks of flats that already exist. At present, there are many housing improvement schemes absorbing large sums of public money, more in hope and faith than in scientific knowledge of what will work. We have monitored 17 blocks of flats 'improved' by hopeful measures such as landscaping and security devices, only to find that vandalism is vastly more common after the expenditure than before it. Our task has been to devise a disadvantagement score for blocks of flats which is simple to apply because it merely counts how many of the 15 designs are at fault. It measures how badly the block has been designed, and points to precisely those features which are in need of modification. The success of the rehabilitation can be forecast by knowing how much it will improve the disadvantagement score, and then tested after completion by seeing how far it has reduced litter, graffiti, vandalism, etc.

Design-disadvantagement research has brought many people's understanding of problem estates into sharper focus. Local housing authority officers, who work face to face with the great Utopian blunder, are often constructively receptive to our recommendations, as also are many policemen, ranging from beat officers on problem estates to Sir Kenneth Newman, Commissioner of the Metropolitan Police. After a discussion with us at New Scotland Yard, Sir Kenneth arranged a seminar for senior police officers in our study area, who summed up our presentation as follows: 'In a way we already know all this from our experience on the beat, but you have crystallised it scientifically, and we shall now look at it with new eyes'.

Some people, however, may be uneasy about the role ascribed to design, as it conflicts with their ideas on the culpability of social phenomena such as unemployment, private versus council ownership, or managerial inefficiency. We have been at the receiving end of many such objections during the course of the research, and have subjected them to scientific tests in Chapter IX to distinguish those which have a factual foundation from those that are plausible but erroneous. Private blocks, for example, have an average disadvantagement score that is over twice as good as council blocks, so ownership is not independent of design. None of the factors studied detracts from the conclusion that design can be a powerful influence for bad — and also presumably for good, if different designs were used.

None of this is to be construed as a claim that design is the only factor in the prevention or promotion of social breakdown. On the contrary its influence is bound to be differentially offset or reinforced, diverted or distorted, by innumerable other factors. But in spite of all these disturbances, known or unknown, it nevertheless shows through as having an effect. Even if the effect were small, it could still be extremely valuable in practical terms. Design modification would need to bring about only a 10 per cent drop in levels of litter, graffiti, vandalism, excrement and the number of children in care to achieve more than all the Utopian efforts of government over the last 40 years. In practice, however, we expect it to achieve far more, including a spin-off in the reduction of stress and trauma, mental illness and crime.

II | Utopia Accused

The twentieth century in Britain has been split in two by a great revolution in housing. The first half of the century was dominated by the age-old system of natural selection, which left people free to secure the best accommodation they could. The second half has embraced the Utopian ideal of housing planned by a paternalistic authority, which offered hopes of improved standards but also ran the risk of trapping people in dwellings not of their own choosing. Unfortunately, Utopia is not automatically synonymous with progress, and much of our planned housing is proving to be retrograde – the scene of many kinds of social malaise.

The photograph opposite shows Oak and Eldon Gardens, Birkenhead, a Utopian block of flats designed with every kind of expertise, safeguard and subsidy that officialdom could command. Yet even before it had been fully paid for, it had to be declared uninhabitable and condemned to death. It heralded a spate of similar demolitions, either because of structural defects or because the block became a behavioural sink, or frequently for both reasons.

Blocks like this are not only financial disasters; they are also human disasters that sear many lives with traumatic experiences. First there are the pre-Utopian residents, many of whom have been ruthlessly evicted from their little terrace houses, and sometimes mentally scarred by this process as severely as by the loss of a spouse or the loss of a limb. Then there are the hopeful new flat-dwellers, who suffer all the stresses and tensions of seeing their block degenerate into a place they are ashamed of and fearful to live in, until they too are forced out to make way for a second round of Utopia. Nor is there any guarantee that this second round will not, in its turn, blight further lives. Housing authorities do not yet understand the failure of Utopia well enough to be sure of avoiding mistakes in future.

It is hoped that this book will help to fill the gap in understanding, as the research results it describes are drawn from accurate factual observations subjected to scientific tests. It is sad and surprising that neither of the two mainsprings of our modern Utopia – Garden City and

PLATE 1. Failed Utopia. The last wing of a massive complex of flats embodying many officially recommended design features such as 10 storeys poised on concrete stilts, internal corridors, flat facades and flat roofs. When built, a brochure was circulated to local authorities showing it as a Utopian ideal to be imitated. Yet it proved unsalvageable and hundreds of imitators were also condemned to a short life. (Oak and Eldon Gardens, Birkenhead)

Radiant City—had any scientific background whatsoever. On the contrary, both were based upon intuitive beliefs and prejudices, embellished by unsupported theorising and made contagious by sincerity, enthusiasm, fine phrases and attractive sketches. They were carried into action by such powerful propaganda that they have become deeply embedded in our way of thinking, and difficult to dislodge.

The Garden City Movement was pioneered by Ebenezer Howard in 1898. He lived in London and disliked it so much that he believed everyone should be transferred to small new towns of under 30,000 people, with garden-like layouts and easy access to the countryside. So perfect did he consider his vision to be that he precluded any changes made by the residents—a degree of authoritarianism which prompted Jane Jacobs to comment in her book *The Death and Life of Great American Cities* (1961), that garden cities would be very nice for docile people who never had any plans of their own.

Le Corbusier approved of the garden image but not the low density that went with it. His Radiant City, introduced in 1923, would retain high densities by piling dwellings up in 24-storeyed blocks of flats (apartment buildings), which would allow 95 per cent of the site to be devoted to landscaping. He believed that the sharing of building and grounds would promote a strong community and social life.

Both these prescriptions for how people ought to live were adopted in the USA from the 1920s but Britons continued to pursue the kind of housing they wanted individually. Semi-detached dwellings with front and back gardens proved immensely popular, and a few early garden city experiments, such as New Earswick, Bournville and Port Sunlight, may well have owed their success to the fact that they followed the design fashion of their times fairly closely.

It was the housing shortage created by wartime bombing that turned the nation's mind towards Utopian rebuilding. The New Towns Act of 1946 was a triumph for the Garden City movement, and its authoritarian stance was greatly extended in the following year by the Town and Country Planning Act, which decreed that henceforth all changes in land use should be subject to planning control. Actual building did not make much progress for several years, and a great deal of interest was taken in the Lansbury Estate, built in the bombed East End of London as a showpiece for the Festival of Britain in 1951. It included not only houses but three-storeyed flats, which were to prove the thin end of the wedge for the pattern of inner city reconstruction. So it came about that the main model for these areas was not the successful house with a garden but the tenement block with its disastrous record in places such as the Gorbals, the most notorious slum in Glasgow. Stated baldly, like this, the choice seems incredible, but decked up in the language of Radiant City – 'the tower block glittering above the greenery' – it appealed to the official mind.

Jane Jacobs – an American view

As blocks of flats began to multiply, a groundswell of criticism began to emerge, but was largely ignored. In America, which had a headstart in the Radiant City stakes, the problems were more serious and the first major exposé was a book destined to become a classic: *The Death and Life of Great American Cities* by Jane Jacobs in 1961. Although it was concerned more with streets than with buildings, it laid important foundations for insight into why certain kinds of housing prove to be deleterious.

Jane Jacobs demonstrated the essential falsity of planning theory by instancing areas possessed of all the supposed virtues, which were nevertheless disintegrating, and supposedly unviable areas which were spontaneously upgrading. Impressed by this contrary evidence, she advocated the most basic of all scientific principles: the need to observe the facts and to discard theories at variance with them. She also argued that it was not enough to observe what was bad about cities and then invent what might be a good substitute. The existing good should also be observed, to act as a constructive model, and 'good' should not merely be equated with aesthetic appearance but should focus upon what actually worked to promote a stable social structure.

Practising what she preached, Jane Jacobs observed successful city neighbourhoods and distilled the essence of what they shared in common. They proved to be close-textured, high-density assemblages of mixed land uses, where many people live within walking distance of many destinations and there is constant coming and going on foot along a dense network of streets. This pattern works naturally to ensure the emergence of a firm social structure. People passed on the sidewalk (pavement) come to be known by sight, and this leads to a web of public acquaintanceship, in which roles are known and talents can be called upon by the community without invading people's private lives. Degrees of congeniality can be savoured and personal friendships can mature naturally, without forcing the pace. The overall result is a complex system of interlocking levels and circles of acquaintanceship, which gives the community a clear knowledge of its accepted mores, and hence practical guidelines for behaviour – an essential framework for stability.

A strong, stable social structure is also the aim for new planned developments, but Jane Jacobs showed the very designs that are alleged to create it are the barriers that preclude its emergence. The segregation of land uses into large units, such as Radiant City developments with spacious grounds, extensive parks, huge schools, big shopping precincts, industrial estates and cultural complexes, means that few destinations are within walking distance. Cars are needed for most purposes, but people passing each other at high speed behind glass are deprived of natural opportunities to build up a web of public acquaintanceship. Housewives, in particular, may become very lonely, but in order to develop friendships they have to take the risk of inviting strangers into their homes; gradualism is largely eliminated. In these circumstances the circle of contacts tends to remain small and the prevailing atmosphere is one of anonymity. There is no accepted set of social mores, which means that some people agonise over what is acceptable behaviour while others, at the opposite end of the scale of temperaments, find no constraints to curb their excesses.

Jane Jacobs believed that the contrast between these two extreme types of area makes a striking impact upon the bringing up of children. In the successful areas the streets are peopled with friends and acquaintances who know the accepted mores and keep a responsible eye on children playing on the sidewalk. Their involvement is reinforced by 'eyes on the street' from the windows of the buildings — people who find it interesting to watch a busy scene full of familiar figures. Such a neighbourhood is self-policing and mothers do not fear to allow their children out into it as they grow beyond the toddler stage. This gives them a wide range of adult examples on which to model their behaviour, and helps them to become successfully integrated into the adult community.

How different is the experience of youngsters in Radiant City. Mothers are more fearful about letting them out into an anonymous world of strangers with unknown standards of behaviour. Children encounter only a restricted range of adult models to imitate, and much of their time is spent in situations where the ratio of adults to children is very low: the school-room, the playground, the wardened play centre, and the gang territory of the housing estate. Frustrated by constraints intended for their safety, they pick up most of their behaviour patterns from their peers — the immature leading the immature into the generation gap. Unlike the street children, who are taught to respect private property, the estate children live in an environment where the distinction between public and private is blurred by shared grounds that extend right up to private windows, and by internal common areas that extend right up to private doors. There are no 'eyes on the lawn' and no spirit of self-policing to curb the youngsters when they test their powers too far. Indeed, there is no clear idea of what 'too far' may mean.

Although Jane Jacobs' work was full of penetrating insights, it was not taken seriously by policy advisers in the British Ministry of Housing and Local Government, now the Department of the Environment. In 1961 there were still too few post-war housing estates for her message to be inescapably self-evident, and there was still a chauvinistic attitude that American problems could not happen here. Probably, too, the Ministry's housing and sociological research staff were anxious to defend their pro-tenement recommendations, as they still are, 24 years later, while the government of the day had a different concern at the forefront of their minds: the housing shortage. Delays due to planning had perpetuated the war-induced shortfall, and the top priority was more dwellings at all possible speed. Blocks of flats were seen as the quickest solution and large government subsidies were granted to stimulate this form of building. In fact, the taller the block, the more lavish the rate of subsidy. At the same time, generous density standards were imposed, and in retrospect the resulting estates can be seen as a cross between the worst features of Radiant City and Garden City – high-rise combined with low density. *High rate – low density?*

Pearl Jephcott – a British perspective

Utopian estates multiplied rapidly during the 1960s and the growl of complaint gradually became more audible. High-rise, as the most conspicuous innovation, attracted the most explicit criticism, with the result that from 1968 housing subsidies to local authorities ceased to be proportional to the number of storeys, although flat-building was still favoured. In the second half of the decade, the Joseph Rowntree Memorial Trust took an important constructive step by funding Pearl Jephcott and Hilary Robinson to enquire into the views of the residents themselves. They investigated new high-rise blocks in Glasgow and published their results as a book entitled *Homes in High Flats* (1971). This interesting study was mainly based on nearly 1,000 interviews in 168 multi-storey blocks rising at least six storeys and served by lifts. Spontaneous comments made by the tenants were classified as shown in Table 1.

Taken as a whole, the 'likes' slightly outweighed the 'dislikes', (although in fact four times as many specific items were criticised as approved). The balance of likes was greatest for the dwelling interior, as subsequently found elsewhere, but dislikes predominated in relation to the block. These were, first and foremost, the lifts, followed by loneliness and isolation, the entrances, vandalism, inadequate laundry provision, noise, poor maintenance, and refuse disposal problems. Graffiti was not mentioned, but the research workers found it sufficiently conspicuous to merit a special study. Some blocks were clearly better

TABLE 1 *Residents' comments on their multi-storey homes in Glasgow*

Aspect assessed	Number of tenants expressing liking	dislike	Dislike percentage
Dwelling	838	493	37
Block	485	701	59
Estate	529	492	48
Total comments	1852	1686	48

what people actually dislike – block – estate

than others; some people spoke appreciatively of good sound-proofing and quiet.

With respect to the estate as a whole, likes and dislikes were nearly evenly balanced. However, two-thirds of the reasons for liking the estate were not based on the estate's own characteristics, but on accidents of their location near to good transport and facilities such as shops or schools, or in a pleasant district, or near relatives. The majority of the criticisms dealt with the same criteria in estates that lacked them, and a further 21 per cent complained of too many noisy children without proper play space.

The spontaneous-dislike percentages were all large enough to inspire a certain measure of distrust for the Utopian environment, but a different picture emerged from the answers to the question '*On the whole*, are you satisfied with living here?' 90 per cent said 'Yes'. This must have given great comfort to the Ministry of Housing and Local Government advisers who had maximised the trend towards flats, but there are cogent reasons why it should never have been taken at its face value. Chief among these is the fact that it was based on Glasgow.

Pearl Jephcott described the typical Glasgow dwelling as a 60-foot-high stone tenement blackened by the years. Although well built, its interior had often broken down beyond repair, and it often lacked basic facilities such as a fixed bath or shower, or an indoor toilet. Many consisted of one room and kitchen, where families were grossly overcrowded and where housework was arduous. Every drop of hot water might have to be heated on a coal range, and all the coal would have to be humped up flights of stone stairs. Each staircase was approached by a draughty doorless passage which also led through into a muddy, sunless courtyard shared by all the tenements on the four surrounding streets. Who, coming from such a harsh environment, could fail, *on the whole*, to prefer the cleaner, more spacious and more labour-saving modern flat? But that does not mean that the new blocks are truly satisfactory or that a deaf ear should be turned to the widespread criticism of them. If the survey had been conducted in London instead of Glasgow, there would no doubt have been plenty of people to say: 'I wish I were back in my old nineteenth-century terrace house'.

The Glasgow study was not fully scientific because it did not overcome this limitation of relativity. Although nine other estates in England and Europe were visited in the company of housing officers, architects, sociologists and community development workers, there was no time to conduct interviews with residents and obtain opinions that were strictly comparable with those of the Glaswegians. Another problem is that while residents may have a very clear insight into what is wrong, they do not necessarily understand how to put it right. For example, one of the additional estates studied by Pearl Jephcott was the Brandon Estate in Southwark, which has also been included in the present research. In 1983 its residents thought that the top priority was to mend all the glass broken by vandals until it was pointed out that £40,000 had been spent on glass the previous year, only to be promptly vandalised again.

Another type of survey that has intrinsic interest but remains defective for applied purposes, is a recent study of traditional Mediterranean settlements, to see which design features have survived over time. These are then recommended as being of value for Britain and elsewhere — a non sequitur which leaves out a vital scientific ingredient. Apart from their survival, there is no independent test of whether, how or why they can be considered good. It might well be that their virtue lies solely in their adaptation to the Mediterranean climate.

Oscar Newman — Defensible Space

The most scientific research to date is the project described by Oscar Newman in *Defensible Space*, in 1972. Its findings are fully in harmony with those of Jane Jacobs and have sometimes been regarded as a development of her work, but this fails to do justice to a brilliant concept which was quite independent in its origin and approach.

While Jane Jacobs took a broad view of whole streets and varied land uses, Oscar Newman focused on purely residential sites. To avoid any risk of bias in selecting his evidence, he opted to study all the public housing projects (council estates) in New York, a total of 169 estates comprising about 4,000 blocks of flats and many houses, accommodating approximately half a million people.

He also introduced the idea of a specific test measure to serve as an index of the goodness or badness of each block. For this purpose he chose levels of crime and vandalism, and was able to obtain much better statistics than normally exist in this field. New York had a special housing police force consisting of 1,600 men, and while they may not have been conspicuously successful in catching criminals or preventing crime, they kept excellent records of what crime occurs and its exact location. For example, a note would be made as to whether a smashed light was in the lobby, or on the sixteenth floor, or out in the grounds, etc.

Newman's aim was to discover which design features attracted the most crime or vandalism, and to do so precisely he used the statistical method of correlation. While Jane Jacobs' work had been mainly descriptive, Newman's was also quantitative, which gave added value to his evidence. As he identified the designs that seemed to encourage crime, Newman advanced three unifying principles that explained how crime was made easy to commit and difficult to prevent: *anonymity, lack of surveillance* and the presence of *alternative escape routes*.

Anonymity is the impersonal character of areas where a community structure has failed to develop and people know few other residents, even by sight. This makes criminals feel secure in the knowledge that they will not be identified, and are hence free to prowl through the buildings and grounds looking for illicit opportunities. The householder is robbed of the power to question and deter intruders, as they are in no way suspicious or distinguishable from genuine residents. And the community cannot co-operate to challenge even obvious wrong-doing because they have no experience of everyday interaction and do not know whether they can rely on other residents to be on the side of the law.

Jane Jacobs attributed anonymity to low-density layouts. Oscar Newman specified four other causes. The first is the sheer size of the block or estate. If these are small, the number of neighbours is manageably few and acquaintanceship begins to build up. But the more numerous they become the more difficult it is to know everyone, and in large buildings all attempt to do so is abandoned. Anonymity feeds on size.

The second cause of anonymity is a different way of looking at size: the number of people using the same entrance. A block may be large enough in overall size to produce an anonymous society, but if it is internally partitioned into self-contained sections served by separate entrances, the residents of each section may be few enough for acquaintanceship to develop, and override the anonymous tendency of the building as a whole. Oscar Newman found that this design—the number of dwellings per entrance—had a stronger correlation with crime levels than simple undifferentiated size. He has also stressed that it is numbers, and not densities, that are important. Density, per se, emerged as irrelevant.

A third cause was the number of storeys in the block. The more people are spaced out on different levels, the less they interact and the more anonymous the building becomes. This means not only that more crime takes place on the higher floors, but also that the building as a whole becomes more vulnerable to criminal violation.

The last cause of anonymity concerns the degree to which the grounds and the common parts of the buildings are shared and defended by different households. This carries an echo of Jane Jacobs' reference to public and private property, but is much more precisely defined in a sequence from private space through semi-private and semi-public to public space, with increasing anonymity as the degree of sharing widens. A single household with its own garden is in no doubt of its right to control its garden space, and because this right is recognised by the community at large, it has the confidence to challenge people who intrude upon it. In this non-anonymous atmosphere intrusions are likely to be few. Where spaces inside the buildings or out in the grounds are clearly shared by just a few households who know each other sufficiently well to care for them co-operatively and take any necessary action to defend them, intrusion may also be substantially deterred. The larger and more anonymous the degree of sharing, the less defensible the space becomes, and criminals perceive it as easier prey. These important variations in layout are referred to jointly as spatial organisation.

The principle of *surveillance* has a connection with what Jane Jacobs termed 'eyes on the street'. Veterans of World War II described their biggest fear and frustration in battle as lack of visibility, and Newman showed that visibility is an essential ingredient of residential space. Criminals like to operate unobserved in screened and secluded places, but the householder feels safer and more in control of his territory if he commands a clear view of the approaches to it. The community at large can then act as a watchdog, making crime less likely in areas that are in public view.

The level of surveillance varies according to type of corridor. Newman pointed out that external corridors, on the outside of the building, are open to public view from the street, and can also be seen from the windows of the flats opening onto them. They are less attractive to criminals than internal corridors with flats on both sides, which make them invisible from the street and also from the flats, which have no windows onto internal passages.

The position of the entrance also helps to determine the level of surveillance. Those flush with the street were found by Newman to be least vulnerable to crime; those which are set back are more vulnerable; and those which face away from the street are most vulnerable of all. Radiant City designers have often favoured an approach-path winding through the greenery, but Newman found it dangerous. Not only was public surveillance precluded but landscaping with trees and shrubs provided good cover for lurking muggers.

The third principle, *alternative escape routes*, allows criminals to be more audacious, as, even if they should be detected at work, they feel confident of being able to lose themselves in a network of outlets. In pursuit, the housing police experience many frustrations by losing track of where their quarry has disappeared. Newman found that the chief kinds of escape route affecting crime levels are interaccessible lifts, staircases and exits, and as these increase in number, so too does crime.

Crime levels would be highest in blocks where the design combines all three of these alienating mechanisms: anonymity, lack of surveillance and multiple escape routes. The appalling degree of lawlessness reached in New York's worst concrete jungles is indicated by Oscar Newman's mention of two armed guards permanently on duty at a local library.

Not content with demonstrating a strong association between design and crime, Newman went on to establish whether the link was causal. If one or more of the implicated design features were improved, would the crime rate fall? This was tried, with positive results. Newman's work had opened up design modification as an important new weapon in the fight against crime.

Newman's critics

Design modification reduces crime — Is it temporality & the new — shows move come?

In Britain his research was received with mixed feelings. It rang true to people such as housing officers and policemen whose daily work brought them face to face with the pressure of problems in estates of flats, but it also provoked a backlash from the decision-makers who had advocated them. The social services, too, found it hard to stomach a rival expertise claiming to alleviate problems which they saw as their own domain, and joined in the chorus of argument seeking to discredit *Defensible Space*.

The chauvinist feeling of 'this is an American problem', and the belief that socio-economic causes were stronger than the influence of design, led the Home Office to conduct a study intended to refute Newman's thesis. But when the evidence from 52 London housing estates was analysed, it proved the opposite. The preliminary report in 1976, by Andrew Sturman and Sheena Wilson, noted that only one socio-economic factor proved more powerful than design: the density of children. This confirmed Jane Jacobs' observations on the need for a high ratio of adults to children and led to a trend among housing authorities to reduce child densities in high-rise blocks. Unfortunately it was allowed to overshadow a further conclusion in the report, i.e. that if child density were constant, design was seen to exert a differentiating influence, and as a result there was an unfortunate neglect of design modification. The same neglect was apparent in the Home Office's final report by Pat Mayhew, in 1980. Design features were still seen to be significantly correlated with vandalism, but were discounted in practice because child density was correlated more highly. Some local authorities, however, felt that two forms of attack would be better than one, and a few successful design changes have been implemented.

The belief that 'it couldn't happen here' has had to be abandoned, and there is growing evidence that similar designs can breed similar problems in a great diversity of countries. Oscar Newman has been called in as a consultant in Holland, Finland, Russia and China. The Puerto Rican government found that their first five estates of flats bred so many problems that they abandoned that type of solution in favour of self-help housing schemes. Professor Emrys Jones of the London School of Economics studied Venezuelan urbanisation on behalf of the United Nations (1964) and found that areas of housing erected by squatters developed a more stable social structure than large estates of flats, where tenants were liable to shoot the rent collectors. Bulgarian geographers who listened to a presentation of our design-disadvantagement research at Lancaster University in 1983 commented on similar manifestations in their own country, and South African officials have sought information from both Oscar Newman and the Land Use Research Unit. To date, similarities have been reported from five continents, and although this does not mean that Utopian designs are inevitably disastrous, it does suggest that they have a widespread tendency to generate problems. Since this tendency is cross-cultural, it may well spring from something very fundamental in human nature.

Design and human evolution

The Dragons of Eden, by Carl Sagan (1977), deals with the human brain in the context of the evolutionary history of the animal kingdom and recognises four major phases of development, each of which continues to function in its own cerebral layer, and each of which would have implications for home-making.

The first—pre-reptilian—component consists simply of bundles of nerves to regulate bodily functions and purely instinctive home-making behaviour. A limpet manufactures a protective shell. A snail creates a mobile home. A shrimp burrows into the sea-floor.

The second – reptilian – component brought increased power to interact with other organisms, through ritual behaviour, social hierarchies and aggressiveness. Aggressiveness assisted the development of territoriality whereby an animal secures control over an area large enough to provide its needs.

In the third phase, birds and mammals developed warm-bloodedness and endocrine glands, with an intensification of consciousness through feelings and emotions. Experience of cold and pain, fear of attack and care for the young stimulated more elaborate home-making such as nests, beaver lodges or elaborate burrows.

Finally, the primate-human neocortex is associated with an upright stance, permitting a greater inflow of sensory information with better manual dexterity, reasoning, foresight, concern, and ethical understanding. In home-making terms these powers are reflected in innovativeness, individuality and adaptability.

Each major addition overshadowed the earlier parts of the brain so that we tend to ignore them, but we do so at our peril; we are adaptable but not infinitely adaptable. However, in the matter of housing we are discovering our adaptive limits very slowly through trial and error, and during the Utopian epoch both the trial and the error seem to have been on a more massive scale than the discovery.

Throughout most of human history our inbuilt guidance system has led us to produce a shelter with an adjoining piece of territory, and to impress it with distinctive marks of identity. The decoration, the garden layout, the boundary fence, the name plate or other signals proclaim the residence of a unique family rather than a faceless unit among the masses. Even when division of labour passed the initiative to builders and architects, there was no conflict with the territorial imperative as long as people remained free to accept or reject what was on offer. Designs that incorporated defensible territory and scope for the occupants to make their mark proved popular and were repeated, while those that denied these needs proved hard to sell and were discontinued. Natural selection was still in command.

However, when the power to make one's mark was taken from the individual and vested in authority, it began to be exercised on a different scale. Individual planners and architects cannot be blamed for this, as they too were following the human instinct to make one's mark as impressively as possible. They created designs that unified whole estates, and because the mark of the individual household was seen to interrupt the unity, it came to be regarded as wrong. Blocks of flats can minimise such 'intrusions', and this may be part of the reason why they have commended themselves during the Utopian epoch.

In historical retrospect we can see other examples of the association of the tenement with lack of individual power, whether that lack be due to poverty, despotism, or other causes. The very poor of nineteenth-century London, for example, were crowded together in shared 'rookeries', formerly the homes of affluent single families. Many housing trusts assume that flats are good enough for the recipients of charity. The USSR decides, every five years, on a single residential design to be built throughout the country – and it is invariably some kind of tenement block.

Utopian design

All these arguments converge upon the conclusion that the trouble in Utopia may be due to Utopian design itself and, if that is true, a change in housing policy is essential. However, the last thing we need is to jump into a new enthusiasm that is no more supported by evidence than the present one. Evidence is the keynote. The research mind must be open to factual evidence and not closed by some predetermined ideology.

The ideology of the official design recommendations existed at two levels. In a broad general sense it was *environmental determinism*, the belief that if the environment is changed, human behaviour will also change. In a more specific sense it was the Radiant City/Garden City dogma – the belief that if the environment is changed in the ways prescribed by these ideologies, human behaviour will improve and human happiness increase.

When the evidence began flooding in that the prescribed designs were not producing the postulated benefits, their advocates had the choice of several interpretations. One logical course would have been to retain the belief in determinism while acknowledging that the Radiant-Garden brand of it was not successful and seeking more effective alternatives. What the DoE housing research staff chose to do was just the opposite. They renounced determinism, asserting emphatically that architecture cannot influence people, and went on recommending the same designs. This ploy was a masterly stroke in self-preservation. It absolved them from blame for any ill effects of their designs, it rescued them from the admission of error, and it provided them with a dirty word, determinism, to fling at critics who had the temerity to suggest that the designs really were disadvantaging and that alternatives would be more beneficial. In one bound they went from determinism to *possibilism*, namely that it is perfectly possible for everyone to be good and happy regardless of the nature of the environment and, if they were not, it was because they were problem people. The concept of 'sink estates', populated by the dregs of humanity, followed in the wake of this volte face.

In reality, both the original determinist ideology and the possibilist rebound are over-simplifications. Human beings are all individuals, and react in different ways. At one end of the spectrum there are a few who will always rise above adversity, no matter how appalling their environment, while at the other end there are a few who will always be sluts or criminals, even in ideal conditions. This could mean that design acts as a sliding scale. The worse it becomes, the more people it affects adversely, and the more intense becomes the atmosphere of social malaise.

The sliding scale concept is *probabilism* which is not so much an ideology, as a willingness to see what degrees of environmental influence are revealed by factual evidence, and it was with this principle in mind that the Land Use Research Unit embarked upon its scientific study of housing.

A scientific approach

The research aimed to advance the frontiers of knowledge about housing design in several ways:

— Firstly, it explored whether there were additional design features, over and above those identified by Newman, which could be recognised as disadvantaging.

— Secondly, it investigated whether these features are associated with forms of social malaise other than crime which had already been demonstrated by Newman and the Home Office. It selected six forms of malaise in order to see whether they were all related to the same design features or whether different features seemed to provoke different kinds of human response.

— Thirdly, it compared the design features of the pre-planning era with those that have been introduced under centralised guidance since 1948. Even if modern designs are bad, that does not necessarily make them worse than those they replaced, and independent evidence is needed in order to make a judgement.

— Fourthly, it assembled a wide variety of non-residential features of

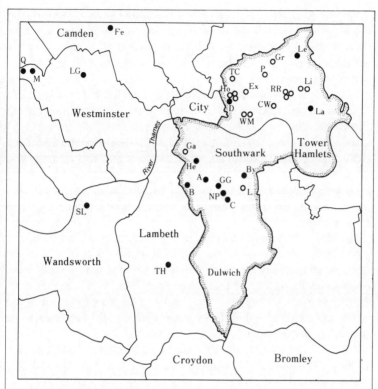

FIG. 1. Location of Southwark and Tower Hamlets. White circles show blocks of flats monitored before and after housing improvement schemes: CW − Clearbrook Way, Ex−Exmouth Estate (Chater House), Ga−Gaywood Estate (Prospect House), Gr−Greenways Estate (Lister House), Ho−Holland Estate (Bernard, Brune and Carter Houses), L−Ledbury Estate (Bromyard House), Li−Lincoln Estate (Gayton and Sleaford Houses), P−Portman Place, RR−Rhodeswell Road, TC − Tomlinson Close, WM − Watney Market (Colstead and Melwood Houses). Black circles denote other estates mentioned: A−Aylesbury, B−Brandon, By−Bonamy, C−Camden, D−Denning Point, Fe−Ferdinand, GG−Gloucester Grove, He−Heygate, La−Lansbury, Le−Lefevre, LG−Lisson Green, M−Mozart, NP−North Peckham, Q−Queen's Park, SL−Surrey Lane, TH−Tulse Hill.

the environment, and socio-economic factors such as poverty and unemployment, in order to ascertain whether any of these might be exercising an influence as well as, or instead of, design.
— Fifthly, it moved from the scientific discovery of facts to the practical recommendation of design improvement, not with the aim of enforcing an alternative to current design guides, but to help people become more informed and able to escape from the tyranny of having their housing choices made for them.

These various research aims require a large body of evidence assembled with a painstaking regard for accuracy, and consequently the survey was conducted in a way that compels its own high standard of discipline: large-scale mapping. The map not only ensures that no blocks or houses are omitted; it also places them in the context of all the other land uses in the vicinity.

The area to be mapped had to be large enough to avoid bias due to local idiosyncrasies and permit any basic trends to emerge, and we therefore chose the two London boroughs with the most council flats: Tower Hamlets with 1,782 blocks and Southwark with 2,263 (Fig. 1). Blackbird Leys in Oxford, which was included for comparison, contained 54 blocks, giving a total of 4,099, approximately the same number as that studied by Newman.

The design data and the test measures were collected independently for each block and then compared to see whether any particular design features showed any tendency to repel or attract the various forms of social malaise. 'Tendency' is the operative word: this is a study of probabilities and not inevitabilities. Living in a high-rise block does not force all its inhabitants to become criminals, but by creating anonymity, lack of surveillance and escape routes, it puts temptation in their way and makes it probable that some of the weaker brethren will succumb. By the same token it increases the probability that others will be victimised.

If design features can really be disadvantaging, then the worse the design, the larger the percentage of people who will have their lives blighted by it. It is a tragic thought that Utopian designers, with their idealistic intentions, have tipped the balance sufficiently to make criminals out of potentially law-abiding citizens, and victims out of potentially secure and happy people.

III | The Evidence

Can the design of buildings really lead to social malaise among the in-habitants? And if so, how can it be proved? There is no ready-made armoury of social-malaise tests equivalent to the fingerprints or blood tests of crime detection, and we have to pioneer new kinds of fair and unbiased evidence.

Verbal testimony is one kind of evidence which can give invaluable insight into what oppressive design means in terms of human experience. We have interviewed 224 people, and talked informally with others, but we could not rely entirely upon verbal information because it would have taken too long to interview a sufficient number in all 4,099 blocks.

Another kind of evidence is official statistics, but unfortunately these are not collected by blocks, and cannot be related to design features. Census enumeration districts, for example, usually contain a mixture of dwellings of different designs. Some unpublished figures are catalogued by addresses, but London authorities are sensitive about high levels of social malaise and withhold information that may be available elsewhere, e.g. figures for truancy, suicide, divorce or juvenile de-linquency. Other types of evidence, such as wife or baby battering, bullying, perversion or corruption, would be unreliable as, like crime, they undoubtedly have a 'dark area', which has not yet come to light. In view of all these difficulties we are most grateful to Southwark's Social Services Department which took a great deal of trouble to provide in-formation on children in care while safeguarding confidentiality.

In the main we have relied upon a third kind of evidence: material clues that could be objectively observed in each block of flats. As we could not afford time to lie in wait for incidents to happen, we chose types of malaise that leave behind visible traces: litter, graffiti, vandal damage and excrement. It will be shown that all of them have been on the increase over the same period as the vogue for flats, and are therefore potentially design-dependent forms of abuse.

Interestingly, these measures were echoed in a perceptive study of Castle Vale, a town-sized development for 25,000 people in

Birmingham – winner of a 'Wide-awake Trail' Competition organised by the Civic Trust and the *Daily Mirror* in 1981 to encourage environmental awareness among school children. Castle Vale was opened in 1965 with full benefit of planning, including 11-storeyed and 16-storeyed blocks, but by 1981 it had become so unpopular that one third of its dwellings were empty. Children and parents were asked what they considered the worst and ugliest features of the estate. Those mentioned most frequently were vandal damage first, closely followed by graffiti, and litter third. In addition there were other problems associated with children.

Children appear to play a crucial role in social malaise. People who have been brought up to abstain from litter, and who would never think of committing graffiti and vandalism, do not suddenly change their habits when they move into flats, but they may find it difficult to rear their children to the same standards of behaviour. Something about flats, as opposed to houses, is commonly perceived as being 'unsuitable for children' or as making it 'difficult for mothers to supervise their children's play.' Babies, toddlers, primary school-children and teenagers all suffer from the lack of appropriate training in fitting into society. This does not mean that adults are immune to detrimental designs. They may suffer severely from the traumas of unsuccessful parenting, marital breakdown or mental illness. They are also subjected to environmental insults such as noise, lack of privacy, isolation, fear of fire, and all the stresses entailed by the constant vigilance needed to avoid attacks upon person and property. But it is with the youngsters that widespread malaise begins, and we therefore feel justified in concentrating upon test measures that are particularly related to children.

Litter

Litter-dropping is a lapse in social behaviour which has become increasingly common as flats have multiplied. By 1958 it had aroused enough public concern to lead to the passing of the Litter Act, but legislation has not stemmed the tide. In our study area, litter is found in 86 per cent of the 4,099 blocks, compared with 20 per cent of 1,800 single-family houses surveyed in Tower Hamlets and Southwark. Furthermore, most of the littered house-gardens are located opposite blocks of flats; litter is much rarer in streets which are entirely houses.

There is little doubt that littering characterises flats more than houses and it is easy to see why. In houses with gardens children can spend their formative pre-school years under close parental supervision. The

Litter in flats because of lack of gardens?

garden is a safe place where toddlers can gain the self-confidence that comes of venturing out alone while knowing that help is immediately at hand if needed. They learn to care for the home territory, partly through the natural impulse, at this age, to imitate parents, and partly by being taught, until litter abstention and litter clearance become engrained habits.

In blocks of flats these child-rearing advantages are not available. A mother has a different range of options—all unpalatable. She can keep her children safely indoors, which deprives them of energetic exercise to let off steam. She can let them play on the balcony, with the risk of a serious fall. She can let them loose in the corridor, where their noise may drive the neighbours mad. Or she can allow them out into the grounds, where she cannot always be supervising them, and where they pick up bad habits from other unsupervised children. Some parents succeed, against all the odds, in teaching their children not to litter. Others do not, and litter may be ever-present. Children then see it as the norm, not as an environmental insult—an attitude which is probably permanent.

This illustrates the point made earlier, that the effect of design is not deterministic but probabilistic. Flat-dwelling does not force people to become litter louts, but it makes it more probable that some will be.

As successive age-groups of litter louts are bred, their collective activities become too much for the remaining litter clearers. An old lady living in a slab block in Tower Hamlets described how at first she had regularly scrubbed the corridor and staircase, only to find them promptly relittered and fouled by dogs. Her sense of responsibility was strong, and she continued the abortive cleaning for a whole year before finally giving it up as useless.

It seems that litter levels in blocks of flats depend on the relative dominance of abstention, clearance and discouragement. Where the residents mainly abstain from littering, any chance piece of rubbish is likely to be whisked away immediately, and the block is rated as *litter-free*. Where there are rather more litter-droppers and fewer litter-clearers, a small amount of litter tends to lie until the arrival of the official cleaners. It is usually fresh-looking and is recorded as *clean and casual*. Where litter droppers are in the ascendant, even official cleaners may be hard to recruit and desultory in their work, so that litter remains long enough to become trodden, stained and dust-covered. It accumulates in quantity and may decompose objectionably. It is classified as *dirty and decayed* and may sometimes become a health hazard. There are some blocks where refuse collectors refuse to collect, and we have even come across a case where rubbish was used to conceal murdered bodies.

Excrement

It was soon recognised that excrement ought to be mapped separately from rubbish. The incidence of faeces was mapped for all 4,099 blocks and proved to occur in 7.5 per cent of them. Observation of urine was added at a later stage, and mapped in Tower Hamlets only, where it occurs in 43.9 per cent of blocks. It was originally thought that both kinds of excrement were deposited by dogs, but in fact human excreta are also included. There seems to be a contribution from children, as urine and faeces are commoner in blocks adjacent to play areas, especially where the design makes it difficult to reach home in a hurry. It also seems likely that urine is contributed by alcoholics who, with their high liquid intake, have frequent need to relieve themselves. Tower Hamlets has been described by social workers as 'the meths capital of England', because drunks tend to drift there from all over the country, and hence there may be a disproportionately high percentage of polluted entrances. Houses, by contrast, have very low percentages at the entrances: 0.0 for urine and 0.1 for faeces.

Litter, faeces and urine have been mapped in a standard location in each block: inside the common entrances and within a radius of three metres outside them. If different entrances have different ratings, the worst one for each test measure is used for the record.

Graffiti

Graffiti scrawls are another phenomenon that has multiplied synchronously with flats. Its increase has been accompanied by the publication of books about it in recent years, and it has also come into prominence as a subject of tenant concern. It is found in 76.2 per cent of the 4,099 blocks as compared with 1.2 per cent of the houses. It is largely the work of children; Celia Redknap, in a Nuffield-sponsored research project on entrance design (1983), found that 'children's graffiti' occurred in 70 per cent of graffiti-ridden entrances.

Graffiti can be interpreted as a way of making one's mark in an anonymous environment that offers little in the way of more legitimate opportunities to do so. Houses with gardens offer scope for expressing individuality, but flats are constrained to be exactly like each other. There, housewives frequently react by displaying beautifully laundered curtains to signal that the household rises above the general squalor of the block as a whole, but this does not serve for teenagers, who are passing through a phase of needing to make their own independent mark. School success may be hard to come by in huge inner-city comprehensives, and many hobbies are ruled out by lack of garden space, so some teenagers may be reduced to making their mark literally, in the form of writing on the wall, and younger children, ever imitative, may add their quota.

It takes much longer to remove graffiti than to inscribe them, and hours of cleaning may be set at nought within minutes. The would-be cleaners are discouraged and graffiti abound. They may well be a more permanent and consistent test measure than litter, as litter can be misclassified if surveyed immediately after sweeping while graffiti may yield only to redecoration, a much rarer occurrence.

Graffiti may range from a single scrawl to a dense coverage of many surfaces. It would be too time-consuming to count or measure, and has been recorded in three simple classes: *graffiti-free*, occurring *either inside or outside the building*, or *both inside and outside*. The 'either/or' class usually consists of sparse graffiti while the 'both' class is more copious. Graffiti are commonest in and around the entrances, but may be recorded anywhere inside the ground floor and anywhere on the outside of the block.

Vandalism

Vandal damage has also been on the increase, as demonstrated by police statistics on malicious damage. It may be a more aggressive way than graffiti of making one's mark and hitting out at life's frustrations – a flat-dweller's version of taking it out on the cat. If so, it may be justifiable to deduce that stresses are greater where vandalism is more frequent, and consequently the presence of damage helps single out the more stressful design features. As it overlaps with crime it could be a useful indicator of whether our social-malaise measures run parallel to Newman's crime measure. The majority of crimes in the United Kingdom are committed by young people, and vandalism is particularly concentrated among youth, so it too fits our criterion of being concerned with children and teenagers.

Like graffiti, damage is recorded from anywhere in the ground-floor interior or anywhere on the exterior of the block. Additionally, it is observed in detached features such as fences, pramsheds or garden benches. A count is made of the number of *types* of target; broken glass for example, is counted as one, regardless of the number of broken panes. Despite this broader locational sweep, vandal damage affects only about half as many blocks as graffiti, 38.8 per cent, which is in keeping with

TABLE 2   *Frequency of the test measures in blocks of flats*

	Total study area	Tower Hamlets	Southwark	Blackbird Leys
Litter	86.1	96.8	78.3	57.4
Graffiti	76.2	87.0	69.1	18.5
Vandal damage	38.8	49.9	30.7	9.3
Children in care	(30.4)	—	24.6	—
Urine	(22.9)	43.9	—	—
Faeces	7.5	7.8	7.3	0.0

Figures are blocks with each kind of malaise, expressed as percentages of all blocks. Estimated percentages are shown in brackets.

its more extreme nature. The percentage in houses is 1.9 per cent, and it tends to be restricted to houses close to flats.

Frequency of occurrence

The relative frequency of the six test measures is shown in Table 2. They maintain the same order in all three areas, but Tower Hamlets always exceeds the average while Southwark falls somewhat below it and Blackbird Leys is markedly below. As urine was surveyed only in Tower Hamlets, and children in care only in Southwark, their respective percentages are not typical of the study area as a whole, and have to be adjusted to make them properly comparable. The reasoning behind the method of adjustment is explained in Appendix I, and the estimates obtained are included in Table 2.

Fig. 2 shows the same breakdown of test measures in both houses and flats; the contrast is very clear. Litter is still the commonest in houses but it is only one-sixth as common as in flats, and the disparity is even greater with the other measures.

The figures for houses are calculated by dwellings whereas those for flats are calculated by blocks. Not every household in the block contributes to the squalor, but they all have to endure it, and the more responsible they are the more ashamed they feel of the abuse of their shared space. House-dwellers are less vulnerable in this respect. Any anti-social residents are spoiling mainly their own space and impinge upon fewer neighbours.

Excrement appears to be completely taboo in the entryways of houses,

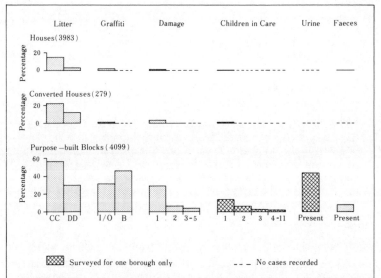

FIG.2. Eighteen bar graphs showing the frequency of six test measures in three categories of dwelling. The frequencies are expressed as percentages of (a) 3,983 houses, (b) 279 houses converted into flats and (c) 4,099 purpose-built blocks of flats. CC−clean and casual litter. DD−dirty and decayed litter. I/O−graffiti either inside or outside. B−graffiti both inside and outside. 1,2,3-5−number of types of vandal target. 1,2,3,4-11−number of families with children in care. A broken line means none. The shaded areas are percentages obtained by mapping Southwark only for children in care, and Tower Hamlets only for urine pollution. All the test measures are least common in houses and most common in blocks of flats.

and the concept of taboo suggests a way in which the different test measures may be linked together. In problem-free areas, British culture regards all of them as taboo, but when society breaks down, some taboos may be flouted more readily than others. It seems that they are breached in a set order, from the weakest to the strongest.

The taboo against litter appears to be the weakest. Litter dropping is generally regarded as inconsiderate rather than vicious and there are fewer sanctions against it than, say, vandalism. Where there is no firm social structure to defend an accepted set of mores, litter dropping may well be the first lapse, so litter becomes the most widespread form of abuse.

Graffiti is usually resented more than litter, and the taboo against it

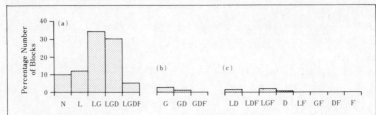

FIG.3. Sixteen possible combinations of litter (L), graffiti (G), damage (D) and faeces (F). N=none. The five commonest combinations are those where more serious abuses do not occur in the absence of less serious ones (group a). Group b consists of the same normal combinations disturbed only by the absence of litter; these blocks may have been swept just before being surveyed. The eight least likely combinations, (c), occur in only 3.9 per cent of blocks.

would be upheld more tenaciously. It is unlikely to occur in blocks that are still resisting litter. Vandalism, as the third commonest form of abuse, would probably occur where litter and graffiti both have a foothold and excrement would come later than all three. However, the taking of children into care and urine pollution would probably occur before faeces in the entrances.

There are 16 possible combinations of litter, graffiti, damage and faeces – the four measures that have been mapped throughout the whole of the study area. If they were distributed purely by chance, each of the 16 would occur in roughly the same number of blocks, but Fig. 3 shows this is not the case. The five commonest combinations (group a) are those where the more serious abuses occur only where the less serious ones are already present, supporting the taboo hypothesis. These account for over 92 per cent of all blocks. The second commonest group, (b), consists of the same combinations, disturbed only by absence of litter. These blocks were probably swept just before they were surveyed. The eight least likely combinations, (c), occur in less than 4 per cent of the blocks. Their rarity suggests that the test measures are reasonable criteria, not too seriously disturbed by caretaking activities, and capable of revealing a relationship with design if it exists.

IV | The Suspects

Following the analogy of a trial we can see designs as suspects lined up for identification. What are their descriptions? Are they of good character? Do they keep bad company? Do they have alibis, i.e. are they present where the test measures are worst or do they stand aside from involvement? Are they ringleaders, or accomplices, or innocent parties?

In describing the suspects we want to spare non-technical readers as much jargon as possible, but there are two indispensable terms: *design variable* and *design value*. A variable is a broad category of evidence that can vary in its detailed manifestation, and the specific variations are its values. For example, 'number of storeys' is a variable, the values of which range from 'two' to '27' in the area of survey. A variable is found in all blocks of flats but its values differ from block to block.

Fifteen suspected variables are listed in Table 3 (page 33). The eight marked with asterisks are variables investigated by Newman and the other seven are additional suspects identified by our study. Four are related to characteristics of the block or the dwelling, four are related to channels of circulation round the building, three are related to aspects of the entrances and the remaining four to features of the grounds.

We originally intended to adopt Newman's definitions of his variables and values, but in practice they had to be elaborated a little. Newman was dealing with a few standard types of building, and it was natural for him to write fairly interchangeably of block type and design type. The Home Office study could do the same as it used mainly four types. But we could not follow suit as our 4,099 blocks are incredibly varied. In Tower Hamlets alone there are at least 1,250 different combinations of design values and Southwark probably has an even wider range. This necessitates a breakdown by individual designs and some of Newman's variables had to be adapted. For example, he divided horizontal circulation into internal and external corridors and did not compare these with the small landings found in walk-up blocks without lifts. However, British landings are not restricted to walk-up blocks, and therefore we have compared all design features catering for horizontal movement in the block.

Detailed definitions have been compiled to ensure that each value of each variable would always be identified consistently. We are also concerned with giving the designs a human face by explaining how they might be deleterious, and recounting the independent opinions of 74 people interviewed in Tower Hamlets.

The interviewees were asked to say what they thought about their blocks or estates. They were given absolutely no clue as to which designs were suspected, in order to see which would be mentioned spontaneously, and whether people would be in favour of them or, like Newman, against them. The range of spontaneous comments was extended by showing people their local large-scale maps, and finally Newman's variables — plus overhead walkways — were mentioned by name to elicit prompted comments. Table 3 includes first comments only; repetitions at the prompt stage are excluded. Each interviewee is counted once as for, or once as against, or sometimes twice if they expressed contrary viewpoints for different reasons. It is of interest that four times as many comments were critical of the designs as in favour of them.

Number of storeys in the block

Whenever it is suggested that housing design may have a detrimental effect, the first response of the general public is 'high-rise'. Tall buildings seem to be as conspicuous in the mental landscape as they are in the townscape. However, it was only the second most frequently mentioned by the Tower Hamlet interviewees; the first was spatial organisation, embodying the desire for individual gardens.

High blocks are regarded as creating anonymity because they segregate people at different levels instead of allowing the normal interactions that take place on the street when houses are on the ground. The anonymity produces feelings of loneliness and isolation, and, according to Dr Eileen Coats, a general practitioner in Tower Hamlets, may induce neuroses. Because many of her patients requested medical certificates to support their applications to be rehoused, she took an interest in the type of housing which they found intolerable, and observed that whereas slim point blocks (tower blocks) seemed to induce neurosis, massive slab blocks were more often associated with complaints about vandalism and crime. Other reasons cited for the undesirability of tall buildings are fire risk, lift breakdown, fear of being attacked in the lifts, inability to have open windows because of the strong winds engendered by the block, and difficulties in supervising children's play.

TABLE 3 *Suspected design variables and interviewees' comments*

	Spontaneous comments		Prompted comments		
	For	Against	For	Against	Total
Size variables					
Dwellings per block*	2	31	3	11	47
Dwellings per entrance*	—	3	—	12	15
Storeys per block*	10	45	4	5	64
Storeys per dwelling	—	—	nm	nm	—
Circulation variables					
Overhead walkways	1	30	—	6	37
Interconnecting exits*	—	2	3	13	18
Vertical routes (lifts and staircases)*	—	2	—	2	4
Corridor type*	5	35	2	10	52
Entrance characteristics					
Entrance position*	3	—	2	—	5
Entrance type	—	—	nm	nm	—
Blocks raised above stilts	1	14	nm	nm	15
Blocks raised above garages	5	8	nm	nm	13
Features of the grounds					
Spatial organisation*	15	54	1	6	76
Blocks in the site	—	—	—	—	—
Access points	—	10	nm	nm	10
Play areas	25	24	nm	nm	49
Total	67	258	15	65	405

* Variables identified by Newman
nm Not mentioned as a prompt by the interviewers

In addition, 31 people voiced criticisms of the common parts of the block without specifying precisely which. Some of these may have been covered by the subsequent prompting on exits, vertical routes and corridors, so they are not shown separately. Stilts and garages are combined as one variable for testing.

It may seem surprising that 14 people defended high-rise blocks, but most had already criticised them on general grounds before expressing the reservation that tower blocks are better than slab blocks and can be quite satisfactory for certain types of tenant. These would be working singles or couples, much of whose life is spent elsewhere in a satisfying

way, and who use the flat as a base rather than a total living environment. High blocks are not recommended for families with children or
old people, which may mean, in practice, most of the people living in
them.

Number of storeys in the dwelling

In New York larger flats for larger families are provided by extending
the floor area on the same level. This contrasts with the British vogue
for maisonettes, which are designed on two floors to give a more house-
like atmosphere. Each block was mapped as consisting either of flats,
or of maisonettes, or as a mixture of both. None of the interviewees
made any comment on this variable.

Number of dwellings in the block

Another aspect of design that attracts a great deal of public criticism
is size. Large developments are described as anonymous, packed with
humanity in the mass but lacking scope for the individual to establish
his own unique identity in a functioning community. It seems to be no
accident that the concept of 'identity crisis' has emerged during the trend
towards increasing scale and a more impersonal atmosphere in the places
where people live.

The interviewees stressed the size difference between point blocks and
slab blocks; buildings of the same height may contain very different
numbers of flats and taller buildings do not necessarily house more
people. The points are characterised by isolation and slabs by greater
invasion of privacy. Inadequate soundproofing allows tenants to overhear
neighbours' conversations, and naturally they fear that their own private
lives are being listened to. Yet this does not mean that neighbours can
be summoned in time of trouble. Instead they learn to disregard what
they hear, and so become desensitised. In 1983 in Exeter, a girl was
trapped in her flat by an intruder for ten hours and repeatedly raped at
knife-point, but her screams were ignored by her neighbour who merely made the standard response of turning up the radio to drown the
unwelcome noise.

Number of dwellings served by the same entrance

In criticising large size, the interviewees were mainly thinking of a large

PLATE 2. A concentration of objectionable features in Southwark's Heygate Estate. Excessive height was promoted by government subsidies and excessive length by official encouragement – one of the Department of the Environment's design awards for 1979 was for a building half a kilometre long. The long slab block contains 222 dwellings, and is more anonymous and disliked than the 99-dwelling point block in the background, even though the latter is five storeys higher. The ground-floor garage design means that residents cannot observe or control access to ground-floor entrances, and numerous overhead walkways form a network of escape routes for criminals. Note anti-vandal lights at fifth storey.

number of dwellings in the same block, but in the survey we have also recorded the number of dwellings served by any one entrance. Some blocks are divided up into self-contained sections, each served by its own separate entrance. This restricts the number of people going in and out, and increases the likelihood of their being able to recognise each other. Other entrances may serve a whole block and still others may serve several blocks linked together by overhead walkways. In the Aylesbury

PLATE 3. The Gloucester Grove Estate, Southwark, consists largely of two-storeyed maisonettes in high-rise blocks. Its graffiti-laden internal corridors continue as overhead walkways linking 916 dwellings via round service towers that contain lifts, staircases, refuse chutes, etc. The separate towers have been officially promoted as a fire precaution, but they appear to multiply fire risk, as children frequently ignite the contents of the refuse chambers. The ground-floor flats have been given miserly *semi-private* gardens, set in landscaped *confused* space, resulting in an overall *semi-confused* spatial organisation. A recent 'improvement' exercise failed to change any of the 14 deleterious design variables here, and its social problems persist.

Estate in Southwark a single entrance gives access to no fewer than 2,268 dwellings without having to emerge at ground level en route. The number of dwellings served is a design variable that covers a vast range in the degree of anonymity experienced, and also in the number of alternative escape routes.

PLATE 4. The positions of lifts and staircases are marked by differences in fenestration, and by breaks in the roof line to accommodate winding machinery. In large blocks it is officially required, as a safety measure, that any vertical route should be accessible from at least one other, either in the same block or in an adjoining block reached by an overhead walkway. This interconnectedness of vertical routes, and consequently of exits, multiplies escape routes for criminals, and also intensifies anonymity by enlarging the number of dwellings served by any one entrance. (Tower Hamlets)

Oscar Newman found dwellings per entrance to be the most influential factor in encouraging or abating crime, but it appeared rather too subtle an idea to be widely recognised by our interviewees. Only three people mentioned it spontaneously, but more found it meaningful when prompted. Once it was recognised, people expressed strong views against having a large number of dwellings per entrance; the advantages of knowing one's neighbours and being able to identify intruders were clearly perceived.

Number of overhead walkways

Overhead walkways were mapped as the number of raised bridges radiating from the block. They clearly increase the escape-route options for criminals and also help foster anonymity. Everyone who commented condemned them, complaining especially of the noise and congestion caused by children playing on them and apprehensiveness about strangers using them. It was spontaneously remarked that walkways increase crime by enabling offenders to dodge from block to block, and at the time of the Peckham riots in 1981 the rioters and looters were quickly able to lose themselves in the ramifying North Peckham Estate, where 72 blocks are all linked together by walkways. One person condemned walkways but also expressed the reservation that friends living in adjoining blocks might object if their short cut via a walkway were removed.

Number of interconnecting exits

Another design variable providing alternative escape routes is the number of interconnecting exits. As with the number of dwellings served by an entrance, few people recognised the implications spontaneously but more did so when prompted. Three of the interviewees suggested that more exits were desirable as they provide more people on the alert for wrong-doers, but it is difficult to see the logic of their argument as dispersing people among several exits must attenuate the duration of surveillance, compared with blocks where all the traffic is concentrated into one. The fact that the role of interconnecting exits is not generally recognised spontaneously may account for its not always being properly thought through.

Number of interconnecting vertical routes

Escape routes are also provided by the presence of numerous lifts and staircases, collectively termed vertical circulation channels or vertical routes. We have counted the total number that can be reached from any dwelling on the way to any exit; it is greatly increased where overhead walkways give access to exits in different blocks. Criticism was mainly focused upon lifts. These seem to attract more intruders and vandals than staircases because they offer an easy ride, and they are also feared by residents as a prime area for attacks upon the person. A Tower Hamlets councillor described how she was sexually menaced in the lift of Denning Point block, and one of the lifts on the Brandon Estate in Southwark has repeatedly been the scene of rape.

Type of corridor

Horizontal circulation channels include shared balconies and external corridors running along the outside of the building, and landings and internal corridors running through the inside. Newman considered this distinction important in terms of surveillance as the outside features are visible both from the street and from the windows of the flats, whereas the inside features are not visible from either direction. We believe that anonymity is also relevant, and have distinguished landings and short balconies where the inhabitants of four or fewer dwellings can more easily become known to each other than in either type of longer more impersonal corridor.

Residents are keenly aware of corridor problems, which received more mentions than even the more publicised size factors. Internal corridors were picked out as particularly objectionable and described as more like an institution than a home. Although many of the flats have spyholes to identify callers, these do not provide surveillance of the corridor as a whole, and there is clearly a great deal of tension and fear due to the fact that residents have to open their doors blind, without knowing whether they are emerging into a dangerous situation. It is not uncommon to find a definite reduction in the frequency with which people venture out. They may feel trapped in their flats, and it is not surprising that they find the corridors 'prison-like'. The lack of surveillance also leads to undesirable forms of children's play. The walls, ceilings, doors, and sometimes even the floors, are covered with graffiti, and noise may be magnified to intolerable levels as in an echo chamber. Internal corridors are also described as a haven for vandals, and they clearly induce a great deal of unnecessary stress and hostility, as well as the high crime levels demonstrated by Newman. Conversely, single-loaded corridors (having dwellings on only one side), with their better surveillance, were said to be less anonymous and to suffer less damage.

Position of the entrance

Oscar Newman found that the position of the entrance to the block had

PLATE 5. Older blocks contrast strongly with those of the Utopian period. They are lower and smaller, with only a few flats served by each entrance. A door of normal domestic size signals that this is private residential property. It faces the street, and is slightly set back in 'grounds' which, although miniscule, are clearly walled and railed, pointing up the single access point, and denying any hint of confused space for indiscriminate public use. Such design features are respected, with greater cleanliness and less vandalism and crime than their Utopian successors, but unfortunately these older blocks continue to be demolished.

a marked bearing on the incidence of crime, with the degree of vulnerability increasing from those flush with the street, through those that are set back from the street but still visible from it, to those that are located in the interior of the estate. This is a variable which most of the interviewees had not thought about, but those that did respond disagreed with Newman's findings. They said that street entrances were abused by passers-by who vandalise them and use them as urinals. They also believed that thefts and violent crimes were more likely to occur on the streets than in the more secluded grounds of estates. This difference of opinion has been resolved by the facts, in the next chapter.

Type of entrance

We also mapped entrance type as being either communal only, which would seem to be more anonymous, or communal for upper floors with

PLATE 6. Entrance design in the Aylesbury Estate, Southwark. No door was provided for this gaping aperture, which leads into a twisted passage without proper visibility, and offers a short cut through the block for outsiders. Such entrances often face inward into the estate instead of outward onto the street and, as the graffiti demonstrates, they do not command respect.

separate doors for ground-floor flats, which would seem to afford more individual identity. With the benefit of hindsight, it would have been desirable to subdivide the designs with separate front doors into those that were protected by individual front gardens and those that opened directly into communal territory.

Blocks raised over concrete stilts or rows of garages

Oscar Newman suggested that blocks designed with wings allowed residents to keep the entrance under surveillance better than flat-fronted

PLATE 7. This block has communal entrances for the upper storeys and individual external doors for ground-floor flats. Shared gardens are a basic principle of Utopian layouts, but here the shared lawn could easily be divided up to give each ground-floor dwelling its own front garden: the presence of individual front gardens profoundly improves the value of individual entrances. Oscar Newman showed that surveillance is improved and crime levels lowered in buildings with small wings, as here. The external corridor design also improves surveillance, both from the dwellings and from the street.

blocks. Celia Redknap in 1981 found that entrances which cannot be seen from ground-floor flats in the same block are twice as likely to be polluted by urine and three times as likely to be vandalised as those entrances which *are* observable. We have mapped two other features that preclude surveillance of the entrance: buildings on stilts and blocks with the ground floor occupied by garages. It is only very rarely that either of these designs accommodates any flats at ground level.

Although the stilt design is rare, it is more obvious to people than the number of dwellings served by one entrance; it received the same number of comments but more of them were made spontaneously. It was felt that pram sheds under the block were unsafe because their owners cannot see them, and consequently do not use them, while refuse chambers also tend to be vandalised. The stilt design was consequently disapproved of as wasting space, and also, presumably, money.

Garages occupying the ground floor under the block received diverse

PLATE 8. Concrete stilts, like ground-floor garages, impede surveillance. Residents would have to see down and round corners to observe who is entering their block. The space between the stilts is often intended for parking but residents do not feel their cars would be safe, and prefer street parking. Pramsheds behind the stilts are also vulnerable and frequently unused. As well as the graffiti, there is excrement between the stilts in the centre of the picture and it can also be shown that crime rates rise in buildings on stilts. Fortunately, the additional cost involved in providing this feature has led to its eclipse in recent years.

comments. Some people complained that there were too few of them, but others objected to their poor layout and location which prevented surveillance from the flats and opened the way to serious vandalism. Adverse comments were also made on other types of garaging. Underground car parks were particularly disliked, and said to be disused, except for processing stolen cars. A multi-storey park serving the Lefevre Estate in Tower Hamlets was also too hazardous to be used. Fortunately, both these designs are very rare, and they do not obstruct surveillance of entrances as garages under the block do. Other people mentioned open parking space. Most preferred this to garages but a few were concerned with conflicts between parking and play-space needs.

Spatial organisation

We now turn from the design variables of the building to those of the grounds, which between them attracted one-third of the total number of comments. Oscar Newman considered the spatial organisation of the grounds to be very important, but his detailed method of classification proved so cumbersome that he has dispensed with it in subsequent research, while still applying the recommendations derived from it. We have tried to find a simplified essence of it, and have also separated out three specific components — the number of blocks, access points and play areas — to map in their own right. Even so, spatial organisation remains a complex variable which presents certain difficulties.

Spatial organisation means the arrangement of the grounds in ways that encourage or discourage their control and maintenance by the residents. The inside of the dwelling is *private space*, where upkeep and behaviour are under the control of the occupying household. The street outside is *public space* for everyone's use. Upkeep is the local authority's responsibility, and behaviour is kept in civilised check by the presence of pedestrians (or, on a deserted street, their potential presence at any moment). Both private and public space can be thought of as 'self-policing' because they incorporate naturally-functioning forms of control. Between the two, however, there is a buffer zone which may or may not produce a self-policing social structure, and it is the varying types of buffer zone that make up our spatial organisation variable.

The best type of buffer zone is *semi-private space* controlled by a single household, although visible to others. Its three essential features are house windows giving surveillance over the territory, house doors giving direct access out into it, and perimeter fencing that clearly signals the line where the household's property begins. Each family knows its territorial control is assured and exclusive. They tend their own gardens responsibly and respect other people's. No-one goes through the gate without having business with the occupants, and failure to go straight up the path to the front door is immediately noticeable as suspicious behaviour. Children are brought up to follow the same mores, and not to intrude inside other people's fences; toddlers who try to are promptly hauled back. All these conditions combine to produce a high probability of a cared-for environment and a low probability of criminal intrusion.

A less satisfactory type of buffer zone is *semi-public space*, where there is enforced sharing of territory. No household can exercise individual control, but the total number of households is small enough to co-operate in tending and controlling the territory. The upper limit is not simply a number but depends on the way the grounds are arranged. The perimeter is securely walled or fenced, with a gate on one side only

PLATE 9. Confused spatial organisation implies grounds shared between different blocks, with a supposed maximisation of use. One of the Disadvantagement Team has walked past the confused-space lawn above twice daily for 16 years, without once seeing anyone using it. If it were divided into individual gardens for ground-floor flats it would be available for family use of many kinds. (Southwark)

(or occasionally two gates on the same side), so that there is no opportunity for strangers to take short cuts through, and the only people present are the residents themselves and those who have business with them. The filtering out of unrelated strangers makes it easier for the residents to come to know each other by sight and develop a degree of acquaintanceship sufficient for workable joint control of the territory. Usually there is only one block of flats, but there may be up to four small blocks arranged round a courtyard or in some other close and mutually observable cluster. Intruders are still conspicuous, but less so than in semi-private space, and crime may be rather more common.

The least satisfactory buffer zone is *confused space*, shared by too many people to permit natural, unconscious self-policing. The absolute number need not be very great if the spatial layout admits a large number of strangers. This occurs when there are gates or gaps on different sides of the site, providing short cuts for the public at large. It is also fostered by designs which fence off the grounds from the block as strongly as from the street, or by extensive greens which the public perceives as parks rather than as residential property. Outsiders feel no compunction about passing through the estate or even through the blocks, and as they cannot be distinguished from residents, criminals feel safely anonymous while the inhabitants feel vulnerable. It is difficult or impossible to develop a social structure based upon mutual trust or responsibility, although the community may to some extent be organised artificially if it happens to include someone with exceptional qualities of leadership, or is run as a housing co-operative.

Apart from confusion as to whether the grounds are public, confused space embodies another kind of confusion. There are no clear signals indicating which part of the grounds pertains to each block. In the absence of separate fencing it is rarely possible for tenants to care for the land adjoining their dwellings as their efforts are often promptly vitiated by other people's litter, dogs, or undisciplined children. All care and control has to be surrendered to the housing authority, which may or may not exercise it efficiently.

Originally, each block was classified as a single type, which necessitates extra terms, such as *semi-confused* and *row blocks* for cases where the front grounds differed from the back, and a separate designation was reserved for the surrounding area. This approach has been superseded by a three-digit code which makes estate survey easier in practice. The first digit indicates whether the space in front of the block is semi-private (1), semi-public (2) or confused (3), and the second digit gives similar information for the back. The third digit shows whether the abutting land is at least partly confused space (3) or wholly satisfactory (0) i.e. a public road or properly enclosed land uses. Thus, semi-confused would be 310 or 313, while row blocks would be 230 or 233. Some of the 18 possible combinations can result from design improvement.

Only a few of the interviewees referred to the spatial layout of the grounds as a whole. The majority were specifically concerned with the concept of individual gardens *vis-à-vis* shared grounds. In fact this aspect alone received more comments than any other design, even the number of storeys. Houses with gardens were picked out on the map as examples of the most successful design, and the desirable qualities that were stressed were privacy and direct access from the dwelling to one's own ground. The dream of the Englishman's castle was clearly in the ascendant; semi-private is what most people want.

As with number of storeys, about one-fifth of the comments contained the opposite view but once again these proved to be mainly special

PLATE 10. This site is shared by more than one block – a four-storeyed maisonette block can be seen on the left. A facet of the site's confused spatial organisation is the fact that it provides short cuts to five different flanking roads, two visible here, with no proper fencing. A third access route is from behind the camera, under the stilts of the high-rise block there. In the foreground is a children's play area. Attracting hordes of anonymous children, this is associated with a deterioration in all our test measures. (Southwark)

reservations. They did not refer to the semi-private space of house gardens, but to the semi-confused space of gardens for ground-floor flats. These were not considered successful if the blocks were too high, as upstairs tenants may drop things into them. Often this is merely dust, which can be unpleasant enough, but sometimes there are heavier objects, which can be dangerous. In one instance a discarded cooker was tipped out of a high window. Naturally, ground-floor residents fear to use their gardens in such circumstances. With lower blocks, however, upstairs tenants know that the source of ejectamenta can easily be identified, and this is normally a sufficient deterrent. The gardens are safe to use, and greatly appreciated.

Number of blocks sharing the same site

One way to measure the extent to which grounds are shared is to count the number of blocks occurring inside the boundary of the same site.

The term 'site' is usually, but not always, synonymous with 'estate', but some estates are too complex to be coherent spatial units. For example, a new estate may be named as the extension of an older one on the other side of a busy shopping street, and apart from the name, the two have nothing in common, and are better analysed as separate sites. A site is therefore an area of housing bounded by public roads or by effective physical barriers separating it from other land uses or other housing sites.

The number of blocks within the site boundary is not a characteristic which had occurred to our interviewees as having relevance to the quality of life, and no-one commented on it, either spontaneously or after having it drawn to their attention.

Access from the street into the grounds

An aspect of spatial organisation which was specially singled out by interviewees was the need for a distinct boundary round the grounds, with a limitation of access points, in order to prevent all and sundry from trespassing on residential property. The presence of strangers was thought to dilute contact with fellow-residents and to cause increased problems of litter and vandalism, while too-easy access outward to the roads was considered dangerous for children playing in the grounds. Our original intention was to record the number of gates or gaps in the site perimeter, but some estates had whole sides left unfenced, and to maintain parity we settled for counting the number of sides containing at least one access point. Because of the configuration of the more complex sites this variable proves to extend up to a value of six sides.

Play areas

The last of our design features was also added in response to concern expressed by interviewees: the provision of play areas. Play areas and open space received the fourth most mentions after spatial organisation, block height and corridor type, and the chief complaints were that they were inadequate in amount and poorly arranged. The perception of inadequacy is of great interest as open space occupied 21 per cent of Tower Hamlets as compared with under 13 per cent as the comparable national figure (i.e. tended open space as a percentage of all settlement). There is clearly no absolute shortage, so what is the reason for the perceived shortage? Dislike was expressed for large quantities of amenity space that served no real purpose and was not, for example, laid out for children's play. At the same time, however, there seemed to be a desire for more landscaping, presumably of a different character from that which already exists. It was thought that play areas should be positioned in the middle of the estate so that they could be kept under surveillance from the surrounding flats, yet if noisy play was located near blocks containing old people, it caused stress and often real suffering.

These conflicts of interest would hardly arise with houses with gardens, where occupiers can please their own taste in landscaping and keep their children under surveillance, while old people have their own buffer zone that helps to insulate them from child noise, broken windows, etc. In a shared estate, however, it is difficult to please everyone. The mapping of play areas was intended to show whether they are desirable or undesirable on balance.

General comments

As compared with the 436 comments on design there were 137 comments on other topics of concern to the interviewees: lack of facilities such as clubs, lack of community spirit, the presence of an undesirable type of tenant, the location and age of the building, and the limited powers of tenants to exercise control. These things will be touched upon later. They are separate from design although not necessarily unconnected.

A comprehensive picture of design in the study area is given in Fig. 4a. There is a separate graph for each of the 15 design variables, in which the horizontal axis is marked with the range of design values, and the percentage number of blocks with each value is drawn as a vertical column. Reassuringly, most blocks are concentrated at the low end of each

---

FIG.4. Frequency distributions of values of the 15 design variables, (a) by blocks and (b) by dwellings. The non-numerical values are labelled as follows. Storeys per dwelling: F−flats, M−maisonettes, Mx−mixed. Corridor type: L−landings, B−balconies, E−external corridors, I−internal corridors. Entrance position: F−flush with the street, S−set back, I−inside the estate. Entrance type: C−communal only, I−individual and communal. Stilts and garages: A−absent, P−present. Spatial organisation: a−semi-public multiple small blocks, b−semi-public single block, c−semi-confused single, d−confused single, e−semi-confused multiple, f−confused multiple, g−row blocks. Play areas: N−none, C−children's, H−hard-surfaced games areas, B−both types.

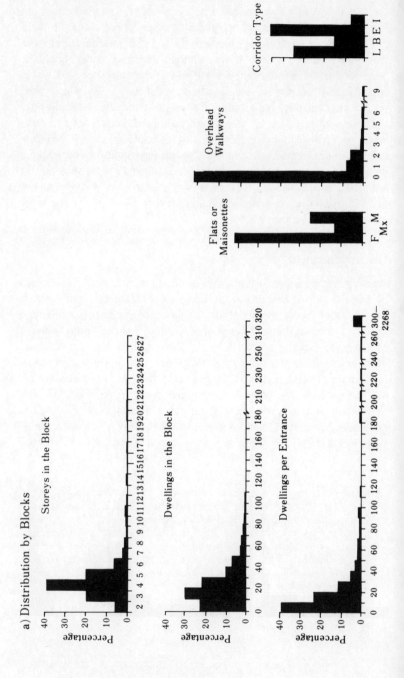

a) Distribution by Blocks

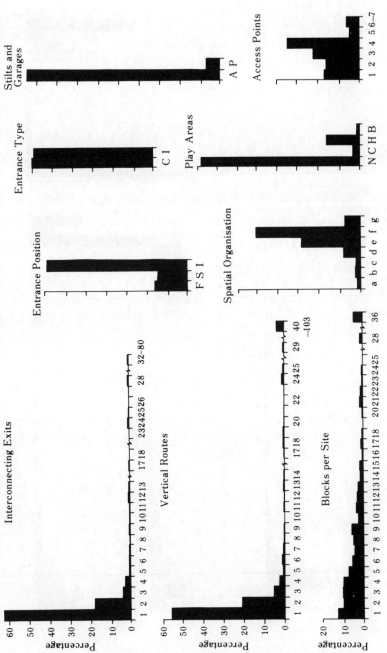

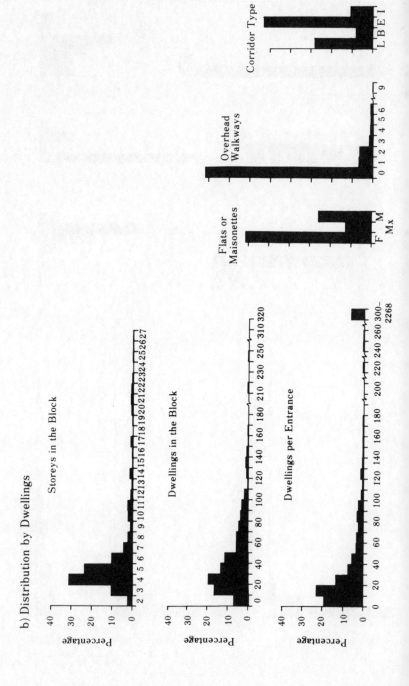

b) Distribution by Dwellings

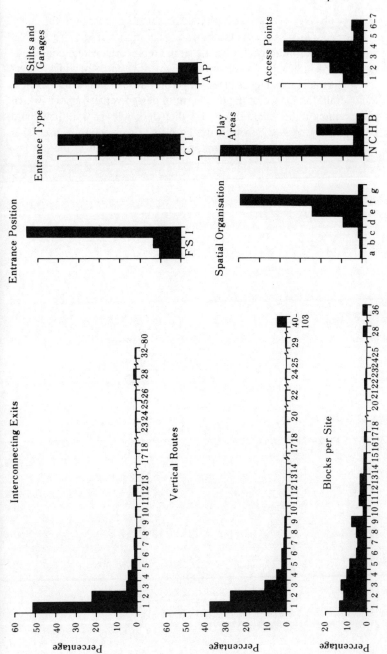

scale, with very few at the high and presumably most harmful end.

However, in some cases the blocks at the high end are larger, so it is possible that more people reside in the more detrimental conditions than Fig. 4a indicates. To test this we have drawn Fig. 4b, which counts dwellings rather than blocks. This shows only a small shift in the balance; the overall dominance of the less harmful design values remain, which is something to be thankful for. Bad though conditions are, they could be so much worse—if, in fact, design does affect social malaise. This is the crucial question which we are now ready to put to the test.

when ~~when~~ dwellings as applied to blocks is counted trends stay similar .... larger blocks are, therefore, not more likely to suffer.

V | Case for the Prosecution

The evidence has been assembled and the trial can begin. Attention must now be focused upon the technical analysis on which the case depends. There are 15 suspects charged with contributing to various forms of social malaise and we have to establish whether they are guilty or not guilty.

The case advanced by the prosecution takes the form of trend-line graphs in which design values are marked along the horizontal scale and percentages on the vertical scale. Trend lines are drawn to show how each test measure increases or decreases as a percentage of the blocks having each successive design value.

We can interpret the trends by comparing them with four simple cases, drawn in Fig. 5. These are imaginary extremes, but they illustrate what to look for in the real graphs. The first one, (a), assumes that the design has no effect whatsoever, so that each test measure occurs in the same percentage of blocks regardless of how the design changes. This results in horizontal lines. The second one, (b), assumes just the opposite, that design has maximum effect. In this case the best design value would be completely abuse-free and the trend lines would fan out from zero. Graphs (c) and (d) repeat the same two assumptions, but also allow for other influences that introduce seemingly random fluctuations. If these are very strong they may mask the effect of design completely.

Dwellings in the block

As the sharing of territory by different households is regarded as the basic reason why flats generate more problems than houses, the most obvious suspect is the size of the block. Its trend lines are shown in Fig.6, which is a mine of information, providing six different clues.

The *first* and clearest clue is the fact that all six lines tend to rise from left to right, showing that as block size increases, more blocks are affected by each kind of social malaise. The trends are disturbed by fluctuations, but compared with the simplified cases in Fig. 5, they are clearly most like (b), where design has maximum effect.

55

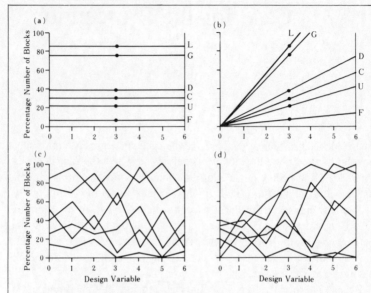

FIG.5. Idealised trend lines for four contrasted cases. The horizontal axes represent design values, and the vertical axes show what percentage of the blocks have each type of abuse. In (a) the design has no effect upon abuse, whereas in (b) it is the sole influence. Cases (c) and (d) are similar to (a) and (b), but disturbed by the presence of other factors. L−litter, G−graffiti, D−damage, C−children in care, U−urine, F−faeces.

The *second* clue is the relative magnitude of the six measures. From the top of the graph to the bottom their order is litter, graffiti, vandal damage, children in care, urine and faeces. For the most part they rise in harmony, an arrangement which fits the idea that civilised niceties disappear in a definite order. Mild taboos are broken by more people than stronger ones, and it will be seen later that the same order is maintained by all the other designs.

The *third* clue is the fact that the trend lines do not begin at zero. Even though smallest blocks are the best, they are by no means abuse-free. Possible reasons may be that even the smallest blocks are worse than houses, or that other design variables are encouraging abuses that would not occur on the strength of block size alone, or that non-design factors are exerting an influence.

Fourthly, the trend lines are not completely smooth. Irregularities are most likely where there are only small numbers of blocks. At each design

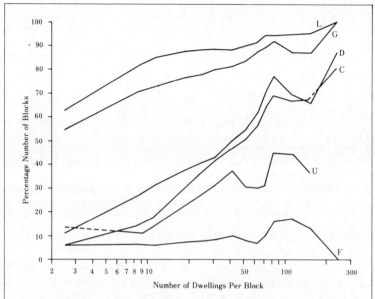

FIG.6. Trend lines for the number of dwellings in the block. All the test measures are commoner in larger blocks, but as there are fewer of these, the lines are less regular. The urine line is shorter because maximum block size is smaller in Tower Hamlets.

value some of the blocks are abused, shown by the space below the trend line, and some are abuse-free, shown by the space above the trend line. Where there are only a few blocks it may be quite accidental whether they are abused or abuse-free. Large numbers of observations, on the other hand, are likely to represent the proportions accurately, and there are standard ways of combining adjacent sets of observations to smooth out minor irregularities on the graph and clarify its basic trend. A slight smoothing of this type has been used here and is explained in Appendix I, but a few irregularities remain. The faeces curve tails off in the largest blocks, which number only eight.

The *fifth* clue is the steepness of each trend line which can be measured as the range between the lowest percentage and the highest. The range figure answers the question 'What percentage of the largest blocks have abuse problems additional to those occurring in the smallest blocks?' Table 4 shows that the range figures are substantial.

However, it might appear from Fig. 6 that the various forms of social

TABLE 4   *Range of abuse due to differences in size of block*

	Lowest %	Highest %	Range
Litter	62.7	100.0	37.3
Graffiti	54.5	100.0	45.5
Damage	11.2	87.5	76.3
Children in care	5.8	80.8	75.0
Urine	11.0*	45.2*	34.2
Faeces	6.0	17.6*	11.6

Note that the adjusted figures for children in care and urine do not affect the magnitude of the range (Appendix I).
* If the smallest percentage does not occur with the smallest blocks or the greatest percentage with the largest blocks, a more extreme percentage is quoted, provided that it is within two steps from the relevant end of the trend line.

malaise do not increase as fast as the number of dwellings in the block. This is a misleading impression as the graph shows only how many blocks are affected and not the increasing intensity of abuse within each block. Graffiti, for example, is no more than an occasional scrawl in the smallest blocks, but is a copious cover of many surfaces in the largest.

Is the increase merely proportional to the larger populations in larger blocks? If there are 10 times as many dwellings it would be only reasonable to expect 10 times as much litter, etc., and in that case it could not be argued that design was having any effect. To clarify this point it is necessary to calculate abuse levels per dwelling as well as per block, and this has been done in Fig. 7.

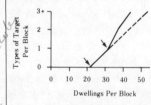

FIG.7. Vandal damage related to the number of dwellings per block. The number of types of target actually attacked (solid line) increases faster than the pro rata number predicted from the number of dwellings (broken line). Individual acts of vandalism (not shown) appear to increase even faster than types of target.

If we take all blocks without vandal damage, we find that their average size is 22 dwellings, whereas blocks with one type of target have an average of 32. This is an increase of one target per 10 dwellings, a rate which, if population size is the only factor, should be maintained, as shown by the broken line. In reality, however, there is a faster rate of increase, shown by the continuous line and, clearly, population size is not a sufficient explanation. The design decision to concentrate people

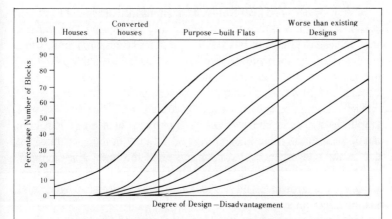

FIG.8. Stylised S-shaped growth curves for the six test measures. The commonest types of abuse arise where designs are only slightly disadvantaging and spread rapidly to all blocks. The less common, more serious, abuses begin where designs are worse and spread more slowly. They would not spread to all blocks unless designs became more disadvantaging.

in larger blocks is at fault.

This conclusion is reinforced by considering the 1,800 houses that we surveyed in inner city locations. Only 12 cases of vandal damage were observed, yet if the *same* number of dwellings were to be crowded into blocks with 50-60 flats, there would be over twice as many targets attacked, and each target would be more extensively damaged.

The *sixth* and last clue is gleaned from the shape of the trend lines. The top pair appear broadly convex, the middle pair are straighter and the bottom pair somewhat concave. This draws attention to the concave-convex, or S-shaped, curve that is frequently used to represent natural or economic growth. If the height of a growing tree, for example, is graphed throughout its lifetime, the curve progressively steepens in a concave arc as its youthful growth accelerates, and then progressively flattens in a convex arc, as its growth slows down in old age. Could it be that the growth in the frequency of abuse with increasing block size has some affinity with the classic S-shaped growth curve?

Fig. 8 consists of six stylised curves showing how this pattern of growth might apply to the six test measures used in the trial of housing design. The lines are spaced out from left to right in order of litter, graffiti, damage, children in care, urine and faeces, and are progressively flatter in the same order. The later forms of social malaise are not only slower to appear, but also slower to grow once they do appear. Two vertical lines enclose the range of block sizes found in the research area, while the outer zone to the right corresponds to blocks larger than 317 flats, and that to the left corresponds to houses. In the relevant central section, the litter and graffiti lines occupy the convex upper part of their S-shape, damage and children in care occupy the straighter middle part, and urine and faeces the lower concave part. A faint resemblance to this pattern can be seen in the trend lines of Fig. 6, not only in the curvature, but also in the convergences and divergences of the lines. For example, graffiti progressively overtakes litter, while urine and faeces diverge from damage. The growth of the various measures appears to have some quantitative similarity to growth in general.

Thus, in varying degrees, all six clues in the trend-line graphs indicate that building size is guilty, as charged, of contributing to social malaise. The differences between smallest and largest blocks show that the contribution is substantial and it is also clear that various kinds of abuse develop in the sequence suggested by the taboo hypothesis. So although the effect of design is considered probabilistic rather than deterministic, the probabilities are beginning to correspond with certain broad regularities.

Dwellings served by each entrance

Is building size operating alone, or does it have accomplices among the other suspected design variables? We next examine another suspect which Oscar Newman found to be even more culpable in promoting crime: the number of dwellings served by each entrance.

Some blocks are divided into self-contained sections shared by fewer households than the block as a whole, and the most finely divided blocks are only about half as likely to be abused as the smallest whole blocks. At the other end of the scale, where blocks are linked together by overhead walkways, the number of dwellings accessible from a given entrance is expanded to include those in neighbouring blocks. Consequently, the trend lines for this variable are steeper, and the range figures are greater, even than those for block size, and its malign influence seems clear. Not only is a verdict of guilty strongly indicated, but it also seems possible that this design is a ringleader among the 15 suspects.

Fig. 9a shows that the trend lines are clear and steep up to a design value of about 85 dwellings per entrance. This accounts for 87.5 per

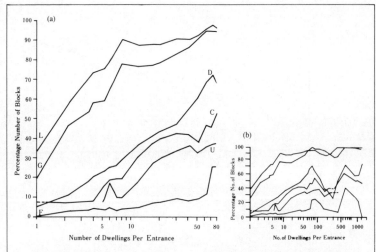

FIG.9. Trend lines for the number of dwellings served by each entrance. The large graph shows a fairly steady increase up to 80 dwellings, which includes 87.5 per cent of all blocks. The small graph shows irregularities where the remaining 12.5 per cent are spread thinly over a wide range of values from 80 to 2,268 dwellings. These are mainly blocks of varying size linked together by overhead walkways.

cent of all blocks, most of which are free-standing without walkways. The remaining minority is thinly spread over a wide range of values from 85 to 2,268 dwellings, and 88 per cent of them have walkways. In some cases the total number of interaccessible dwellings is made up by small inter-linked blocks and in other cases by large ones and the influence of the block size may be responsible for irregularities that are more conspicuous on the graph than the small numbers of blocks warrant. This is why they are shown on a smaller inset, Fig. 9b.

Number of storeys in the block

The most notorious suspect is the height of the building, the trend-line evidence for which is shown in Fig. 10. While there is a clear rise from left to right, the overall range is not quite so large as for either of the two size variables already found guilty. At 41.1 per cent, the mean range is only the third highest (Table 6).

The trend lines are less irregular than those for dwellings per entrance, suggesting that this suspect is a smoother character. A scale consisting

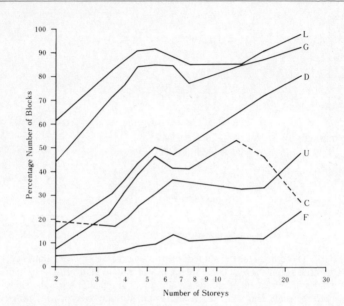

FIG.10. Trend lines for the number of storeys in the block. A general increase in each test measure is interrupted at 5-6 storeys, where child densities have been reduced in buildings with lifts. The children-in-care line falls abruptly in the highest blocks, probably because the social services have arranged transfers for families with the most serious child problems.

of whole storeys is somewhat coarser than one based on individual dwellings, and this may be the reason why minor fluctuations do not show up. However, there are noticeable dips at about six storeys, which probably reflect a definite disturbing factor. The Home Office found only one factor strong enough to disturb the effect of building height: child density. Oscar Newman found two: the ratio of teenagers to adults and the proportion of single-parent families with female heads on welfare. All three seem to be different ways of measuring a factor also identified as detrimental by Jane Jacobs: a low ratio of adults to minors.

Housing authorities have reduced the number of families with children in high-rise blocks, if only by not moving fresh families in when existing ones move out. Children are still housed in the lowest four storeys, which are regarded as a walk-up layer, and teenagers are still permitted at all levels as they can manage the lifts, but as teenagers grow into adults, child pressure is definitely alleviated. In blocks of five or six storeys, the relatively child-free upper floors are reflected in a flattening of the trend lines; above this an actual drop occurs. However, it is shortlived. The troughs set each trend line back to a lower level but do not stop their continued rise thereafter as the design continues to worsen. Child density appears to affect absolute frequencies but does not mask the differential between good and bad design values.

We still have to account for two more fluctuations in individual trend lines. One occurs at the end of the children-in-care curve, which follows the damage curve up to 12 storeys and then dips sharply down. This may reflect the special efforts made by social workers to have families with known child problems moved out of the worst blocks. The other deviation is the fact that the urine curve is slightly higher at two storeys than at three. This does not seem explicable in terms of child density, and may perhaps be an accident due to the presence of alcoholics. Little can be concluded about it on the strength of a single design. It may be that people in a state of inebriation are desensitised to the normal restraints of social mores, and pollute blocks that would not normally be abused.

In spite of these disturbing factors, the trend lines for building height testify that this suspected design, too, is guilty as charged. Its range of influence is smaller than the two variables already discussed, so it does not live up to its reputation as the worst feature of modern design, but it may be that the range was greater before the drive to reduce child densities. If so, its notoriety as the leading suspect may have been more justified a decade ago.

Storeys in the dwelling

Maisonettes, with two storeys in the dwelling, are intended for larger families and probably have higher child densities than single-storeyed flats; they are definitely worse abused. Fig. 11 shows that blocks with mixed layers of flats and maisonettes are intermediate for four of the test measures but worst for children in care and urine pollution. It may be that the mixed design causes the noise and hassle of numerous children to impinge at close quarters upon childless households that find it hard to tolerate. Elderly people may no longer have the stamina to cope with boisterous youth and resent bad behaviour that was rare in their own young days when there was no plague of flats. There may also be single people or childless couples who have no experience of anti-social mores in their own families, and whose nerves may be frayed by the relent-lessness of the impact. They may attempt to admonish children in ways

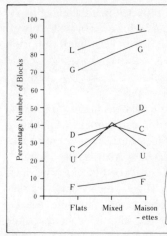

FIG.11. Trend lines for the number of storeys in the dwelling. Four measures worsen from flats to mixed blocks to maisonettes, but children in care and urine both peak in mixed blocks. Children are not necessarily worse behaved in mixed blocks, but they impinge more closely upon childless households, which may lead to more official complaints and care orders.

that have been successful in other times and places, only to unleash a spate of insolence and render themselves targets for future malice. Their complaints may be the last straw for parents who are themselves tense with the trials of family life in flats, and children may have to be placed in care, not because the mixed design encourages worse abuses than maisonettes only, but because it maximises confrontation. The problems of sharing residential space are all the more acute when the residents have no basic community of interest.

Community of Interest is the title of a book by Oscar Newman, who advocates segregating people by their lifestyle. He has demonstrated the new lease of life that accrues to older people when they escape from the badgering and hectoring of mixed communities to live in apartment buildings with people of their own generation. Conversely, the parent and child age groups benefit by shedding censure and constraint. But child densities have also been increased and children are deprived of a range of adult models who could help them integrate into adult society, so it may be that the immediate solution will have adverse side-effects for the maturing generation. This dilemma is completely outflanked in streets of houses where a mix of generations can co-exist successfully because each household has recognised and respected territorial autonomy.

Overhead walkways, interconnecting exits and vertical routes

Fig. 12 shows clearly rising trend lines for the number of overhead walkways linking blocks together above ground level. Walkways not only

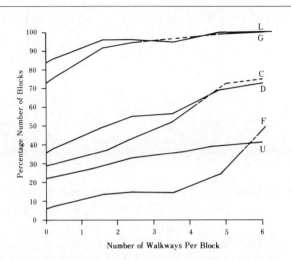

FIG. 12. Trend lines for the number of overhead walkways radiating from each block. The absence of walkways is preferable to their presence. The children-in-care line exceeds the damage line where there are five or more walkways, possibly because families with child problems have been transferred from high buildings to lower blocks with walkways.

function as escape routes in themselves, but also increase the range of three other variables. More dwellings become served by any one entrance, more exits become interconnecting, and so do more vertical routes. The combined effect is to knit blocks of dwellings together into a great communal anthill riddled with passages, which intensify anonymity and escape routes (Table 5).

TABLE 5 *How walkways affect other design variables*

| | Maximum value of the variable in blocks | |
	Without walkways	With walkways
Dwellings per entrance	317	2268
Interconnecting exits	24	80
Vertical circulation	24	103

The trend lines for interconnecting exits and vertical routes (Figs. 13 and 14) are less regular than those for most of the preceding variables. However, they are mostly quite smooth up to a value of five, which includes the majority of the blocks. The subsequent fluctuations repre-

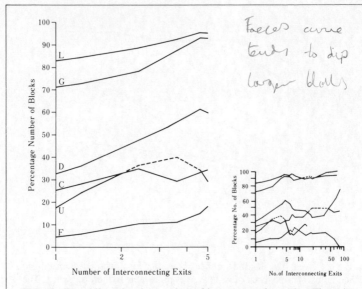

FIG.13. Trend lines for the number of interconnecting exits. There is a general increase in abuse up to five exits, which includes 89 per cent of all blocks. The other 11 per cent are spread over values of 6 to 80 exits, and the irregularities may be due to the fact that these are mainly blocks of varying size linked together by overhead walkways.

sent only 11-14 per cent of the blocks, and are far lesser disturbances numerically than they appear visually on the graph.

Dwellings per entrance, interconnecting exits and vertical routes all have large irregular dips in their trend lines at the worse design values, which are largely made up of blocks with walkways. The interlinking of different numbers of blocks of different sizes may account for the fluctuations and there may also be a side-effect of the policy of reducing child densities. As the policy is directed specifically at tall blocks, its effect upon other variables would be incidental, producing dips that are more uneven and spread out, and hence more conspicuous.

The same three variables are also alike in the tailing off of the children-in-care curve. This feature, too, matches the curve for number of storeys and may reflect the policy of removing problem families from the highest blocks. Other characteristics in common are non-conforming curves for urine pollution and a sudden drop at the end of the faeces curve; the latter irregularity seems to occur in the same few blocks in each case.

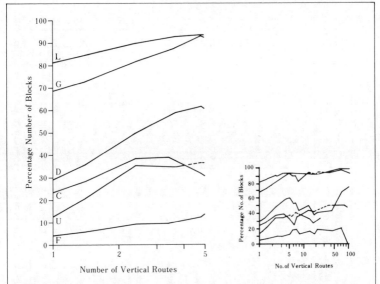

FIG.14. Trend lines for the number of interconnecting vertical routes: lifts and staircases. The general increase of up to five routes accounts for 86 per cent of the blocks. The irregularities in the other 14 per cent may reflect the fact that these are mainly blocks of varying size linked together by overhead walkways.

Table 6 sets out the range figures for each test measure and each design and also, in the last column, the averages of the six ranges. Although the other designs have somewhat lower mean ranges than the three leading size variables, they are still substantial, especially overhead walkways.

All these things add up to the undesirability of anthill designs riddled with walkways, passages between exits, lifts, staircases and ramps. Fortunately, however, the worst excesses of all these variables can be cut by a single solution: the removal of overhead walkways.

Corridor type

Corridors also contribute to the anthill effect. They are classified on grounds of anonymity into short balconies and landings, and longer external and internal corridors, and, as expected, the shorter types are the less abused (Fig. 15). They are also classified on grounds of surveillance into external balconies and corridors, and internal landings and corridors, but here the expectation is not wholly fulfilled. Internal corridors are

TABLE 6 Ranges between lowest and highest test-measure percentages

	Litter	Graffiti	Damage	Children in care	Urine	Faeces	Mean range
Size variables							
Dwellings per block	37.3	45.5	76.3	75.0	34.2*	11.6	46.7
Dwellings per entrance	67.2	80.1*	70.4	44.4	55.6	28.3	57.7
Storeys per block	36.3	48.3	65.5	47.0*	30.9*	19.1	41.1
Storeys per dwelling	10.5	17.0	14.3	13.2	21.2	6.5	13.8
Circulation variables							
Overhead walkways	16.1	27.5	36.6	52.0	19.8	44.0	32.6
Interconnecting exits	16.7	23.5*	42.8	25.4*	12.5*	13.7*	22.4
Vertical routes	18.3	28.9*	46.2	27.6*	21.8*	17.5*	26.7
Corridor type	16.0	19.9*	24.8	27.6	23.1*	12.3	20.6
Entrance characteristics							
Entrance position	1.7	6.6*	8.5*	17.7*	13.3*	3.0	8.5
Entrance type	9.4	10.9	10.8	13.4	11.0	2.8	9.8
Stilts and garages	0.3	4.9	10.0	2.6	17.6	4.1	6.6
Features of the grounds							
Spatial organisation	30.4	41.1*	33.4	26.4	46.4	9.3*	31.2
Blocks in the site	20.3	34.6	9.7*	19.7	−22.9*	8.7	11.7
Access points	19.8	24.5	24.3*	28.9	35.0	15.1	24.6
Play areas	4.2	9.0	11.1	9.9	7.3	1.1	7.1

* Range calculated from a lowest or highest percentage that refers to a design value that is not quite the best or worst. See Appendix I.

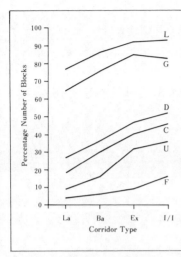

FIG.15. Trend lines for corridor type. Landings (La) and balconies (Ba), with up to four dwellings, are less abused than long external corridors (Ex) or the combined class of internal and intermediate corridors (I/I).

worst, as expected, but internal landings are the best of all. This suggests that anonymity is a stronger influence than surveillance.

Why should landings without surveillance have less abuse than balconies with surveillance? It may well be that blocks with internal landings are more likely to be defended by entrance doors, while those with open balconies are merely served by gaping apertures. A door appears to be an effective physical or psychological defence of residential space and Celia Redknap has shown that entrances with closed doors were eight times as likely to be litter-free as those where doors had been removed. They were 10 times as often graffiti-free, three times as often damage-free, and four times excrement-free. Blocks with long external corridors are also less likely to have doors than those with internal corridors. They more readily admit passing drunks, which may help explain the steep rise in the urine curve. (Door/hole is a now a sixteenth variable.)

Intermediate corridors, having potential surveillance on one side only, prove to be worse abused than any other type. In practice, they do not seem to have surveillance from either side, as their dwellings are windowless and they face away from public observation from the street. There are few of them and consequently they have been absorbed into the internal corridor category.

The mean range for corridor type is 20.6 per cent. This is rather less than for vertical routes and interconnecting exits, but the trend lines are steadier, and corridors certainly loomed larger in the minds of our interviewees. Perhaps if we had counted the actual number of dwellings

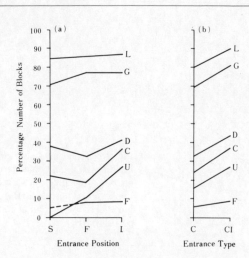

FIG.16. Trend lines for entrance position and entrance type. Entrances positioned inside the estate (I) are worse than those facing the street. Those flush with the street (F) are generally worse than those set back a little (S), but better for damage and children in care. Blocks with communal entrances only (C) average better than those that also have individual front doors to ground floor flats (CI), but the graph does not show a discovery made elsewhere: if individual doors are fronted by semi-private gardens, abuse levels fall below those for blocks with communal entrances only.

per corridor instead of using a break point of four, there might have been a bigger contrast between the smallest and largest values of the design. This would have yielded a larger range and reflected the residents' concern more faithfully. But even without this refinement, the evidence on corridors strongly reinforces the conclusion that 'small is beautiful'.

Entrance position

The fact that entrances are less abused when provided with doors turns attention to other aspects of entrances. Oscar Newman investigated entrance position and found that those located *flush with the street* were safer than those *set back* a little, which were, in turn, safer than those *inside the estate* and screened from the view of people on the street. He showed that the distance from the street to the entrance is a rough measure of the risk of being mugged en route.

For our present test measures, however, the role of entrance position is less clear cut. In the first place, there are 366 blocks which have entrances in at least two of the positions, and a whole range of testing was required before deciding how they should be classified. It emerged that mixed blocks with any entrances flush with the street were best included in the flush category, while those with a combination of set-back and inside-the-estate entrances were best included with inside the estate.

A second source of confusion is the fact that entrance position does not have the same effect on all the test measures. For vandal damage, which comes closest to Newman's crime and vandalism measure, his findings are confirmed. Flush with the street is definitely the best and inside the estate definitely the worst. The same order holds good for children in care. For all the other measures the set-back position proves the best, while flush with the street is variable. It is intermediate for litter, faeces and urine and marginally the worst for graffiti (Fig. 16a).

On balance it seem that a set-back entrance is to be recommended, but in view of the result for vandalism, it should not be set far back.

Entrance type

Entrance type is the next design to be considered. We expected separate front doors for ground-floor flats to be better than communal entrances for all dwellings but this has proved to be untrue for every test measure (Fig. 16b).

This is the first and only case of a shared design feature being better than one giving autonomy to separate households, and it demands explanation. One possibility is the fact that two-thirds of the blocks having only communal entrances have advantageous short corridors whereas 80 per cent of those with individual front doors have disadvantageous long corridors. It may be that the more powerful corridor design is overshadowing any benign tendency inherent in separate entrances.

Another possible explanation is that individual doors would be superior if they opened into semi-private front gardens, allowing each family to control its own territory. In practice, however, there is usually no separate territory to control; the doors open directly into common space. The absence of any buffer zone at all appears even less satisfactory than the shared buffer zone of hallways and staircases separating dwellings from communal entrances. In this context the individual front door seems to be the beginning of a good idea which does not work because it is incomplete. If it can be completed by adding front gardens with fences and gates it might prove successful.

This idea has been tested in the Mozart Estate, Westminster, where individual front doors are fronted by a much better approximation to front gardens than is normal in Tower Hamlets or Southwark. There the abuse levels associated with separate doors are substantially lower than those in blocks with communal entrances only, and the anomaly is resolved.

Wandsworth Council has recently introduced fully fenced and gated front gardens for ground-floor flats in the Surrey Lane Estate, Battersea. This has apparently caused a marked change in children's behaviour. Instead of merely assembling in anonymous hordes, they have to come through the gate and ring the door bell for friends, and consequently they talk to parents and become more integrated into the community. A different atmosphere has developed, with positive side-effects such as a better use of play areas, where both adults and children now gather. It seems quite likely that if entrance type had been mapped in conjunction with gardens, its mean range would have emerged as greater than the 9.8 per cent shown in Table 6.

Blocks raised above stilts or garages

Fig. 17 shows the effect of lifting the residential part of the block up above ground level by means of concrete stilts or ground-floor garages. In most cases these features exclude dwellings on the ground-floor, and residents cannot see who goes into the entrance, so lack of surveillance may be responsible for the fact that the presence of stilts or garages attracts more abuse than their absence. Fig. 17 demonstrates that stilts generally have a worse effect than garages, perhaps because the latter afford a reason for residents to frequent them, which may substitute to some extent for the lack of surveillance from windows. Car owners not only visit garages to take the car out and put it away, but also spend longer periods washing and repairing their vehicles and loading or unloading them. This may provide opportunities for public acquaintance-ship to develop, leading people to keep a watchful eye on neighbours' garages as well as their own. Garages have the lowest mean range of all the designs, but even so they appear to double the risk of urine pollution in the entrances, possibly because their blank faces give the block an impersonal air which fails to signal that people's living space is being violated. There may also be a higher rate of vandalism than could be observed. Westminster Housing Department stresses the need

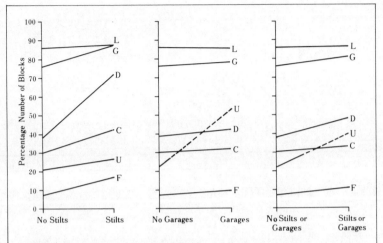

FIG.17. Trend lines for stilts designs, garage designs, and the two together. The absence of these features is better for all test measures.

for quick repair of damaged garages, not only to protect their contents but also because doorless spaces are used for rubbish dumping and become a health hazard.

Garages in blocks of flats are particularly hazardous when they are designed as two infacing ranks with no external surveillance. On the notorious North Peckham Estate, garages of this type are often used for bringing stolen cars and motor cycles in order to indulge in the sport of setting fire to them. Outfacing garages, like external corridors, do not quite plumb the same depths, but they too must be pronounced guilty, and so must the concrete stilt design.

Spatial organisation

Like Newman we found spatial organisation important but difficult to survey. The three-digit method described on page 46 was not available during the original research, when the clearest result involved the nine categories in Fig. 18. The mean range is 31.2 for purpose-built flats but increases to 48.2 when inner-city houses are included to represent semi-private space.

Semi-private house-gardens are clearly the best, followed by former semi-private turned semi-public as a result of converting houses into small

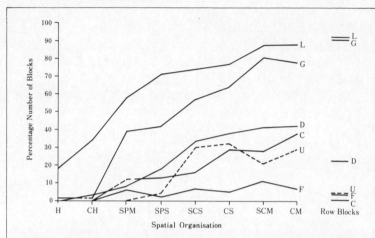

FIG. 18. Trend lines for spatial organisation. The graph begins with houses (H) and converted houses (CH) where each form of social malaise except litter is negligible. For purpose-built blocks, the test measures generally increase from semi-public multiple sites (SPM) to semi-public single-block sites (SPS), to semi-confused single-block sites (SCS), to confused single-block sites (CS), to semi-confused multiple sites (SCM) to confused multiple sites (CM). Row blocks are shown in a separate column as they do not fit the normal sequence; nor does urine which is shown as a broken line.

numbers of flats. For both of these the only appreciable form of abuse is litter, as shown in Chapter VII.

Purpose-built blocks are grouped in seven classes. Six of them are single-block and multi-block variants of semi-public, semi-confused and confused space, and in general the single-block classes precede the multi-block in the order listed. There is, however, a notable exception; multi-block semi-public sites prove to be better than any kind of single block. When these are checked on the map, they prove to contain two, three or four small blocks oriented at an angle to each other, and occasionally arranged round a courtyard. They are all visible from the street, which ensures some degree of surveillance by the public, but even more important in surveillance terms is the fact that residents can see both outward and across the site, and observe who enters the grounds and buildings. This recalls the fact that Oscar Newman thought windows in projecting wings afforded better surveillance than flat frontages.

Surveillance is also technically possible among the buildings of multi-block semi-confused and confused sites but in practice it rarely ameliorates the test measures, which are worse than in single-block sites. It appears that these blocks are larger and more anonymous so that surveillance is less effective. People do not generally watch out for other blocks, although they still do so for their own if they can observe the entrances. The importance of such surveillance was specifically tested by Celia Redknap who classified entrances according to whether they were visible from windows or doors of ground-floor flats in the same block. Observable entrances were three times as likely to be litter-free and twice as likely to be graffiti-free and damage-free; they are also only half as often polluted by excrement. Unfortunately, about a quarter of the entrances she surveyed were designed to be invisible from any resident's dwelling.

The remaining type of spatial organisation, blocks arranged in a contiguous row, is separated from the rest in Fig. 18, as it does not fit consistently into the overall sequence. Among the seven purpose-built classes they are best for numbers of children in care, second best for the two kinds of excrement, third for damage, and worst for litter and graffiti. It may be recalled that they have a hybrid form of spatial organisation. For example, some are semi-public at the front and con-fused at the back – which may account for the inconsistency. They could, perhaps, be redeemed if the common space at the back were fenced off as semi-public spaces serving separate blocks.

Confused space can easily be divided into single-block, semi-public space, and then subdivided into semi-private front and back gardens for ground-floor dwellings. Semi-private space is inappropriate below high-rise, where anonymous upstairs tenants may drop heavy objects. Low-rise tenants refrain from doing so, as they know they would be identified; even eight-storeyed maisonette blocks have only three dwellings above the bottom one. This height is exceeded by only 5.5 per cent of the blocks, so semi-private gardens could become the norm.

Blocks within the site boundary

As spatial organisation is a complex variable, some of its simpler com-ponents have been studied separately. The first of these is the number of blocks sharing the same site. It has already been demonstrated that single-block sites are generally a better form of spatial organisation than multi-block, which is confirmed by Fig. 19, but the trend is not as clear as with other design variables, and urine pollution shows a definite decrease as the number of blocks increases. It is suggested that alcoholics

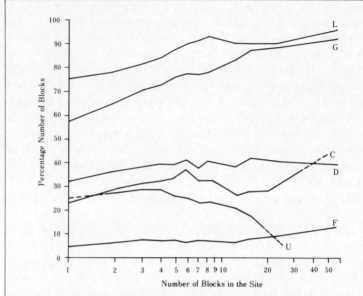

FIG. 19. Trend lines for the number of blocks per site. Urine is an exception to the general rise in abuse with larger numbers of blocks.

may be responsible. Drunks may tend to relieve themselves in nearby entrances accessible along the road rather than exercising the control needed to seek out greater privacy in the interior of the estates. This would mean that the larger the site, the greater the number of blocks that are relatively protected. Another deduction is that if drunks urinate in blocks of relatively good design, they raise the urine percentage, but if they pollute blocks of bad design they affect the percentage less, as these are more likely to be abused by children and animals in any case.

It has several times been suggested to us that dogs, rather than alcoholics, may be responsible for the anomalies in the urine curves, but the curve now under discussion seems to belie this idea. Dogs would have to be very discriminating indeed to urinate consistently less in multi-block estates, especially as they appear to be defecating more in the same ones. It is asking a lot of a dog to differentiate between the two types of excretion. A simpler answer is that dogs are better controlled in blocks where their owners are also able to control other forms of social malaise, and most likely to run loose in the worst estates. They appear to reinforce existing trends rather than cause substantial deviations from them.

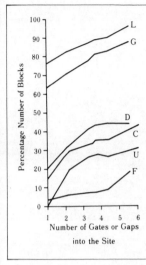

FIG.20. Trend lines for the number of sides of the site which contain an access point from the street. One access point is a better safeguard against abuse than several.

Table 6 shows that the mean range for the number of blocks per site is only 11.7 per cent, which ranks eleventh out of the 15. However, if the anomalous negative trend for urine pollution is set aside, the mean range increases to 18.3 per cent, which is very close to that for corridor type. This suspected variable should definitely be considered guilty.

The effect of numerous blocks would probably emerge as even stronger if all blocks were the same size. As it is, the block is a very rough and ready unit of measurement. It cannot discriminate very sensitively, as the 'best' value is one block regardless of whether it is large or small. Similarly, the 'worst' sites may consist of either tiny or gigantic blocks. Consequently, the percentage values are derived from a mixture of good and bad, and the trend lines are flatter than the importance of the variable would predict. Nevertheless, they clearly show that one-block sites are to be recommended. The phrase 'small is beautiful' applies to estates as well as blocks.

Access from the street

Another component of spatial organisation is number of access points in the site perimeter. These can influence whether outsiders take short cuts across the site and increase the number of people contributing to levels of abuse. The trend lines in Fig. 20 show a smooth steady increase from one to six sides with access points. The mean range is roughly

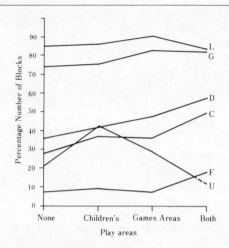

FIG.21. Trend lines for play areas; absence is better than presence. Urine pollution peaks in blocks adjacent to play areas for small children. Litter and graffiti peak near hard-surfaced games areas for older ones. Damage, faeces and children in care peak where both types of play areas occur.

the same size as those for interconnecting exits or vertical routes. This suggests that if the site were securely walled with only one gate, there would be an appreciable drop in the various abuses.

Play areas

The final design variable to be tested is play areas. In spite of the pressure of demand for them, Fig. 21 shows that they are far from being an un-mixed blessing. Their absence is better than their presence for every test measure, presumably because they attract a high density of unsuper-vised children. The various types of play area differ in their effect upon adjacent blocks. The simplest trend is for damage, the probability of which increases when children's play areas are introduced, increases again with hard-surfaced games areas for older children, and reaches a still higher percentage where both age ranges are served. The children-in-care curve is fairly similar. The two excrement curves decline with older playground users, but litter and graffiti peak with teenagers' play provision.

It seems clear that the demand for more play areas in residential estates

TABLE 7 *Relative influence of the fifteen designs*

	Mean range
Strongest designs	
Dwellings per entrance	57.7
Dwellings per block	46.7
Storeys per block	41.1
Overhead walkways	32.6
Spatial organisation	31.2
Spatial organisation including houses	48.2*
Intermediate designs	
Vertical routes	26.7
Access points	24.6
Interconnecting exits	22.4
Corridor type	20.6
Blocks per site (excluding urine pollution)	18.3
Weakest designs	
Storeys per dwelling	13.8
Blocks per site	11.7
Entrance type	9.8
Entrance position	8.5
Play areas	7.1
Stilts and garages	6.6

Figures are mean ranges (percentages) for the six test measures in the 4,099 purpose-built blocks of flats.

* The spatial organisation figure shows the increased range obtained when the semi-private space of house gardens is taken into account. On this basis all the other mean ranges would also increase, in varying degrees (see Chapter VII).

is misconceived. Children can hardly be benefiting if they are learning to litter, bedaub, vandalise and pollute the play area environs, and if they also run a greater risk of having to be placed in care in blocks with play provision nearby. The demand should be refocused on the need for more houses with their semi-private gardens, the conversion of shared grounds into semi-private garden space, and the provision of play areas for the full age range in public parks outside the estate.

Summing up the trend-line evidence

There are 90 individual trend lines and almost all of them show an upward trend, indicating a strong tendency for all six kinds of social malaise to worsen in precisely-known design directions. Table 7 summarises the mean ranges of the six measures, grouping the designs according to their strength.

The five most powerful designs are dwellings per entrance, dwellings per block, number of storeys, overhead walkways and spatial organisation. These, it is submitted, are the ringleaders of the anti-social design gang. The last two may appear to be less powerful than the first three, but this is not necessarily so, as they lead from behind and increase the effect of other suspects. If overhead walkways were removed completely, the worst excesses of dwellings per entrance, vertical routes and interconnecting exits would be curtailed, and if residential space were reorganised to best advantage, the worst values of blocks per site and access points would also be damped down. Bad designs reinforce each other, and this will have to be taken into account when making practical recommendations.

Another general observation is that the test measures always follow the same descending order of magnitude in all 15 of the trend-line graphs. There is only a minor degree of overlapping, and this is mainly in the case of children in care or urine, which were both mapped for one borough only. From this regularity of pattern we can deduce that the various forms of social breakdown tend to occur in a set order as design features worsen to the successive degrees of depravity needed to undermine each social taboo in turn. The effect is a general one, exercised by all the designs, and it is not a question of different designs being responsible for different kinds of behavioural lapse. Design variables appear to exert the same kind of demoralising influence, and the values within each variable affect the degree of demoralisation.

The prosecution rests its case. The contribution made by each suspect to the various forms of social malaise has been demonstrated and the defence is now invited to cross-examine.

VI | Cross-examination

Even an apparently cast-iron case may sometimes break down under cross-examination, and it is now only fair that the case made out against the 15 design variables should be exposed to objections raised by critics. In this chapter the main criticisms that have been made during the course of the research are given a hearing, together with the evidence we have explored to see whether they might be right.

Question 1

> Some of the design variables are a matter of size. Might this perhaps be a sufficient explanation in itself? A large block accommodates more people, who are bound to produce more litter, graffiti, vandal damage, etc, so the test measures may have no real connection with design as such.

This argument seems reasonable, but so too did all the arguments in favour of the new, spacious and green Utopia which has proved so disastrous. The main burden of this book is that reasoning in the abstract can be very misleading. There must be a foundation of fact and reality to argue from, and if we test Question 1 against factual evidence, it does not stand up.

Fig. 7 has already demonstrated that vandal damage increases faster than pro rata in relation to the size of the block. Fig. 22 is a similar example for numbers of children in care. If we take all blocks without children in care, we find that their average size is 21 dwellings, whereas blocks where one household is affected average 35 dwellings. This is an increase of one household per 14 extra flats, and the broken line shows the additional number to be expected on a pro rata basis. The continuous line shows that the actual increase is faster. Blocks with 60 dwellings have 50 per cent more families with a child problem than would be predicted from the number of dwellings alone, and if these buildings had been designed as a larger number of smaller blocks, or better still

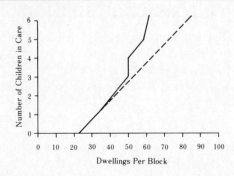

FIG.22. Children in care related to the number of dwellings in the block. The broken line shows the predicted increase as block size increases, while the continuous line shows that the actual increase is faster than the pro rata prediction. Blocks having 50 dwellings have either three or four families with children in care. The number of families predicted for 80-dwelling blocks already occurs in 60-dwelling blocks.

houses, the incidence of children in care would probably have been negligible.

In a wider context we can point to the fact that Southwark's population has decreased by two-thirds since earlier in the century and Tower Hamlets' by three-quarters. Much of the loss was intentionally planned on the assumption that lower densities would improve social conditions, but this they have signally failed to do. On the contrary, almost every measure of social malaise one can think of, from litter and graffiti to mugging and murder, has risen as population has fallen. Whatever the explanation may be, the pro rata hypothesis is definitely untenable.

Question 2

> Have you related the measures of social malaise to the age of the building? Surely the problems you describe are related to obsolescence. Old, cramped buildings without a single blade of grass in sight are wearing out and becoming un-suited to modern lifestyles, and it is not surprising that they give rise to problems.

The obsolescence argument is another superficially reasonable hypothesis — so much so that it has been the mainspring of planned demolition and comprehensive redevelopment. New, green and spacious estates are now legion, providing plenty of factual evidence against which the hypothesis can at last be tested. Is age really a determining factor?

Dates are known for 2,711 blocks, including about 86 per cent of all blocks in Southwark and 42 per cent in Tower Hamlets. Fig. 23a shows their age distribution. Approximately one quarter were built during the first half of the century, and three-quarters during the following 30 years.

Fig. 23 (b-e) show what percentage of the blocks in each age group have litter, graffiti, damage and faeces. The graphs are rather variable, but they certainly do not show the steady decline of abuse over time that the question assumes. On the contrary, the very oldest blocks have the best record for litter, damage and faeces, while those of the 1950s, 60s and 70s are worse. Old blocks may be obsolete in the sense of needing new wiring, heating systems, or kitchen and bathroom fittings, but there is no reason to believe they are worse than modern blocks in terms of community structure or user behaviour. The age hypothesis is not substantiated.

The question of age can be tested further by examining modern blocks designed better than the normal modern idiom. It so happens that there are 15 blocks in Southwark built during the early 1980s, when financial constraints and recognition of the high-rise problem have led to lower, smaller designs. These have much smaller abuse percentages, showing convincingly that it is design and not date that is associated with the various test measures. Nor is it a matter of new blocks not having deteriorated as yet. Some of the late 1970s blocks were mapped when they were equally new, but their worse design was accompanied by worse abuse. The age hypothesis can be discarded completely.

Question 3

> You are suggesting that people's behaviour is determined
> by the housing they live in. Isn't it more likely to be a
> response to bad social conditions such as poverty?

First, let us stress that we are not dealing with determinism. Even in the best housing there may be people who choose to behave badly, and even in the worst there are those who maintain impeccable standards. Bad design does not determine anything, but it increases the odds against which people have to struggle to preserve civilised standards.

Having said that, we agree that poverty sounds a very reasonable influence upon our test measures. We have never claimed that design explains everything, and the trend-line graphs show clearly that it does

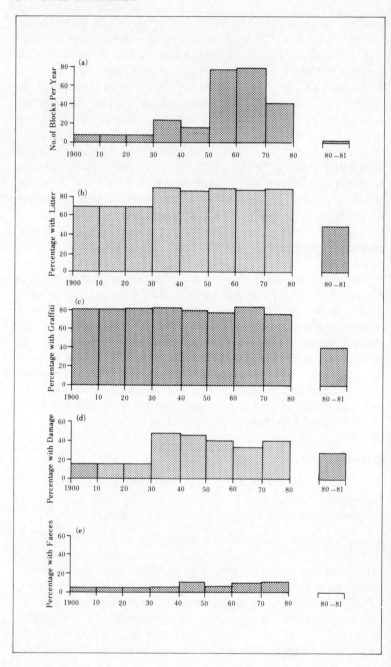

not. There is plenty of room for other factors to play a part as well, and Question 3 asks whether they play an even stronger part than design.

To test this idea we need to relate both design and poverty to the same test measures in the same blocks. The data source for social conditions is the Population Census, which unfortunately does not give figures for individual blocks. It groups them in enumeration districts which normally include a mixture of blocks and houses. Occasionally, however, an enumeration district consists of a single large block or several smaller ones of the same design, and if we select these we can make the comparison. There are 90 such blocks in Southwark, and while this is too few for drawing trendlines it is quite sufficient for correlation.

Correlation measures how closely two phenomena agree with each other. If litter increases as poverty increases, then the correlation is positive, but if opposite changes predominate, the correlation is negative. If the changes are sometimes in the same direction and sometimes in opposite directions, there is no correlation. Positive or negative correlations are regarded as significant when they are strong enough to be more than a purely chance effect.

The Population Census records affluence and poverty in terms of six socio-economic classes. If poverty is the reason for a high incidence of litter, graffiti, vandalism and faeces, as the question assumes, then we should expect to find these test measures positively correlated with the percentage of the population in the three poorest social classes: skilled manual workers, semi-skilled and unskilled. Conversely, we should expect the three more affluent classes, professional, intermediate and skilled non-manual, to be negatively correlated with the test measures.

These expectations are not fulfilled. The three more affluent groups are significantly correlated with the various forms of abuse in a positive and not a negative sense, while the three less affluent groups are not significantly correlated with any of them. This suggests that poverty should be ruled out as a cause of the abuses.

We can apply a different test by singling out a special group that has, by definition, become poorer than it was previously: pensioners. If pensioner poverty is a cause of social breakdown, then the more pensioners

---

FIG.23. Dwelling age related to the incidence of abuse. Graph (a) shows the age distribution of blocks of known date, and (b-e) show the percentages of each age group that have litter, graffiti, damage and faeces respectively. Older blocks are not consistently worse than newer ones but the 15 better-designed 1980s blocks show a noticeable improvement.

there are among the population, the more common we should expect each form of abuse to be.

This expectation, too, proves to be false. The prevalence of pensioners is negatively correlated with the various test measures; the more pensioners present, the less common are all these problems. Old people are a force for good in the community, perhaps because they increase the adult presence and reduce child density. It also has to be remembered that pensioners belong to an age-group which had the advantage of being brought up in houses and they retained their standards of behaviour after becoming flat-dwellers. If it were not for a substantial pensioner presence the concrete jungle would be even more fearsome and degrading than it is.

Question 4

Unemployment is also a form of poverty, and a very demoralising one, which is widespread in the type of inner-city area you have studied. Isn't it more likely to be a cause of social malaise than architectural design?

Unemployment is significantly related to litter and graffiti but not to vandal damage or faeces. It may be that children in families without work are taught greater care of material goods when they cannot easily be replaced, and perhaps the cost of keeping pets may have to be dispensed with. Unemployment is more weakly correlated with graffiti than four design variables, but is marginally the strongest in the case of litter. Overall it appears to be of less significance than design, and its popularity as the supposed source of all kinds of ills seems to be overdone. Unemployment was just as widespread during the Great Depression of the 1930s and the poverty associated with it was even more severe than now, but it was not then accompanied by a great upsurge of litter, graffiti, vandalism or excrement. These things all multiplied during the postwar boom period, and although they have continued into the present depression, they are not caused by it.

Perhaps we should stand the unemployment argument on its head. Is joblessness another form of social malaise that *follows* from the existence of misconceived design? In broad terms the answer is no. There is a world recession accompanied by high unemployment as there was in the 1930s when design was quite different. But if we look at the more detailed distribution of unemployment we find high concentrations in inner cities with post-war housing estates, and we have to ask, 'Why there?' We can envisage a chain reaction in which badly-designed blocks of flats make children less easy to bring up and more likely to become anti-social and uncontrollable. When they go to school, they may well resist educative control and be unwilling to learn, giving the school a reputation as a blackboard jungle and reducing its ability to compete for good teachers. The combination of a high proportion of resistant pupils and a low proportion of gifted teachers leads to poor educational standards and low employability. This is not an improbable sequence of events, so that even if it had been proved that unemployment was a proximate cause of vandalism it would not rule out design as an ultimate cause.

Question 5

> The Home Office (1976) found child density to be the one socio-economic variable that is correlated with vandalism more strongly than design. Doesn't this mean that if families with children are taken out of blocks of flats, design will lose its sting completely?

Local authorities have already reduced child densities in high blocks, so this idea can be tested. An ideal test would be before-and-after surveys of all blocks where all families with children are removed over a short period. Unfortunately, this is impossible to arrange, and we have to make do with inferences from our existing data.

Child densities have gradually been reduced in high-rise blocks, partly because some resident children have grown into adults and partly because families with children are not introduced into flats becoming vacant above the fourth floor. This means that the taller the block, the lower the child density is likely to be, and if it is really the strongest factor, the trend lines ought to decrease from five storeys on. This is not what happens. There is indeed a dip in the trend lines from about five or six storeys (Fig. 10), but it does not continue; the upward direction is resumed. With fewer children the trend becomes geared to a lower baseline, but it does not reverse its overall slope. This indicates that for our 4,099 blocks, number of storeys is a stronger influence than child density, important though the latter is.

The child-density hypothesis can be tested in a different way using census data in relation to the 90 blocks in Southwark mentioned earlier. Two measures of density are the ratio of children under 15 to adults aged 20 or more and the ratio of young people aged 10-19 to adults. These are the nearest age approximations that census data permit. Single-parent

TABLE 8 *The significance of child density*

Child density measure	Litter	Graffiti	Damage	Faeces
Children under 15 as a percentage of adults over 19	*	***	•	•
Young people, 10-19, as a percentage of adults over 19	•	***	•	•
Single-parent families with female heads as a percentage of all households	*	**	**	•

• Not significant	**	Highly significant
* Significant	***	Very highly significant

The table uses data from 90 blocks in Southwark (see text).

families also contribute to high child densities by reducing the number of family adults, and those that are headed by females are likely to have a higher child to adult ratio than those headed by males.

Table 8 shows that child density, unlike poverty, has some relationship with three of the test measures surveyed for all 4,099 blocks, but even so, six of the 12 correlations are not significant, and two more, for litter, are barely significant. Although child density is quite closely related to graffiti, some of the design variables, and also the combined effect of all the designs taken together, are related even more closely. The Home Office studied four designs and found child density to be more strongly correlated with damage than any of them. We have studied 15 designs, and have found child and teenage densities to be *less* strongly correlated with damage than most of them. However, the apparent discrepancy is easily resolved. It is precisely because the perceptive work of the Home Office highlighted the detrimental effect of child density, that density reductions have subsequently taken place and with it, reductions in the power of density as a factor. Frances Reynolds, in a report to the Joseph Rowntree Memorial Trust (1983), has also demonstrated the importance of high child densities and their weakening influence as the children have grown up.

We have tried to place the child-density factor into perspective by means of a scattergram (Fig. 24). We have taken the average child density for each of the 44 wards in Southwark and Tower Hamlets, and plotted it against the corresponding ward average for 'abuse' (i.e. a combination of litter, graffiti, damage and faeces). The lower limit of the scatter has been sketched in as a line rising from left to right. On the

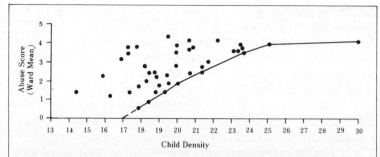

FIG.24. Child density related to abuse score. Child density is plotted along the horizontal axis. Children under 15 are expressed as a percentage of adults over 19 in each ward (1981 population census). The abuse score, a combined measure of litter, graffiti, damage and excrement, is plotted on the vertical axis. Where children are over one quarter as numerous as adults (right hand side of the scattergram), blocks of flats are likely to be badly abused. As child density decreases (towards the left) abuse scores become more varied, reflecting the influence of design. Child densities above 17 per cent (one child to six adults) are not recommended for flats.

right of the graph, child densities are high and are associated with high levels of abuse regardless of design. Moving towards the left, child densities decrease, and permit decreasing abuse levels in the better designed blocks. But they do not bring abuse down in the worse-designed blocks. Abuse remains related to design irrespective of low child densities.

The conclusion is that high child densities are important and can mask the effect of design. The Home Office did invaluable work in promoting density reduction. It should not, however, have gone as far as regarding its significant correlations with design as of no importance. Now that the unmasking has been carried out, design is shown as very important indeed, and the Home Office has subsequently asked County Constabularies to reconsider it as a contribution to crime prevention.

Question 6

> Perhaps the worst-abused blocks are simply those where problem families are concentrated.

None of the local authorities in the study area will admit to having 'sink' estates for problem families. Perhaps they do, but there is some evidence for just the opposite: a dispersal policy based on the hope that unstable families will be less of a problem if they are thinly spread. 'Respectable' families in Southwark complain bitterly about the intrusion of 'rough' elements, and a GLC housing officer has described to us how a single problem family can degrade the quality of life for all the other inhabitants of the block; this has led to the resettlement of offenders in houses with gardens, so that their anti-social behaviour impinges on fewer other people.

Indeed, in 1983 Oxford City Council commissioned an enquiry by I. V. Green into its housing allocation policy but no evidence was found of a grading system to identify households suitable for better or worse accommodation. Prospective tenants expressed more reservations against Blackbird Leys than any other estate, but the main body of their comments focused on the type of housing available, and the presence of flats emerged as a reason for the area's unpopularity. A second factor was the distorted age structure with its high child density resulting from the initial allocation policy, which may also have been partially responsible for the estate's reputation.

Question 7

> Even if there is no definite policy for concentrating problem families, isn't there a tendency for this to happen? The better families would move out of the worst blocks leaving behind the more copeless people who lack the initiative to find a better billet. And newcomers are most likely to be deprived families who are too desperate for accommodation to refuse offers in notorious blocks.

It may well be that there is some kind of multiplier effect reinforcing the bad reputation of certain blocks or estates. But if so, the important question is, 'What created the bad reputation in the first place?' Could it be design? If so, the matter of reputation is not a prime cause, but only part of the mechanism by which bad design results in objectionable user behaviour.

It seems to be true in general that the worst-designed blocks have the worst reputations, and it is therefore of interest to study an estate where a bad reputation has arisen independently of design. Omega Estate in a Midlands city is the anonymous name given for reasons of confidentiality to an area which has been intensively studied by Frances Reynolds. Omega is much better designed than most estates in Tower Hamlets or

Southwark, as it consists largely of houses with relatively few, and relatively innocuous, blocks of flats. It gained its bad name from its initial association, in 1957, with 'immigrant' workers from Wales, Scotland, Ireland and other parts of England, and also from the largely mistaken belief that slum clearance tenants had been dumped there. Once labelled as a problem, the estate was unable to escape this image, and Frances Reynolds has demonstrated how its reputation is reinforced by exaggerated press reports of any incident associated it. Some tenants say they are ashamed of giving their addresses, as they feel that the name of the estate disadvantages them in job applications or obtaining normal services. The estate has become the least popular in the city among people seeking council accommodation and, according to Reynolds, it is often the most desperate and disadvantaged people that accept dwellings there.

Omega, therefore, typifies the situation envisaged in the question, where problem people are claimed as causing the various forms of social breakdown, irrespective of design. To complete this line of reasoning, it would be necessary to show that anti-social behaviour is worse than would be expected from the relatively mild design defects, and more in line with the abnormal concentration of disadvantaged households. Here, however, the argument breaks down. The Design Disadvantagement Team has checked the levels of litter, graffiti and vandal damage that exist there, and found that they are not worse than its design features predict and are not intensified by the supposedly problem population.

We recognise that any area may have a few problem families who behave anti-socially in any case, regardless of design, but Question 7 assumes the existence of problem populations on a much wider scale. Always, to date, the critics have taken a broad theoretical stance. They have not produced independent evidence that the inhabitants of any given estate really are problem people, and certainly not that the worst-abused estates are occupied by worse problem people than the moderately-abused areas. Reynolds has demonstrated a concentration of disadvantaged people in the Omega Estate, but she denies that this automatically makes them problem people. On the contrary, she claims that the vast majority of the residents are, and always have been, decent and hard-working – the victims of an ill-deserved estate image rather than its cause.

It is easy for a circular argument to develop. The buildings have problems which the people are unable to cope with. The people are then labelled as copeless, and this label is used to explain the state of the blocks. No independent measure of whether the people really are less capable is ever fed into the argument, which seems, like others that have been mentioned, to owe its appeal to unsupported reasoning. We have been unable to find any properly tested evidence that substantiates the hypothesis, which is in stark contrast to the wealth of evidence we have assembled on how badly-designed blocks make it difficult for normal people to cope. For example, one of the worst estates included in the survey (North Peckham) is the scene of many rapes and muggings, and was also associated with the July riots of 1981. It might well be considered a sink estate full of problem families, but a spontaneous comment by the local community policeman puts it in a different light:

> 'Don't let anyone tell you these people are scum. They are mostly very decent people trying to do their best in very difficult conditions.'

Question 8

> The staff who look after the buildings must have some effect on the presence of litter, graffiti, vandal damage and excrement. Is the presence or absence of a caretaker a significant factor in the distribution of these test measures?

This question may be crossing its wires on cause and effect. It is the blocks with the worst design features that are most likely to lack caretakers, as the post may be too beset by aggravation to attract applicants. A caretaker represents officialdom and may become the butt of all the resentment that has built up against the housing authority. His home may become a target for vandalism and his family may be threatened with violence. No caretaking job is worth that, and so it is the estates most in need of caretakers are least likely to have them.

The Social Science Research Council even questioned in a letter to us (1984), whether the incidence of psychiatric illness may be related to the quality of caretaking! A logical corollary of this might be that psychiatric disorder would be most widespread in houses, where caretakers are not employed at all. The whole caretaker question highlights the ill-wisdom of creating a brand of Utopia which forces people into dependence upon custodians instead of managing their own lives independently.

Question 9

> It often seems that blocks go downhill once they begin to have 'voids' i.e. empty, boarded-up flats. Perhaps the

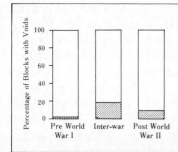

FIG.25. Voids in blocks of different ages. Three age groups are each shown as equal columns, to compare their respective percentages with voids. The oldest blocks have fewest voids, and the inter-war group has the most.

> presence of voids is a stronger influence than design upon the state of litter, graffiti, etc?

We were interested in this possibility at the time of the survey and classified each block as having either 0, 1, 2 or 3 or more boarded-up flats. A total of 232 blocks proved to have at least one, and there is a very highly significant relationship between voids and abuse of the building. However, correlation analysis shows that voids do not exert a stronger influence than design. Their coefficients are weaker than all of the 15 design variables, and must therefore be regarded as a minor factor.

Voids may appear for a variety of reasons. Housing authorities may declare their older properties obsolete, gradually emptying them in readiness for demolition. This seems to be the case in Southwark, where about 90 per cent of inter-war and post-war blocks are publicly owned and the former have substantially more voids than the latter (Fig. 25). However, this policy has relatively little effect on pre-1914 stock, as most of it is owned privately or by housing trusts, and is kept in reasonable repair; consequently it is in demand and has few voids. This suggests that inter-war blocks may be being demolished prematurely and unnecessarily, even though they are better designed than many post-war blocks.

Voids in the newer buildings could result from tenants' rejection of flats on offer in the worst designed blocks, but in general this does not stand up to analysis. Only one variable – number of storeys – is significantly related to empty premises. The evils of high-rise buildings have been so widely publicised that a hard-to-let effect is discernible, but all the other designs are either not significant or negatively significant. This means we must look for a different cause, other than design, to explain the presence of voids.

A strong possibility is the efficiency, or otherwise, of housing management. Westminster, for example, aimed to fill vacancies within a few days, while Southwark was following a procedure for considering applications only once in three months. This meant that if a vacancy occurred soon after an allocation session, the flat was left boarded up for a preliminary three months before even a first attempt was made to let it, and as a result there were over 4,000 unoccupied council dwellings in the borough.

The situation is different in the north of England where the drift of population south has created a dwelling surplus in certain areas. It has been known for tenants to vandalise their blocks in order to make them uninhabitable and force the council to rehouse them in better accommodation known to be available. For them, deliberate damage was the most rewarding strategy they could employ, but this is rarely the case in London where tenants would simply be left to live with unrepaired damage for long periods, and consequently responsible people take good care not to add to the troubles inflicted by wantons.

Question 10

Have you considered the value of facilities such as shops, services, and provision of recreation and entertainment? Surely the inclusion of these in housing estates would help to build up the community structure more successfully.

This is another widely accepted but hitherto untested hypothesis. Among the 4,099 blocks investigated there are 197 which incorporate some kind of facility, and Southwark has been studied in some detail to ascertain how far they are beneficial.

Three sets of trend lines have been drawn (Fig. 26). The first classifies all blocks according to their distance from facilities; whether they are in the block itself, or within 100 metres, or within a distance of 100 to 200 metres, or further away than 200 metres. The second distinguishes whether or not there are facilities within the same site as the block. In both cases the evidence is contrary to the assumption in the question. Far from being a prize feature, a facility attracts outsiders who raise the level of litter, graffiti, damage and faeces above that expected from the residents themselves. Facilities constitute a disturbing factor that interferes with the effect of the 15 designs. Yet they are also design features in themselves, and their power to interfere strengthens the case for an overall relationship between design and the test measures.

However, facilities are needed, and the question of where best to locate

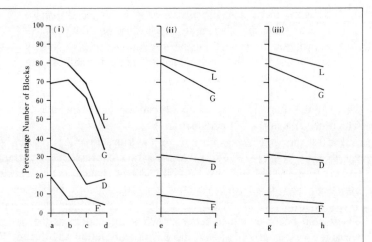

FIG. 26. Trend lines for facilities such as shops, services and community halls. Graph (i) shows decreasing abuse with distance: (a) facility in the block, (b) within 100m, (c) 100-200m, (d) over 200m. Graph (ii) shows a decrease when the facility is outside the estate (f) rather than inside (e). Graph (iii) shows that the distance factor is less influential than location inside or outside the site. Blocks that are closer than 100m but outside the site (h) have less abuse than those which are 100-200m away but inside the site (g).

them has to be considered. It is easy enough to recommend that they should be outside the site boundary where they do not intrude upon residential space, but less easy to argue that they should be 200 metres away from all blocks of flats, as this would require large areas of land to act as buffer zones. The third graph in Fig. 26 is an attempt to resolve this problem by comparing the two distance measures to see which is stronger. The trend lines show that facilities within 100 metres of a block but outside the site boundary have a less deleterious effect than those which are further away but inside, and this indicates that there should be a clear separation of community facilities from the dwellings and their territory. The same thing applies to play areas, which are another type of facility and produce the same detrimental effect upon neighbouring blocks.

Question 11

You seem to have pulled the rug out from under a number of accepted concepts in housing planning and shown that

>design is more strongly correlated with the social malaise
>measures than are other, more expected factors. But you have
>not yet said just how strong the correlations are. Even if they
>are stronger than the other influences, they could still be quite
>weak in absolute terms.

That is quite true, and it opens up a broad aspect of our investigation, which needs a fairly full explanation.

If a test measure always changes in the same direction as a design variable, there is a perfect positive correlation, expressed by a correlation coefficent of $+1.0$. Conversely, if it always changes in the opposite direction, there is a perfect negative correlation with a coefficient of -1.0. If however, the test measure shows no correspondence with design, but becomes either better or worse at random as the design variable worsens progressively, there is no correlation and the coefficient is 0.0. Strong coefficients are near to $+1.0$ or -1.0, while weak coefficients are nearer to 0.0.

Perfect correlations are quite rare, except in laboratory conditions where disturbing factors can be strictly excluded. Even the simplest phenomena may be disturbed by varying conditions. Sound waves, for example, travel 27 miles per hour faster in warm air at $70°F$ ($21°C$) than they do at freezing point.

Housing design cannot be observed in laboratory conditions. It is exerting its influence out in the real world where all sorts of disturbing factors may occur. Fig. 27 shows a clear rise in both classes of graffiti as the number of dwellings in the block increases, but it is not a simple case of small blocks being graffiti-free, medium-sized having graffiti either inside or outside, and large ones having it both inside and outside. At every block size below the largest, there are some blocks with each of the three graffiti classes, and the reasons for this are manifold. Some of the largest blocks may have been newly redecorated and passing through a brief phase of cleanliness before graffiti inevitably reappears. Some of the smaller blocks may have other adverse designs, such as overhead walkways. Removal of families with children, or the arrival of problem families in a dispersal programme, the presence of a 'facility' in the block, scheduling for demolition, or a variety of other factors known or unknown, may all cause deviations from the basic effect of design, and subtract a quota from a perfect correlation coefficient of $+1.0$. In fact the coefficient for graffiti in relation to block size is as low as $+0.193$, even though the trend lines are so clear.

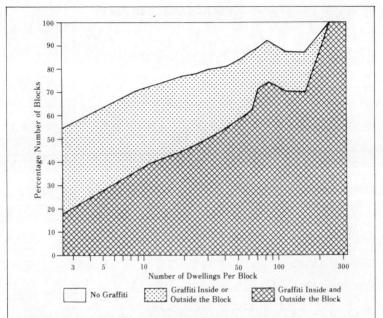

FIG.27. Trend lines for classes of graffiti by block size. With increasing size there is a decrease in litter-free blocks and an increase in those with graffiti both inside or outside. This illustrates what is meant by a probabilistic distribution.

In practice, scientists who study the real world cannot design experiments to exclude disturbing factors, and accept that much weaker coefficients are meaningful in these circumstances than would be valid in a laboratory test of, say, a new drug. This is the difference between a deterministic and a probabilistic approach; in probability terms even a weak coefficient means something if it keeps on recurring throughout a very large body of evidence.

To decide whether a weak coefficient is too strong to be dismissed we use the objective criteria of significance levels. These form a sliding scale that takes account of the number of cases observed. For instance, a given coefficient may be dismissed as a chance effect if it is based on only six observations but accepted as something more than chance if it is based on six hundred. The advantage of studying over 4,000 blocks is that we are alerted to possible non-chance relationships even when their coefficients are very weak.

TABLE 9   *Significance levels of correlation coefficients*

	Litter	Graffiti	Damage	Children in care	Urine	Faeces
Size variables						
Dwellings per block	***	***	***	***	***	***
Dwellings per entrance	***	***	***	***	***	***
Storeys per block	***	***	***	***	***	***
Storeys per dwelling	***	***	***	***	**	***
Circulation variables						
Overhead walkways	***	***	***	***	**	***
Interconnecting exits	***	***	***	***	***	***
Vertical routes	***	***	***	***	***	***
Corridor type	***	***	***	***	***	***
Entrance characteristics						
Entrance position	•	***	**	***	**	**
Entrance type	***	***	***	***	***	**
Stilts and garages	—	•	***	***	•	·:*	**
Features of the grounds						
Spatial organisation	***	**	***	***	***	•
Blocks in the site	***	***	***	•	— ***	**
Access points	***	***	***	***	***	***
Play areas	***	***	***	***	*	•

*   Significant   • Not significant
**   Highly significant   — Negative coefficient
*** Very highly significant

(3654 blocks, exluding blocks above shops and blocks with voids. See Appendix II)

A significant correlation is one that could be expected to occur by chance only once in 20 times; the odds are 19 to 1 against its being a chance effect. A highly significant correlation has odds longer than 99 to 1, and a very highly significant one has odds of 999 to 1, or greater. This means that among the 90 coefficients relating the 15 designs to the six test measures (Table 9) we should expect four or five to show up as significant purely by chance, and one of these might be highly significant. It is unlikely that any would be very highly significant. In reality no fewer than 83 are positively significant and 73 of these are very highly significant. Thus, correlation analysis strongly supports the evidence of the trend lines in showing that the association of poor design with social malaise is a genuine effect, far more consistent than could be expected by chance.

Corroboration, if anything further is needed, occurs in the signs of the coefficients. On a purely chance basis there would be roughly equal numbers of positive and negative results, but Table 9 contains 88 positive coefficients compared with only two negative ones.

The predominance of positively significant coefficients is important but it must be stressed that correlation is a minor method in comparison with trend lines, which are of much greater practical value.

The prosecution has demonstrated the detrimental influence of the design suspects; the defence has not been able to muster convincing counter-arguments. The scene is set for a verdict of 'Guilty', and for the passing of sentence. In the last three or four years some hundreds of modern blocks have been sentenced to death by demolition, but what interests us more is the potential for a better state of affairs in the future. This will be discussed in the next two chapters on preventive measures and corrective measures respectively.

VII | Preventive Measures: Houses

The best blocks of flats are those that are most like houses, and so it is logical to deduce that the most effective way of preventing the various kinds of social malaise would be to build houses and not flats in the future. To be quite sure of this we need evidence from houses themselves, and have therefore examined a sample of 4,172, of which 2,000 are located in our study area, and will be discussed first. They include 1,600 houses in the inner city areas of Tower Hamlets and Southwark, and 400 post-war houses from outer areas: Dulwich in the southern tip of Southwark and Blackbird Leys. Of the 1,600 inner-city houses there are 350 post-war, 350 inter-war, 700 pre-1914 single-family ones and 200 pre-1914 houses converted into flats.

Converted houses are intermediate in design between single-family houses and purpose-built blocks of flats, and they are also intermediate in their litter levels. They are littered nearly twice as often as houses but less than half as often as purpose-built blocks, and there are even stronger contrasts in their levels of dirty and decayed litter.

Graffiti and damage are uncommon in both houses and converted houses, and are generally restricted to those located near flats. No urine pollution was observed and only two of the 1,800 houses had faeces within three metres of the facade; one of them had horse manure, and the horse

TABLE 10 *Percentage abuse levels by dwelling type*

	Single-family houses (1800)	*Converted houses* (200)	*Purpose-built flats* (4099)
Litter	19.8	37.0	86.1
Dirty and decayed litter	4.0	16.5	45.7
Graffiti	1.2	0.5	76.2
Damage	1.9	2.5	38.8
Urine	0.0	0.0	22.9*
Faeces	0.1	0.0	7.5

* adjusted percentage: see Table 2.

TABLE 11 *Litter percentage by building age*

	All litter	*Dirty and decayed*
Pre-1914 conversions, inner city	37.0	16.5
Pre-1914 houses, inner city	23.6	8.0
Inter-war houses, inner city	10.0	0.9
Post-war houses, inner city	20.0	0.9
Post-war houses, Blackbird Leys	21.2	0.9
Post-war houses, Dulwich	22.5	4.1

was actually observed standing with his hindquarters inside the front gate. This illustrates the kind of freak occurrence that may prevent good designs from actually registering zero. In effect there is no significant difference between houses and converted houses for any test measure except litter. Both are undoubtedly better than blocks of flats, and houses are better than conversions.

Are converted houses worse than unaltered houses because of the design change, or simply because they are pre-1914 in date? This can be ascertained by comparing them with houses of the same vintage; they prove to be significantly worse and it seems that even this small degree of sharing makes a difference (Table 11).

Table 11 suggests it is not sufficient to build houses instead of flats; certain types of houses are better than others. It is perhaps surprising that post-war houses, carefully vetted by planners, have much the same litter percentage as pre-1914 houses, whereas those of the inter-war period are significantly better. Just as planned flats have created problems so planned housing seems to have fallen short of the optimum.

Before placing too much reliance upon this single sample of inter-war houses it seemed reasonable to enquire whether others of the same date would show similar characteristics. Three areas were chosen for comparison in the outer London boroughs of Bromley and Croydon and the Buckinghamshire town of High Wycombe. Houses with the standard design features of front gardens more than three metres deep, with waist-high walls and gates have litter percentages ranging from 8.8 to 12.4, close to the 10 per cent figure given in Table 11. The overall percentage for all 900 inter-war houses is 9.9, which is less than half the average of 21.2 for the three samples of post-war houses.

Corroborative figures for pre-1914 dwellings were also sought. The Queen's Park Estate in Westminster proved to have litter percentages of 17.5 for single-family houses and 26.6 for houses converted into flats.

These figures are somewhat lower than for dwellings of the same age in Southwark and Tower Hamlets, but a possible reason for this is that they are smaller, and shared by only two households instead of up to four. This would mean that conversions follow a trend similar to that of purpose-built blocks, in that increased sharing is associated with increased abuse, even though the absolute frequency of abuse is lower. In comparison with the inter-war houses, however, the Queen's Park percentages are still high, which suggests that inter-war design has something to teach us that has generally been ignored. Inter-war housing was the evolutionary culmination of natural selection in vernacular building, the continuing merits of which are evident from our test measures. Yet paradoxically, it has also been the most despised and rejected, and it is important to understand why .

Historical evolution

Architecture established itself independently of building when the ancient world began to produce grandiose public buildings that demanded forethought and measurement. Temples and tombs, cathedrals and castles, palaces and places of mass entertainment were its main preoccupation for many centuries, with a gradual extension of its sphere of activity downward, from the religious to the secular, from the royal to the rich, from the national to the municipal, and so on. There was always a tendency to invest the lesser project with something of the glory of the greater. Nash's terraces, for example, imparted a communal grandeur to houses that were too small to sustain it individually. Even when Victorian villadom achieved an advance into individuality, it was still often invested with significance in the form of details drawn from the cathedrals or fortresses of the past.

Over the same centuries vernacular building was evolving in the opposite direction, upward from the one-storeyed, one-roomed, earth-floored cottage. Unable to afford architects, and for long beneath their notice, it remained in close contact with how ordinary people lived, and gradually came to serve their needs more effectively. It catered for a complex variety of functions: shelter, defensibility, scope for making one's own mark and projecting one's image, opportunities for varied home-based activities, and the relaxed sense of security that comes from living among compatible neighbours. The highly competitive housebuilding of the inter-war period was extremely sensitive to these needs, as each builder responded to the comments of buyers, renters

PLATE 11. The inter-war semi-detached home was the most advanced design achieved by British mass housing before natural evolution was broken off by planning control. Bay windows maximise surveillance of the approaches and the fenced and gated frontages maximise control of the territory. There is scope for householders to make their mark on the streetscape by a variety of garden designs, fencing materials and decoration of the facade, thus avoiding anonymity. (Enfield, North London).

and estate agents in the attempt to make his next round of houses more attractive to the market.

The two decades between the wars saw the two trends approach within flash-point distance. Builders were improving their standards so far upward that the ordinary house began to seem within the proper sphere of architects expanding downward. After World War II, the trends were fused, by virtue of the 1947 Town and Country Planning Act, but the fusion did not give the best of both worlds that was expected. Both architects and builders have been made responsible to planning authorities rather than to clients and purchasers, and consequently they have been deprived of the strongest stimulus to mainstream evolution: direct feedback from occupiers. Even in the private sector this is true to some extent.

Le Corbusier

To understand the form which the fusion has taken, it is necessary to look back to the influence of one man, Le Corbusier. Born in Switzerland in 1887, Le Corbusier was both an architect and a city planner, who became a kind of patron saint to both professions at a formative stage. Planning was just coming out of its chrysalis, and in need of a unifying doctrine. Architecture, despite its millennia of history, was seeking professional status; it was not until 1937 that British law prevented unqualified people from styling themselves 'architects'. Le Corbusier was a powerful polemicist who provided precisely the authoritative rationale that fitted the time, and also had the advantage of leading both professions along the same principles, so that they gave each other mutual support. In so far as Le Corbusier was right, this was an added strength, but in so far as he was wrong, it multiplied the error.

Le Corbusier advocated a break with traditional architecture in favour of a completely new and closely argued concept of design. The basic principle was functionalism: 'A house is a machine for living in'. Functionalism was an integration of ideas on the aesthetics of buildings with ideas on desiderata for family and community living.

On the aesthetic side it laid down that the form of a building should be a simple reflection of its structure and purpose, with clean facades and flat roofs completely free from ornamentation. The structural frame should be explicit, and the windows should be inserted in vertical strips to emphasise it. Materials should be modern—glass and raw concrete—and assembled in modules scaled to suit human stature. And the resulting geometrical volumes should be arranged in balanced clusters to catch up light and shade as components of their design.

Le Corbusier was equally forceful on the human aspect. He had a vision of ideal community living and was convinced it could be created by designs that threw people together. Rooms should be thrown together in open plans, dwellings should be thrown together in tall towers, and towers should be thrown together in vertical cities. Other land uses should be designed into the same buildings as the residences: shops and schools, roof gardens and hotels, theatres and gymnasia—to form a '*unité d'habitation*'. The *unités* were to be set in green parks, and raised up on pillars so that the space could pass uninterruptedly beneath them. They should then be linked together by straight motorways and in order to expedite the birth of this Utopia, ageing neighbourhoods should be demolished in their entirety, to make way for comprehensive redevelopment.

Le Corbusier's vision drew together the various strands of the Modern Movement in architecture and elevated it into the International Movement. It provided a sense of purpose and righteous mission, and gained an enormously powerful hold. It also served the economic end of legitimising contempt for the great arch-rival: the semi-detached mainstream of the inter-war period. Ian Davis in *Dunroamin: The Suburban Semi and its Enemies* (1981) described the orchestrated impact of Corbusian ideology from his very first day as an architectural student. Even before the morning coffee break, the process of indoctrination was inculcating respect for Le Corbusier as the greatest living architect and shame for 'uncivilised' home addresses in suburbia.

Was Corbusian precept valid, or was it mere dogma? Dogma is a theory or doctrine asserted on authority without supporting evidence, and Le Corbusier was certainly not in the business of testing and modifying his designs. Our own testing did not derive from a consideration of Le Corbusier's work, but most of the design features that have failed our tests prove, in retrospect, to stem from his Utopian vision. He was fundamentally right in one respect – that design can affect the character of a community – but whether the effect will be for good or ill is something that can only be determined from factual evidence. Creativity is not enough. It should also be rooted in reality, and this is probably the most vital development needed in contemporary schools of architecture.

Le Corbusier's pre-eminence has placed restrictions on other architects' creativity. It has been taken for granted that their work would be variations upon his theme. This appears to have had a stultifying effect, with the result that British architecture has sunk to a low point in public esteem. It seems unlikely that the trend would have become so monolithic if it had not also been embraced by the planning profession with its power to impose canons of taste to prevent people – and architects – from fulfilling their individual aspirations.

Contemporary appraisal

Corbusianism has been planted very deep in the architectural unconscious, and continues to circumscribe even those who, consciously, are trying to break away into post-Modernism. At present, this is taking the form of Revivalism, with the apparent liberation of going back before Le Corbusier and drawing inspiration from older and more purely British styles. But the favourite among these is the Georgian, which has most in common with the Modern Movement: flat facades, uncluttered rooflines, and grouping into terraces to give added scale.

The Design of Suburbia by Arthur Edwards (1981) epitomises the contemporary reaction. It is a blend of scholarship in modern domestic architecture combined with strong prejudices in assessing it. Prejudice (i.e. an opinion or attitude reached on inadequate evidence) is apparent from the first two sentences, 'Suburbia is a dirty word. This is natural enough, for with rare exceptions, the appearance of Britain's suburbia is at best dull and at worst hideous'. 'Appearance' is the key word; the urban environment is assessed as a scene to be viewed rather than a place to be lived in, and the criteria for quality are visual: contrasts in scale, variety of spaces and unity of floorscape.

The golden age is seen as Georgian and Regency. Edwards explains that their repetitious buildings contrasted with open squares give a pleasing variety to the scene as a whole, whereas Victorian villadom and its inter-war descendants are assemblages of varied buildings in a repetitious scene. The latter is considered vastly inferior because of its jagged restless skyline, the leaking space between houses, the lesser dignity of two storeys as compared with four, the spottiness of flowering trees, the patchy coloration of front walls and hedges, the vague shapelessness of front gardens, the interruptions in the floorscape caused by entryways, kerbs and carriageways, and the ugly clutter of cars and garages. The ideals prescribed for the future are unbroken terraces with flat roofs, grouped to face each other across a smooth wall-to-wall floorscape of grass, with just a few shrubs to afford privacy for windows. A photograph of houses which Edwards approves looks very much like blocks of flats set in confused space, and shows how difficult it is proving to make a real break with the Modern Movement. There is still the same reliance upon emotive phrases to promote one's views, and an absence of hard evidence on what really works for the inhabitants. The latter would be true functionalism, rather than untested abstractions about planes, forms, volumes and spaces.

In complete contrast to *The Design of Suburbia* is the book mentioned earlier, *Dunroamin: The Suburban Semi and Its Enemies* which analyses the denigration of inter-war houses and finds it unjustified. Its authors, Paul Oliver, Ian Davis and Ian Bentley, are well qualified to make an objective study of the semi, because they themselves were thoroughly indoctrinated against it in their student days, but gradually realised the falsity of the criticism. They point out that the semi always was, and continues to be, popular and successful from the resident's viewpoint, and is therefore worthy of serious consideration. Their conclusions are in harmony with our own independent findings, and they develop a fascinating wealth of detail on the actual designs. *Dunroamin* is a book that deserves a wide professional and lay readership.

During its great upsurge, suburbia was dismissed as 'jerry-built', a phrase redolent of professional assessment and accepted by a public unable to judge for itself. There was, indeed, a modicum of jerry-building, but it was quite wrong to assume it was universal, and the phrase began to drop out of use when the semis stood up well to wartime bombing. Moreover, the purpose of the cost-cutting implied by jerry-building was to reduce the price to purchasers and expand the market. The purchaser's irritation when it came to installing a new gutter or damp course was minor in comparison with the benefit of having one's own home. A perceptive epigram has been coined: 'Inter-war semis were cheap without being nasty, while post-war building may be nasty without being cheap'. It is progressively being realised that pre-war jerry-building pales into insignificance in contrast with that approved by planners since 1947. Leaky flat roofs, dangerously loose panels, inadequate reinforcement and hazardous wiring have all emerged as defects of comparatively new buildings.

Scientific appraisal

However, redemption of the semi's reputation is only the first step in encouraging housing evolution to continue from where the semi left off. We also have to specify which of its characteristics are the essential ones. We know from examples of Revivalism that designers select certain features and ignore others that may be more important. They may strain at the gnat of whether railings are Regency or Victorian, and swallow the camel of entrance design. They overlook the fact that Georgian terraced houses had separate entrances spaced out individually, and they group new entrances in pairs, each fenced off from its own garden but not from its neighbour. This is a small-scale relic of the Corbusian concept of forced sharing of territory, and may well be unrecognised by its authors. There are so many architects and planners who have had their experience with blocks of flats that they are unconsciously carrying some of the latter's deleterious features over into the layout of houses. It is therefore necessary to be explicit about the essentials for housing — while also stressing the need for individuality.

What we are *not* discussing is the interior of the dwelling. This has been relatively free from planning fiat and has continued to evolve, so that most people, even in the most horrendous blocks, are reasonably satisfied with their indoor living space. 'I like my flat but I wish it were

PLATE 12. Georgian houses are much admired but are adapted to the lifestyle of a bygone age. Large families with living-in servants did not need to maximise surveillance in order to defend their space, so flush windows and projecting porches were not disadvantaging in the same way as for today's households, which are of unprecedentedly small average size.

somewhere else' is a common sentiment. There are a few unpopular in-door elements, notably the Corbusian open plan and cross-over designs that locate the upper floor of a maisonette over another dwelling instead of over its own lower floor, but criticisms are generally directed outside at the absence of a defensible territory and the resulting lack of surveillance and control. There is a fundamental difference in the surveillance potential of the Georgian terrace and the inter-war semi, and unfortunately it is the former that is being espoused in Revivalism. The Georgian facade has flush windows and a projecting porch, while the semi-detached house has projecting windows and a recessed porch. Each was well suited to the lifestyle of its original inhabitants. The porches of Belgravia offered immediate shelter to people arriving in carriages, and there was no need to maximise surveillance from the windows of houses defended by an army of living-in servants. In a modern servantless family, however, surveillance is much more important, and seems to be best satisfied by bay or bow windows that give a clear view up and down the street as well as across it. Projecting porches are undesirable because they obstruct the view, and recessed porches are more appropriate. Servantless houses also need front gardens to act as buffer zones, so that passers-by can be distinguished from callers actually entering the territory. The recessed porch has the effect of increasing the distance from gate to door, which makes the visitor more observable. This contrast shows why Georgian designs are less suited to be models for today than are the houses of the inter-war period.

Unfortunately, many modern houses seem designed to minimise surveillance. Windows are set flush with the walls, and projections cutting off the line of sight include not only porches but garages, storage compartments, meter cupboards and pramsheds. Frosted or beaded glass may ensure that there is no surveillance, let alone effective surveillance, from the ground-floor front. Doors set into the side rather than the front of projecting porches may have their field of vision cut off by the back wall of the neighbour's entrance hall. Other features which protect front doors from the neighbour's gaze are oblique orientation of the house, offset building lines and small-scale zig-zags in the road alignment. All these features are part of the fashion for visual privacy applied to the outside of the dwelling, where it works in reverse to deprive the occupants of a street outlook. The house has a closed, shuttered face and lacks the surveillance potential that would promote self-policing and stability. Not surprisingly, these disadvantaging features are picked up by the sensitive indicator, litter. Litter is present in 22.6 per cent of houses with sideways-looking doors in Dulwich, as compared with 10 per cent in inter-war houses with front-facing doors and this design is clearly a factor in raising Dulwich's overall litter percentage to the same level as that of ostensibly less desirable areas.

The sideways-looking door is a denial of Oscar Newman's advice to make entrances face the street. Street-facing entrances were almost universal in inter-war houses, but have been progressively repudiated in recent years in favour of off-street enclaves. The enclave is an example of a layout feature of flats adapted to apply to houses, where the

PLATE 13. A 1968 enclave design of eight gardenless terraced houses fronting onto an alley and facing a high bank. Surveillance of the alley is impossible from the front ground-floor windows which are recessed behind projecting porches with sideways-facing doors. The flat roofs frequently spring leaks. (Dulwich)

open squares of the former are replaced by paths, alleys or narrow drives, arranged in an involuted complex. This plan ensures that few, if any, of the doors or windows of the house-fronts are intervisible with the road, and the loss of surveillance is again reflected in an increase in litter. The litter percentage for 88 enclave houses in Dulwich is 26.1, higher than the figure for Victorian and Edwardian houses.

Space syntax

The importance of road frontages as compared with enclave designs has recently been demonstrated by Bill Hillier and his colleagues in a research report entitled *Space Syntax* (1983). It is argued that places, like prose, should be intelligible. The major street system should form a skeletal framework into which the minor streets should fit in a comprehensible way, so that as people move through local areas they are also learning something of the route system as a whole. If the system is highly intelligible, the town would have smoothly graded levels of street occupation from the most frequented to the least frequented areas. The core area would be strong enough to attract many people, and the density would gradually fall off towards quieter side streets. If, on the other hand, the route system is unintelligible, a few places are likely to drain all the street-life away from the rest, and there would be abrupt discontinuities of occupation between overcrowded and deserted areas.

The space-syntax team explored how far the intelligibility of a street layout could be related to graduation of occupation by pedestrians. If the two characteristics could be measured, it might be possible to predict the level of occupation from the form of the street layout, which would introduce more certainty of success into planning. Street occupation levels are easily measured by the standard method of counting the flow of pedestrians past given points but measuring the intelligibility of street layouts is a new challenge which has been ingeniously solved by a scale termed 'integration'. Streets, alleys and other movement spaces are analysed in two dimensions. Lengthwise they are divided into intervisible portions, or lines of sight, and widthwise they are divided into segments of narrowing, broadening or constant breadth. Counts are then made of the number of segments that must be traversed between all possible pairs of sightlines. Places with a low average count have good accessibility and are considered well integrated, and intelligible, whereas those with the highest average are the least integrated. The latter prove to be the labyrinthine rabbit warrens of large modern estates of flats — a statistical conclusion about integration and intelligibility that is often echoed in practice by people trying to make sense of the layout in order to find a specific address.

Hillier found that well-integrated areas permit reasonably accurate predictions of street occupation levels, which prove to decrease gradually in expected directions. Where integration is weak, however, the distribution of occupation is unpredictable and characterised by sudden differences; people do not use the circulation space in ways that might be expected. This discovery makes a mockery of our sophisticated comprehensive planning intended to separate vehicular and pedestrian traffic.

Estates which encourage abuses ranging from litter to crime have been designed on the basis of false prophecies of the movement patterns for whose sake so many other advantages have been sacrificed.

Facelessness

Hillier points out that every segment of well integrated circulation space has at least one building entrance opening on to it. This is an important observation—doorless alleys have always been held in distrust—and it also meshes in with our own concept of facelessness. In 1977, when we first attempted to map design disadvantagement, we questioned why inner-city redevelopment was so often described as faceless, and concluded that it arose from expanses of high walls, fences or iron hoardings, unrelieved by windows. Facelessness seemed to be the obverse of lack of surveillance, experienced from the outside instead of the inside.

Features which make modern houses more faceless than their interwar counterparts include the side wall, the back wall and sometimes even the front wall, as well as grouped garages backing on to the street as a screen to the houses. One trend which exemplifies the problem is the rejection of the corner house in favour of the end house. The corner house looks out on to two intersecting roads over an L-shaped garden fronted by a waist-high or chest-high wall or hedge. This design is not faceless, as passers-by can easily see over the wall which, in the reverse direction, does not interfere with surveillance from the windows. Today, however, the end house has become the norm. It faces only one of the two adjoining roads, and presents the other with two blank side walls, that of the house and that of the back garden.

It is sometimes argued that end windows have to be sacrificed in order to provide sufficient wall space for pictures, bookcases or other tall furniture. These same needs are, however, completely disregarded when wall space is eliminated in order to achieve Le Corbusier's open plan, and the loss of end-wall surveillance can be thought of as a knock-on effect of the open plan design. The open plan has also affected surveillance potential in another way, by giving rise to the see-through house. This affront to internal privacy has had to be redeemed, and unfortunately it has been argued that a view into the back garden is more important than one into the street—another factor leading to frontal facelessness.

Meanwhile, the open plan itself has also proved unpopular. Le Corbusier and his wife did not have children, and he did not understand

PLATE 14. Long high faceless walls have been advocated by the Department of the Environment to screen out traffic noise, but the problems they create appear to outweigh the benefits. There is no surveillance of the street from ground-floor windows and the garden is more vulnerable to intrusion by criminals than back to back gardens. Pedestrians are cut off from help in case of emergency and no-one feels responsible for the grass verge, where litter accumulates.

that a communal area which suits a childless couple may be quite inappropriate for an ordinary family. This defect first gave rise to a great trade in room dividers, followed by a recognition that the missing wall needed to be restored. This has been done only half-heartedly, as yet. The wall is made to extend only part-way across, to improve visual privacy while still genuflecting in the open plan direction. It is a solution which turns a deaf ear to the need for auditory privacy, and does nothing to help economy in space heating.

The garden side wall is also faceless because it has to be made high enough to afford privacy for the back garden, and consequently it precludes surveillance of the street from the back ground floor windows, even though it directly adjoins the public road where surveillance is most needed. Corner houses are said to be more vulnerable to burglary than those with neighbours on both sides, but intruders there have to cross a semi-private front garden where they may be seen as suspicious presences. In the case of a six or seven-foot side wall, the burglar may choose his moment to scale it unseen, and then become immediately screened by it. The supposed defence against intrusion is thus transformed into an asset to the intruder.

Inter-war houses faced each other across a road and backed on to each others' gardens. Earlier terrace designs had needed a back alley and back gate for dustmen and coalmen, but the semi-detached dispensed with these features by substituting side access. Side access had the advantage of being wholly within the occupier's own territory and under his control, and it permitted true back-to-back gardens without external access from the rear. This was an excellent security device, not only against crime but also for keeping toddlers safe. *The Report on the Design of Dwellings Subcommittee* (Ministry of Health 1944) suggested extending side access to terraced houses by means of tunnels between pairs of houses, and another alternative is side access through a garage.

However, this type of territorial defence has been abandoned in favour of orienting successive rows of houses in the same direction, so that the front of one row faces the rear of the next. This is wasteful of land because a path or road is needed for every row of houses instead of every two rows, and it also exposes to public view the high faceless walls of the back gardens. The houses opposite may be spared this view by being made faceless themselves, with their ground-floor windows concentrated towards the rear. The combined effect of these various features is to reduce surveillance and natural policing, while exposing the territory to easier intrusion from the rear.

Gardens, fences and gates

A noticeable post-war trend is a shrinkage of that vital buffer zone, the front garden. To test its effect, garden depth from gate to doorstep has been estimated in three classes: approximately three metres, larger than this, and smaller. Inter-war houses have the least litter and the most deep gardens, while Victorian houses have the most litter and the most small gardens. If garden size is analysed irrespective of age, litter is seen to increase as size decreases, and the same is true of the proportion of dirty and decayed litter. Front gardens should exceed three metres.

Another feature that has been progressively dispensed with is the front garden boundary—a fence, wall or hedge with a gate. Litter is least frequent where there is both a boundary of normal height and a gate. It becomes more common when the fence height is reduced, or the gate

TABLE 12 *Litter related to depth of front garden*

| Garden depth (Gate to doorstep) | No. of houses in sample | Litter percentages | |
		All	Dirty and decayed
Over 3m	850	14.6	2.8
About 3m	420	20.5	3.8
Under 3m	530	27.9	6.0

is omitted, the latter having a greater effect. The combination of a low fence and missing gate is still worse.

Because of the trend shown in the first four items of Table 13, we should expect the last category, fenceless and gateless gardens, to be the worst for litter, but they are not. They are significantly worse than normally fenced and gated gardens but not significantly different from gardens with a low fence and a gate. The anomaly can possibly be explained by the fact that these houses tend to be the best in their immediate area, e.g. private homes of up to five bedrooms in Dulwich, and it may be that pride of ownership fuels anti-litter behaviour in these cases. It is known from elsewhere, however, that fenceless and gateless gardens are unpopular. Residents complain that dogs and children do not respect property, while postmen and milkmen may take short cuts where there are no party fences, and tread on the flowers. Corner-cutting by pedestrians may trample out unsightly tracks across the lawns of corner houses; that which is not bounded is not perceived as semi-private.

TABLE 13 *Litter related to fences and gates*

Type of boundary	No. of houses	Litter percentage
Fence of normal height with gate	1071	15.7
Low fence with gate	189	21.7
Fence of normal height without gate	342	26.6
Low fence without gate	71	42.3
Neither fence nor gate	127	21.3

In one case, a resident who created a boundary signal in the form of a low rockery was prosecuted for violating the designer's non-defensible vision. His neighbours thought it was an improvement, but the planning authority regarded it as a visual sacrilege. A Hampshire councillor received so many complaints about a local ban on walls and hedges that she evolved a standard solution: since flowers were permitted, a row of rose bushes could be planted along the front of the lawn. But how much better it would be to allow freedom to express the territorial instinct and to take it into account as a component in the visual aspect of design.

Car space

Provision for the car is a knotty problem that has evoked a number of counter-productive 'solutions'. One is to group all the garages together, out of sight in a corner of the estate, but this deprives them of surveillance and makes them more vulnerable to criminal attention. A reaction from this is the smaller group, located within sight of the owners' dwellings, but this often obstructs sight-lines between the houses and the road. Council tenants on the more hazardous estates often find it safer to ignore garages altogether and park in the open where the car can be seen from the flat, and certain plans for new starter homes in Southwark are also assuming street parking. This makes the streets difficult to keep clean, and also requires wider roads than would otherwise be necessary. If parking space is to be allocated in any case, it makes better sense to include it inside the front garden where the occupier can keep it clean, rather than out in the street where it reduces public hygiene. It might be better to have sufficient garden depth to park at right angles to the house rather than slewing round to parallel it; this would maximise space for a genuine garden and also offer less obstruction to surveillance. In detail, the relative levels of the parking surface and the main window could be co-ordinated so that sight-lines up and down the street pass well clear of the top of the car.

Better still than parking space within the territory is a lockable garage within the territory, but this too can be designed in a gimmicky way that impedes surveillance. Plate 15 shows a garage design that in-corporates multiple disadvantages. It must surely score low marks for road safety, as the driver has to emerge directly on to the road without being able to see, or be seen by, any pedestrian or vehicle driver about to pass across his bows. It completely eliminates surveillance from the ground-floor front of the house and compels the residents to emerge in-to an alley between garages, deprived of all prior warning of what to expect. At the very least the garage should be set back flush with the front door, and possibly recessed beyond it.

Garage design is a simple matter where the house is double-fronted, and the presence of a garage on one side does not preclude surveillance from a bay window on the other side. The same applies to a single-fronted house with sufficient space for a side garage, but a genuinely narrow

PLATE 15. Faceless houses in Tower Hamlets. The whole of the ground-floor facade is taken up by the projecting garage and the front door, leaving no space for windows or surveillance. There is no buffer zone between the dwelling and the street, and no party fence between neighbours. The seal of planning approval is no guarantee of a satisfactory self-policing environment.

frontage poses a problem. If there is a garage, there is no space for a front room. One possible solution is a slightly sunken, low-roofed garage, and an overhanging front room that remains low enough for effective surveillance, with only a few steps down to the front door if action needs to be taken. To keep down the price of a starter home, the garage could be designed as a car-port, which the occupiers could enclose as funds became available.

The effort involved in getting out of a car to open or close a garage and gate is a factor leading to gateless designs, and since these are undesirable, perhaps some thought could be given to swinging or lifting barriers that can be operated by remote control from the driver's seat.

Making one's mark

Finally, there is the most challenging design need of all: the ability to create a facade and garden space that will not become spoilt as soon as the occupier makes the slightest alteration. House design should satisfy the twin instinctive drives – to control a defensible territory and to make one's mark on it. The uniformity of the terrace appeals to the same instincts in the architect, enabling him to spread his mark over a wider area; a whole square, or estate, or neighbourhood may bear his stamp. He is also able to perpetuate his control over the territory because of the planning ban on changes. But the designer's fulfilment is the resident's frustration, which is all part and parcel of the fashion for large blocks and estates that dwarf the individual and minimise the scope for adapting his home. The grandiose scale has been embraced at the expense of human scale.

'Bring back human scale' has become a familiar slogan, and some designers may be convinced they are applying it by means of tiny gardens, narrow alleyways and exclusive enclaves. But human scale does not mean individual shrinkage trapped in the web of a grander design. It means an arrangement of space that enables human beings to master their immediate environment, and not be enslaved by it. An environment designed for midgets can be just as soul destroying as one designed for giants. Human scale means autonomy for each household, with a garden large enough to be defensible and to accommodate changes that make the resident's mark independently of that of the designer. True professionalism will come when the architect is less concerned with imposing his own vision, willy-nilly, and more concerned with giving satisfaction to the users of his buildings, including the satisfaction embodied in scope to adapt their property to suit their infinite variety of lifestyles and self-images.

Where houses are worse offenders than some flats

The evidence from the study area shows that houses give rise to fewer social-malaise problems than flats, but is this always true? In other areas it is possible to find estates plagued by graffiti, vandal damage and excrement in spite of being wholly or largely houses. Although we have not surveyed such estates in detail, we have been able to visit several of them in the Midlands and North of England, and in every case there seemed to be sound design-based reasons why the social-malaise measures should be worse than those observed in London and Oxford. The defects of facade and frontage identified in this chapter are invariably present in these problem estates, creating conditions of facelessness and lack of surveillance.

It seems that successive official recommendations on housing estates have promoted progressively worse features, in social terms. For example, the Ministry of Housing and Local Government's tenth Design Bulletin (1966) advocates unfenced front gardens and staggered facades to give greater privacy. In our study area, the samples of post-war houses were either relatively early in date, before the worst designs were promoted, or restricted to small areas of later infill. There were no estates that were both very extensive and very recent – a combination which is now recognised by many local authorities as producing levels of social breakdown that exceed not only those in inter-war houses but also those in Victorian houses, house conversions and some of the better designed blocks of flats. Further research would quantify the degrees of overlap in abuse levels between the most deleterious house designs and the most innocuous flat designs.

The observations above stress the fact that it is not sufficient merely to build houses instead of flats. Attention must also be given to the design and layout features of houses in order to ensure that their potential social benefits are properly realised.

Density

Although few people would disagree that properly designed houses are better than even the best designed flats, some critics object that this is purely academic when we cannot afford the space to build houses. They argue that flats pack in more homes to the acre.

The density argument is, in fact, a myth. Flats certainly pack in more litter to the acre, more crime and more vandalism to the acre, and more social malaise in general. But they do not, in Britain, pack in more dwellings to the acre. Densities are strictly controlled by the planning process, and are usually *lower* in modern flats than in the demolished houses that have been superseded. This can easily be proved by comparing Population Census figures for two dates: before and after houses were replaced by flats.

Why does the 'high-rise, high-density' myth persist? In part it is due to an optical illusion. The human eye foreshortens the horizontal distance across the spacious lawns of housing estates but gives full value to the vertical dimension, and when buildings are very tall, the ratio of height to distance can be seriously overestimated. Another reason for the belief is psychological; people feel more crowded when their homes are crated up vertically without direct access to a garden. There is also a confusion between the concept of overcrowding (people per room) with that of density (dwellings per acre). If the former is harmful, the latter is also assumed to be so, although all the evidence on the subject suggests otherwise (see Chapter IX).

A third reason is simply physical. Blocks of flats are bulked up by a substantial amount of space that would not be needed if they were designed as separate houses. Lobbies, liftwells, corridors, pramsheds, service cupboards, refuse chambers and other common parts all help to expand the buildings and create a false comparison with houses. And fourthly, there was also the Department of the Environment's constant iteration of the 'need' for lower densities, which has become a well-worn track in the national consciousness, leading only to unfulfilled hopes.

In 1983 Andrew Chyba of King's College, London, produced a dissertation entitled *The Significance of Common Floor Space Provision to Housing Developments.* He made careful measurements of blocks in eight Southwark estates, and found that up to 18 per cent of their floor space is taken up in common parts that would be unnecessary for houses. This would make room for one extra dwelling in every four or five. Even allowing for normal garden space instead of shared grounds, a decision to build houses instead of flats could have resulted in 10 per cent more dwellings within the confines of the existing estates.

Furthermore, Chyba worked on relatively simple estates. There are many more elaborate designs which devote substantially more space to common areas such as broad streets in the sky, fire-escape features, special service towers for access and water tanks, and a host of useless fragmented spaces left over in between other design features. There is also an appreciable quantity of land in the surrounding area devoted to non-functional amenity spaces such as verges and road triangles, which residents would gladly sacrifice in the interest of more houses with gardens.

The argument based on relative space needs is a hollow one, made all the more poignant for cooped-up flat-dwellers by the fact that up to 15 per cent of their local area has been in a prolonged state of total disuse due to demolition. There is plenty of room for houses, and multiple evidence to prove it.

Cost

Another argument which usually surfaces at this point is that even though we have been mistaken about the space constraint, the case for building houses instead of flats is undermined by the cost constraint. Many people cannot afford to buy houses, and the taxpayer cannot afford to subsidise council houses when flats are so much cheaper.

This, too, is a complete myth. Harold Macmillan as Housing Minister in 1951 did not give the green light to flats on economic grounds any more than density grounds. The key reason was *speed*. Macmillan was seriously concerned to resolve the acute housing shortage that had persisted ever since the war, and to this end he embraced the 1944 Dudley Report with its emphasis on flats and maisonettes. It was almost a case of no expense spared. The building of council blocks was heavily subsidised, and much of the available funding went into the space-consuming common parts. The Ministry of Housing and Local Government's seventh Design Bulletin on *Housing Cost Yardsticks* (1963) calculated that the same accommodation cost at least 20 per cent more if provided in four-storeyed buildings instead of two-storeyed, while in high-rise blocks the cost would be increased by at least 50 per cent.

Council flats have not only been more expensive to build; they also continue to be vastly more expensive to maintain. Unlike houses they require a publicly financed staff of caretakers, cleaners, window cleaners, lift maintenance men, and groundsmen, all of whose workload is increased by the prevalence of litter, graffiti, vandalism and excrement. Ordinary repair staff, such as plumbers, electricians, carpenters and glaziers also have a heavier workload per dwelling, as they have to service the common parts as well. Furthermore, because flats produce more social problems such as children in care, they necessitate expanded social services. These things give rise, in turn, to various tiers of bureaucracy needed to administer the flat-induced officials. There are also additional costs to the police because of high crime levels in flats, to the education authority because of vandalism affecting school buildings and equipment, to the hospitals because of muggings and stress-induced illness, to insurance companies and their clients, and so on. The question should not be whether we can afford houses, but whether we can afford flats. If all their ramifying costs were to be documented, the fashion for flats would be seen as a vast impoverishing influence in our national life.

Nor are flats found to be blameless when it comes to explaining why houses are so expensive. During the 1930s up to 350,000 houses were built each year, and as there was relatively little slum clearance the housing stock was substantially increased. The inter-war semi served a buyers' or renters' market, and there was always a choice available at prices most people could afford. The post-war situation has been completely different, in that supply has always fallen short of demand. Although the peak number of dwellings in the 1930s was exceeded during the 1960s, this was achieved only with the help of lavish subsidies and by giving priority to flats. Moreover, as there has also been a planned demolition of up to 90,000 houses a year, an imbalance has remained, perpetuating a sellers' market. Many people want houses; relatively few want flats; and so the provision of the latter rather than the former has pushed up house prices and profits as a result of excess demand.

It is irrational to argue that we need more flats because houses are too expensive; that is a recipe for continued house-price inflation. What we really need is a bigger supply of houses to restore the balance and reduce inflation. This will allow more people to be satisfied with their housing and more children to be brought up in a satisfactory way. The crowning irony is that even the priority aim of speed, which led to so many undesirable side effects, was never sufficiently achieved. While house-building before the war was constantly able to match demand for houses, flat-building since the war has never been able to do so, in spite of all its new technology.

But this, of course, is an unfair comparison. Pre-war builders were free to get on with the job without the costs and delays imposed by planning, as well as without the design disadvantagement due to ill-informed bureaucratic decisions.

VIII | Corrective Measures: Rehabilitation

'Houses – not flats' is the optimum housing policy but unfortunately it is not universally applicable. We no longer have the resources to sweep away all the disastrous flatted Utopias, and millions of people are fated to go on living in them. The most that can be aspired to is only second-best – rehabilitating the offenders – and even that would not be possible without the new factual insights into the disadvantaging effect of specific designs.

This question of rehabilitation will be tackled in three sections. *Firstly* we have to study the character of the offending blocks to understand what is wrong. This is the equivalent of a psychiatrist's report on a criminal, and involves the development of two new methods of assessment: the *disadvantagement threshold* and the *disadvantagement score*. *Secondly*, we need to evaluate the effectiveness of existing methods of rehabilitation, which can be done by monitoring current housing improvement programmes, as encouraged by the Department of the Environment. These programmes often claim to be modifying design, but in practice they are mostly concerned with modernisation, repairs, replacement of defective parts and landscaping, which merely restore the estate to something like its pristine condition, with all its detrimental designs intact and able to exert the same malign influence that they did from the start. *Thirdly*, we must adapt our new knowledge to form a more constructive strategy of housing improvement, which will tackle the causes of social malaise in a more fundamental way, and with a more permanent effect.

Assessing design disadvantagement

The first step is to find an objective cut-off point for each design variable, so that attention can be drawn to precisely what is wrong with each individual block.

The graphs show that the most logical cut-off point is the lowest and best value of each variable. Unfortunately, this is not practicable. If one

TABLE 14 *Percentage frequency of corridor design by litter class*

Design value	Litter-free	Clean and casual	Dirty and decayed
Landing	23.2 +	54.6 −	22.2 −
Shared balcony	13.8 −	60.8 +	25.4 −
External corridor	8.1 −	58.0 +	33.9 +
Internal corridor	7.2 −	48.3 −	44.5 +
Overall percentage	14.0	56.6	29.4

tries to design a block consisting of the lowest value for every design − two storeys, one block in the site, one dwelling served by each entrance, etc − it soon becomes clear that the building is a house. Most existing blocks simply do not lend themselves to modifications as drastic as this. On the other hand if one adopts a less rigid guideline: 'as low a value as possible', this leaves the upper limit as wide open as before. The graphs have no natural break near the low end of the scale, and consequently we have had to devise a new objective method which is based directly on the statistics. The resulting cut-off point is called a *design-disadvantagement threshold*.

The method of finding the threshold is explained technically in Appendix I, but a simplified description is given here. It begins by setting out a table showing what percentage of blocks with each design value also have the various classes of each test measure. The example given in Table 14 cross-tabulates the four types of horizontal circulation by the three classes of litter.

All classes of litter are found in blocks with any corridor type, but as the majority of the blocks have clean and casual litter, the biggest percentage, reading across, is always the middle column. Reading downward, the largest percentage shifts diagonally, as shown by the arrows, from landings in the litter-free column to shared balconies in the clean and casual column, and internal corridors in the dirty and decayed column. This is a logical decline in litter status as corridor design worsens.

If corridor design had no effect, the number of blocks in each litter class would be a matter of chance. In that case the most probable percentage figures in each column would be the same as the overall percentage at the bottom. For example, the chance figure expected for litter-free landings would be 14.0, but the percentage actually occurring is larger, 23.2, and is therefore marked with a plus sign. All the figures that ex-

TABLE 15 *Better-than-chance and worse-than-chance corridor designs*

Design value	Litter-free	Clean and casual	Dirty and decayed
Landing	*	*	*
Shared balcony	•	•	*
External corridor	•	•	•
Internal corridor	•	*	•

* better than chance
• worse than chance

ceed the chance expectation are marked with plus signs, while those that fall short are marked with minuses. The plus signs show where the weight of the observations lies.

The last step in identifying the disadvantagement threshold is to translate the plus and minus signs into 'better than chance' or 'worse than chance' as follows. In the litter-free column it is better to have a higher percentage than would be expected by chance (plus) but in the two litter columns it is better to have a lower percentage (minus). This means that all three figures in the landings line are better than chance and are marked with an asterisk in Table 15. Conversely, it is worse to have fewer litter-free, or more littered, blocks than chance, and these cases are marked by black spots.

There is a clear transition from better to worse after landings and the threshold line is drawn there. The vertical line separates litter-free blocks, which are worse than expected for all other designs, from littered blocks where the weight of the distribution shifts. Balconies are a little worse than landings, but not bad enough to collect a worse-than-chance frequency of dirty and decayed litter. Both types of long corridor do so, and internal corridors have such a concentration of dirty and decayed, that clean and casual cases are left rarer than chance.

For many of the 15 designs, the threshold level proves to be identical for each of the six text measures, or at least five of them. In other cases it is lower for litter, and progressively a little higher for the other test measures, suggesting that the stronger taboos are not breached until the design worsens. In these cases the lower level is adopted, on the argument that a threshold which keeps litter down will automatically control the other abuses too. However, corridor type is treated slightly differently. Although the litter threshold suggests that only landings are acceptable, all the other test measures include short balconies as well. Short features, whether internal or external, are preferable to long corridors, and as there is no way in which balcony blocks can be converted into landing blocks, the threshold is defined to include both types. The complete list of threshold levels is set out here.

Design variable	Threshold
Overhead walkways	0
Stilts or garages	0
Play areas	0
Blocks in the site	1
Interconnecting exits	1
Vertical routes	1
Storeys in the dwelling	1
Access points	1
Storeys in the block	3
Number of dwellings per corridor	4
Dwellings served by one entrance	6
Dwellings in the block	12
Entrance type	Communal only
Entrance position	Facing the public street
Spatial organisation	Single block or semi-public multi-block

The function of the thresholds is to draw attention to those designs that breach them and need to be modified. These can be listed individually for each block, and their total number in the same block can be used as a *disadvantagement score.*

The disadvantagement score can range from zero in blocks where no design breaches its threshold level, to 15 where all the thresholds are breached. Fig. 28 shows the number of blocks having each score. There are unfortunately few with a score of nought or one, and mercifully few with the maximum of 15. However, the main weight of the score is thrust toward the worse end of the scale, with an average of 8.1. This emphasises the vast number of people who are subjected to highly stressful conditions.

The disadvantagement score can resolve the main difficulty inherent in the trend lines — the fact that social-malaise measures in any given block are affected by all the designs, not merely by the one being tested. The score is a way of finding the combined effect of all the variables and can therefore be expected to even out any anomalies due to one design being overshadowed by others. Fig. 29 shows that this expectation is largely

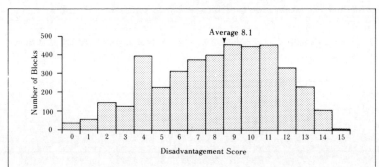

FIG.28. Frequency distribution of design-disadvantagement scores. The 4,099 blocks are concentrated towards the worse end of the scale.

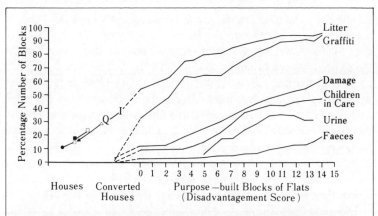

FIG.29. Trend lines for the six test measures in houses (left), converted houses (left-centre) and purpose-built blocks of flats (right). The houses are divided into age groups: circles for inter-war, squares for post-war, and triangles for pre-1914. In each case black symbols denote houses with front garden fences and gates and white symbols denote houses lacking one or more of these features. The converted houses are divided into two groups. Those in Queen's Park (Q) are smaller and less littered than those in the inner city (I). Purpose-built flats are divided into classes with different disadvantagement scores from 0 to 15. As their trend lines reflect the combined effect of all 15 designs they are generally smoother than those for individual designs. The graph as a whole approximates to the theoretical growth curves in Fig.8.

TABLE 16 *Probable levels of abuse in blocks of flats*

Disadvantagement score – selected values	Percentage number of blocks probably affected by					
				Children		
	Litter	Graffiti	Damage	in care	Urine	Faeces
0	55	33	12	10	*	3
3	71	58	17	10	*	3
6	81	64	29	21	15	5
9	90	82	44	40	29	7
12	94	90	53	45	34	13
15	96	95	62	48	*	15
Range	41	62	50	38	>19	12

Figures derived from Fig.29. *see text.

fulfilled by trend lines drawn for disadvantagement scores. As the score increases, each test measure also increases, in a generally smoother way than for the individual variables and the curves conform very well to the theoretical growth curves postulated in Fig. 8. The litter and graffiti curves are markedly convex, the damage and children-in-care curves much straighter, and the faeces curve is more concave. The flattening at the end of the children-in-care curve reflects the tendency to remove families with child problems from blocks with high values of some design variables. The urine curve is the most irregular. As it was mapped in Tower Hamlets only, there are too few blocks with low scores to give a rational result, while the worst-scoring blocks occur in large estates where they reflect the tailing off already described in Fig. 19.

The trend lines for the combined effect of design allow us to predict the most probable percentage of blocks that will be abused at each score (Table 16).

The most horrifying aspect of Table 16 is the top row. Even if drastic design modifications are undertaken to reduce the disadvantagement score to zero, there is still some probability of each form of abuse. The modification of flats is clearly only a second-best solution in comparison with well-designed houses.

On the positive side, however, is the large number of blocks that would cease to have certain forms of abuse if the score were lowered. The maximum scope for this kind of improvement is indicated in the bottom row of the table by the percentage difference between the worst and best blocks. Furthermore, the class of abuse would become less severe. Thus, although 55 per cent of zero-scoring blocks have litter in the entrances, the majority have only a small amount of clean and casual litter.

Disadvantagement scores are useful in persuading housing authorities to take design seriously. For example, our first letter to Southwark Housing Department about our research was brushed off with the comment that design modification is now the accepted wisdom and that our work would have nothing new to offer. Shortly afterwards the Peckham police informed us of a housing improvement scheme for the notorious 12-year-old Bonamy Estate, which proposed an expenditure of over £25,000 per flat, without reducing its horrific average disadvantagement score of 11.3 by even one point. Our next letter contained a factual reference to this disadvantagement score, which produced a very different response. Planning and housing staff visited the Land Use Research Unit, and became convinced that genuine design modification would be beneficial. Councillors, however, refuse to consider this type of modification and propose to 'improve' some of the blocks and replace others by houses of a design that is elsewhere associated with social problems.

There are other examples of how people think they have mastered the gist of Oscar Newman's findings but are actually misinterpreting them. Sheena Wilson, a Home Office consultant, has described how a plot of ground in Liverpool's Angela Street Estate was fenced off as 'semi-private' space for the residents of upstairs flats, but was promptly vandalised, which 'proved that design could not cause crime'. This short statement contains a number of misconceptions. Although she was within her rights to use the term 'semi-private' for shared space which we would call 'semi-public', she was mistaken in applying it to that particular plot of ground, which lacked all the basic mechanisms for exercising shared control. It was not visible from the windows of the upper flats. It could not be entered directly by stepping out of the entrance of the block. And it was just as strongly fenced on the side towards the accredited users as on the sides towards other people. These features undermined the possibility of control and created confused space, where vandalism could be predicted. Sheena Wilson jumped not only to the wrong conclusion that design cannot reduce crime but also to the more profound generalisation that it cannot cause it. In our view the evidence she cites is itself an example of how the creation of a confused-space design did cause the crime of malicious damage the very next day.

Monitoring improvement schemes

Before formulating practical recommendations for design modifications

FIG.30. Frequency distribution of abuse scores. Unlike the disadvantagement scores they are more concentrated towards the lower end of the scale, probably because cleaning and repairs help to keep them down.

we monitored local authority improvement schemes carried out in our study area during the period of research. These covered 17 blocks in nine estates. We wanted to see how far reductions in their disadvantagement scores had been accompanied by improvements in the test measures, and for this purpose we devised an abuse score which combines the design variables. Only the four test measures recorded for all 4,099 blocks were used, to give an abuse score ranging from 0 to 8, as shown here and in Fig. 30.

Litter
None	0
Clean and casual	1
Dirty and decayed	2

Graffiti
None	0
Inside or outside	1
Inside and outside	2

Damage
None	0
One type of target	1
Two types of target	2
Three or more types of target	3

Faeces
| Absent | 0 |
| Present | 1 |

Abuse scores were calculated for each of the 17 blocks before and after the improvement schemes, and it was disappointing to find an overall deterioration. Litter was little changed; most blocks had dirty and decayed litter on both occasions, but three improved to clean and casual status. No block became litter-free. Two blocks had faeces in their entrances

TABLE 17 *Increase in vandalism after improvement schemes*

Type of target	Before improvement	After improvement
Fences	—	2
Windows	5	11
Rubbish chutes	3	2
Electrical fittings	1	7
Doors	1	5
Other	1	1
Total	11	28

Figures are numbers of blocks in which each type of target was damaged.

both before and after.

Graffiti definitely worsened. No block was graffiti-free at either date but four originally had graffiti only inside or outside, while after improvement they all had it both inside and outside.

The worst deterioration was the amount of vandal damage. Before the scheme there were six damage-free blocks and 11 with a single type of target attacked. Afterwards only two remained damage-free and only six had a single target. Nine had two, three or even four types of target damaged (Table 17).

The crucial question is: 'Why should housing improvement schemes lead to a worsening of abuse? Does this not invalidate the claims made for the beneficial effect of design modification?'

TABLE 18 *Components of improvement schemes*

	No. of blocks	Mean disadvantagement score		Mean abuse score	
		Before	After	Before	After
Traffic control/parking	1	13.0	13.0	4.0	5.0
Landscaping	2	12.5	12.5	4.0	5.5
Security devices					
Entryphones	7	12.3	12.0	4.0	4.4
Entryphones with TV	2	11.0	10.0	4.0	6.0
Design or layout changes					
Blocked walkways	2	12.0	12.0	5.0	7.5
Blocked entrances	3	10.7	10.3	4.0	5.3
Communal gardens	4	10.8	10.8	4.8	5.3
Individual gardens	2	10.0	10.0	4.0	4.0

The improvement schemes covered 17 blocks in 9 estates.

Table 18 shows that the second part of the question is based on a false premise. Housing improvement does not necessarily involve design modification, and in fact only four of the 17 blocks had their disadvantagement scores reduced, and then by only one point.

Traffic control involves the installation of sleeping policemen to stop cars and motor-bikes roaring noisily through the estate. One tends to think of ordinary traffic taking short cuts through housing estates, but there may be a different and more dangerous problem. A scheme of this kind at Westminster's Lisson Green Estate was a response to reckless driving by teenagers below the age limit for driving licences. The police had been powerless to take action as estate roads are private in law, and licence-less driving on them is not illegal. It appears that the creation of the estates has deprived the inhabitants of certain forms of protection by live policemen, so that sleeping policemen have been substituted, apparently successfully. However, it may be only a matter of time before the example of the Kick Start motor cycling programme on television causes the sleeping policemen to be perceived as a sporting challenge instead of a deterrent and then the problem may be back in full force. There may be a case for a diametrically opposite solution – the adoption of estate roads as public streets, so that the presence of normal traffic helps create a public presence.

Great faith is also placed in *landscaping*, with its power to lift the human psyche, but in the blocks receiving this treatment, only four out of 22 people interviewed expressed pleasure in the improved appearance. Landscaping did not put a stop to urine pollution in one of the blocks, nor prevent increased vandalism in both of them. It seems, at present, to be purely cosmetic treatment, painting over the surface without touching the dry rot of design disadvantagement underneath. Landscape architecture is a vigorous young profession, capable of making positive contributions towards spatial organisation, and if it can take account of our findings on the layout of estate grounds, it may be able to increase its beneficial effect.

Security devices are in vogue at present, and although they are the most expensive of the various improvements monitored, they have been installed in the worst blocks. As with landscaping, it is instinctive to feel that benefit must accrue from entryphones, as they require callers to speak and identify themselves before being admitted, and some of the interviewees spoke of greater cleanliness and less vandalism, even though the objective before-and-after scores did not substantiate their opinions. Four of the nine blocks showed no change in abuse score and five showed a deterioration; paradoxically, deterioration was worst where the entryphones were backed up with television monitoring systems.

A major problem with entryphones is the fact that they require co-operation among tenants, which may not be achievable in large anonymous blocks. They have proved their worth in places such as Belgravia and Kensington, where the number of dwellings served is less than the threshold of six and it is no coincidence that the most successful of the nine cases monitored were installations serving only 10 dwellings on the ground floors of three blocks in Rhodeswell Road, Tower Hamlets. Here, 80 per cent of the people interviewed considered them a success, and there was no worsening of the abuse scores – although there was no improvement either. In the larger blocks there were cases of people wedging the doors open when they lost their keys, or thinking it a kindness to admit strangers seeking access at the same time as themselves – indications of a lack of established mores.

Entryphones are not immune to malicious damage, and are particularly vulnerable when introduced into blocks already beset by vandalism. Even with the successful Rhodeswell Road schemes, minor cases of vandalism were reported. Improvement schemes are frequently better appreciated by tenants if they have been consulted beforehand and understand the changes that are made, but even the most extensive consultations do not include the young vandals.

Entryphones may also fail because of defects which cause breakdown, which together with the uncooperative behaviour and deliberate damage may completely vitiate the sense of security they are supposed to bring. Some tenants described them as useless, and Oscar Newman has also commented that they are a complete failure in blocks with over 50 residents.

Even if entryphones function, they may fail to produce the expected security because they are based on a false assumption. It is considered sufficient to keep intruders out, and no thought is given to the fact that vandals and criminals are numbered among the residents. These are the blocks that breed anti-social people. They live there, and security devices cannot exclude them. Devices cannot substitute for the self-policing that arises naturally in better-designed areas, although they can usefully reinforce it where it exists.

The remaining types of improvement are more closely related to the design modifications being sought, but they fail to reduce either the disadvantagement scores or the average abuse scores.

The scheme affecting *overhead walkways* has failed because it misinterprets what is needed, and the ideal and the misinterpretation are as different as chalk and cheese. Our recommendation is that walkways should be *removed*, which automatically lops a point off the disadvantagement score and also has beneficial side-effects by reducing high values of three other designs: interconnecting exits, vertical routes and dwellings served by the same entrance. In favourable conditions, one or more of these three may be brought down below its threshold level, which also improves the disadvantagement score, and by implication the abuse score also.

What has happened in practice has not improved the disadvantagement score at all, and has sent the abuse score soaring by 2.5 points — more than any other so-called improvement measure. For economy reasons it was decided not to remove the walkways but merely to block them off by wire barriers. These were easy prey for vandals with wire-cutters, so they failed in their basic function of making each block a self-contained unit, with advantages of safety, privacy and noise-abatement. However, even in their vandalised state they still acted as barriers to law-abiding residents, so their net effect was to allow vandals to squeeze through, undiluted by ordinary citizens whose presence might have kept anti-social behaviour in check. The vandalism of the barriers was accompanied by an upsurge of damage in the blocks themselves, replacing a total of two targets by a new total of seven. Many interviewees felt cheated and resentful, especially as they had been deprived of a convenient access and fire-escape route. This is clearly a case of false economy, which some of the residents condemned as a waste of money, and it illustrates the futility of making 'improvements' without understanding the fundamental reasons for them.

Another inadequate scheme was an attempt to prevent school children taking short cuts through the Portman Place block in Tower Hamlets. This could have reduced the disadvantagement score by one point for suppression of *interconnecting exits*, but did not take the opportunity to do so. Instead, there was a new gate, intended to be closed when children were out of school. However, most of the tenants thought that the gate was positioned on the wrong side of the block, as the side facing the school was still left open, and the children continued to crowd in and congregate on the stairs during breaks and lunch hours.

Individual gardens were fenced off for ground-floor tenants in two blocks. These were greatly valued by the fortunate tenants who acquired semi-private space, but resented as unfair by upstairs residents, and, probably as a result, some of the fences were damaged and rubbish was tossed into some of the gardens. *Communal gardens* for ground-floor residents were also resented at Lister House, where railings were erected to protect ground-floor flats but not extended to cover the communal entrances to upper floors. This may, perhaps, account for the spraying of paint on some of the new garden furniture.

Three other communal gardens, on the Holland Estate, were introduced in full consultation with the tenants' association and actually at their request. They were designated for old people, who used them to sit outside in good weather and regarded them as successful. In two cases it seemed that this facility decreased anonymity and increased surveillance; both vandal damage and urine pollution had gone from the blocks at the time of the resurvey. In the third case, however, there was no such response; on the contrary, vandalism worsened, and both kinds of excrement continued to occur. This block, Brune House, had the worst abuse score before improvement, and it may be that communal gardens are insufficient to make any impact when the disadvantagement is so serious.

There are three general lessons to be learned from monitoring the 17 blocks. The first is that the improvements should be genuine design modifications which reduce the disadvantagement score, and that considerable thought should be given to them to avoid misinterpretation. The second is that the tenants should understand and be convinced of the function of the modifications. There should be no imposition of changes without consultation and agreement. And thirdly, even if the right changes are introduced with the resident's full support, it is necessary to make them quantitatively significant. Table 18 showed that reducing the score by only one point or even less is not enough to make an impact, as it leaves the probability of abuse very high. The present hit-or-miss approach, which creates more disturbance than improvement, needs to be replaced by a more systematic understanding of design and how to amelioriate it.

Recommendations

The principles of design modification will be illustrated by reference to our first practical case, the Mozart council estate, Westminster, which was in need of a housing improvement scheme only six years after completion (Fig. 31). This scheme consisted partly of security devices, which were not generally successful. Locks were vandalised, doors were left unlocked and residents displayed more courtesy in letting strangers in

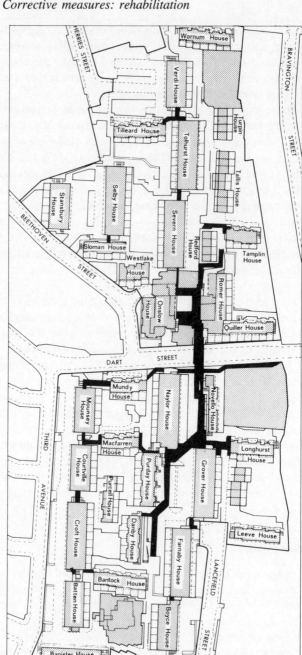

than security-consciousness in keeping them out. A further round of stronger doors and entryphones was contemplated, but it seemed that they too, would be undermined by the difficulty in ensuring that all residents would be security-conscious at all times.

Improved management was also part of the package. Three full-time housing officers and seven people engaged in maintenance were employed at the housing office on the estate, as well as private firms for prompt repair of vandal damage. Together they were highly efficient in removing traces of abuse, and residents were appreciative of their work, but it was also clear that management had reached the limits of its scope without solving the whole problem. The abuse was being made less visible, but not prevented from actually occurring.

Westminster Housing Department had also successfully tackled a few aspects of design modification on other estates and this approach seemed to offer further scope. Consequently, the Design Disadvantagement Team at King's College was invited to look at all aspects of design on the Mozart Estate and to make practical recommendations.

The estate contains 29 blocks of flats and 31 houses. Disadvantagement scores average 12.8, which places it among the worst 4 per cent of all estates studied to date. The average abuse score is 3.9, which is lower than would be expected for a disadvantagement score of 12.8, (thanks, no doubt, to efficient management), but many times higher than the range of 0.1 to 0.3 which is typical of houses in London. The Mozart Estate affords tremendous scope for design modification, and because all the deleterious designs are present, it illustrates all the principles involved. When the modifications have been carried out, it will also yield evidence on the benefits to be obtained.

First principle: Removal of overhead walkways

The Mozart Estate has 23 blocks joined together by overhead walkways and two more linked as a pair. Walkways are the most vicious 'open sesame' making a block vulnerable to outsiders and some of the dwellings of the estate cannot be reached at all without passing through other blocks as they have no staircase of their own. The demolition of the walkways and the provision of staircases where necessary, is an important first step in making each building the preserve of its own inhabitants. Blockage

FIG.31. Plan of Mozart Estate, Westminster. Overhead walkways between blocks are shown in black.

of walkways would not be a satisfactory substitute for removal; apart from the ineffective wire barriers already mentioned we have also seen railings that have been bent to give admittance and seven-foot brick walls which youths have learned to scramble over in their stride.

Walkway removal takes one point off the score of each block that is made free-standing, and another for each one that drops below the threshold for dwellings served by each entrance. One block, for example, ceases to be part of a linked system with 550 dwellings accessible from any entrance and has no more than four served communally. These two types of improvement reduce the estate's average score from 12.8 to 11.7.

Second principle: *Autonomy of the individual block*

Once the blocks have been made free-standing, each one can be separately fenced to form a single-block site. Its boundary wall should have only one gate or gap, to prevent outsiders from taking short cuts across it, and it is helpful if even a mere gap, for cars as well as people, is made as formal as possible, with definite gate-posts.

The whole area of the estate should be taken up by the individual sites; there should be no *left-over pieces of confused space*. These differ from *spaces left over after planning*, as those are outside the estates while these are inside. Their elimination means that people can no longer move diffusely between blocks, but are channelled along public streets or estate roads, where they create a stronger public presence, contributing to public safety.

The Mozart Estate has no fewer than 30 gaps in its perimeter. Some of these need to be closed completely; others can be adapted as the entries to the recommended single-block sites.

Some of the confused space on the estate consists of greens that attract concentrations of hooligans and lead to vandalism, and the police have suggested that they should be fenced off and made inaccessible. This would happen automatically if the estate were completely divided into single-block sites, but since some of the areas are rather large, there is another alternative: to build new houses. About 40 new houses could be accommodated, which would give some of the tenants a chance to better themselves, and would also benefit all residents by diluting the harmful concentration of flats.

Play areas would either be dismantled or included in individual sites. If the residents of a given block wanted to retain a play area, it would be serving a smaller, less anonymous and more manageable group of children. Westminster also provided a playground in a park across the street which, unlike those among the flats, is free from vandalism, probably because the park attracts an adult presence also.

Facilities other than play areas are also best located outside the residential area, both because they themselves are vulnerable to abuse and because they place neighbouring blocks at risk. Both these phenomena are seen in the Mozart Estate. One of the three shops has had to be abandoned and another has had its windows concreted in. Customers of *The Magic Flute* used the entrance of a nearby block as a urinal until it was bricked up, and eventually drunken behaviour led to the pub's closure and to the conversion of the building to a tenants' association centre. It is hoped that the shops can be relocated from walkway level to ground level.

If the layout of the estate is improved in the various ways suggested above the average disadvantagement score would be brought down to 8.3.

Third principle: Reducing anonymity and escape routes in the block

All the modifications suggested so far have been concerned with the reduction of space-sharing among different blocks. The third principle goes on to ameliorate space-sharing problems within each block, which involves reducing the size variables and the degree of interconnection.

The blocks of the Mozart Estate are mostly fairly small. Three are within the threshold for number of storeys and 20 are only one storey in excess, leaving six problem blocks of six to eight storeys. Table 19 shows how average abuse scores increase with building height, the main exception being the seven-storeyed block that contains officialdom in the form of the housing office.

In the north of England, where the drift of population has relieved the pressure on housing, there are successful cases of improvement by lopping off upper storeys to leave two- or three-storeyed houses. This would normally by unthinkable in the home-hungry south, but an episode on the Mozart Estate gives pause to reconsider. Six years after the estate was completed, one of the lifts had to receive major attention, and the cost was billed to the occupants: £1,800 for each household in the block. Their payments were to be spread over ten years, but this is a longer period than the lift remained serviceable in the first place, so there is a constant threat of further liability. As the tallest blocks are the most problem-ridden, there may be a case for reducing them to walk-up height when the next major call for expenditure on lifts occurs. This would

TABLE 19 *Average abuse scores related to some design values –*
Mozart Estate

Number of storeys								
design value	3	5	6	7	8			
abuse score	3.0	4.0	5.5	4.0	8.0			

Dwellings per block				
design value	8-12	15-20	21-30	57-63
abuse score	3.0	3.4	4.5	6.0

Dwellings per entrance				
design value	6	7-20	42	550
abuse score	1.0	3.0	2.5	4.3

Corridor type		
design value	4-9 flats/external	6-12 flats/internal
abuse score	3.0	4.9

Entrance type		
design value	With individual doors	Communal entrances only
abuse score	3.5	4.1

Entrance position			
design value	Set back, facing street	Inside the estate	Both
abuse score	2.0	3.4	4.9

Stilts or garage			
design value	None	Stilts	Garages
abuse score	3.1	4.3	4.5

Overhead walkways								
design value	0	1	2	3	4	5	6	7
abuse score	2.5	2.6	4.1	5.0	6.0	6.0	5.5	7.0

Play areas			
design value	None	Children's	Hard-surfaced
abuse score	3.6	4.3	4.5

Disadvantagement score	10	11	12	13	14
Abuse score	1.0	3.0	3.7	3.9	4.7

simultaneously reduce the number of dwellings in the largest blocks, which is another powerfully detrimental design variable.

Meanwhile, in the absence of such an expedient, block size is best tackled through the dwellings-per-entrance variable. This can be done by dividing the block into separate self-contained sections, either vertically or horizontally.

Long slab blocks can be divided into vertical sections by building walls across the corridors so that each entrance and staircase serves only a few adjacent flats on each floor. The vertical partitions should be continued out across the grounds to give each self-contained section its own walled site and effectively convert it into a separate block. These measures can improve seven variables: dwellings per entrance, dwellings per block, corridor type, interconnecting exits, interconnecting vertical routes, spatial organisation and play-area catchment. It does not necessarily bring all of them right down to their threshold levels, but even without this it would impart substantial benefits.

Horizontal partitioning begins by disconnecting the ground-floor layer of flats or maisonettes from the rest of the building to form individual *quasi-houses* with doors leading into their own front and back gardens.

If the ground-floor flats or maisonettes have separate external entrances the approach paths to the communal entrances can be given side walls, so that the shared space is effectively restricted to the upper floors. If the ground-floor entrances open into an internal corridor there are other possible modifications. One is to separate the communal doors at the ends of the corridors from the staircases leading to the upper floors. Another is to seal off any external access to the ground-floor corridor and divide it up as extra storage spaces to be integrated into individual flats. These flats lose their doors into the corridor, and turn their back doors into front doors, with a garden gate to give independent access.

Some blocks can be partitioned a stage further by installing a separate external staircase giving access to only the first layer above the ground floor dwellings, leaving the existing staircase/lift system to serve the top part of the block separately. Block partitioning would reduce the score of the Mozart Estate to 6.6.

Fourth principle: Improving entrances and streetscape

The purpose of the last principle is to create those features that promote a good social structure in the ordinary, traditional residential road. This not only covers the remaining design variables that pertain to flats but also introduces others that are desirable for houses.

A well-designed house has a front door facing the street and a back door opening into the semi-private space of an enclosed garden with no back gate. The maximum security offered by this simple arrangement is slightly impaired by the presence of a back gate, and more so if the gate opens on to a path or road with a choice of directions or places of concealment. If, as in flats set in confused space, there is no enclosure at all, security is grossly undermined by the presence of two exits affording a through route to outsiders. If, therefore, the block can be enclosed in a site which has no back gate, the second entrance required by fire regulations can sometimes be designed as a back door into the garden, where it becomes less of a liability. If only one entrance faces the street, it does not advertise to outsiders that a through-way exists. If the entrance is closed with a door, it does not offer a casual invitation in the same way as a mere aperture, particularly if the latter is an open arch or tunnel with a direct line of sight through to the other side of the block.

The public entrance to the block should face the street. The Mozart Estate has three estate roads that were formerly public and still remain legal rights of way, connected to the surrounding street system at both ends. Unfortunately, they have been subjected to gimmicky landscaping treatment that undermines their orderly functioning. One has had its pedestrian paths replaced by a series of lumps and ramps of uneven widths, heights and slopes – an uncomfortable obstacle race that forces walkers onto the carriageway. One is divided halfway along its length by a storey-high precipice, with the upper level extended to skirt the lower in a sequence of paths, ramps and raised walkways arranged in a dog-leg layout. The third has marked variations in width, with decorative zig-zag outlines. All these complexities need to be removed and replaced by normal carriageways flanked by continuous footpaths on both sides with proper kerbs and a smooth alignment of front garden walls.

At present many flanking walls in the Mozart Estate are high and faceless. Some are back garden fences for flats on either side of an internal corridor, and may be intended to afford privacy and security. However, there is no privacy in a garden overlooked by upper storeys and little security where a criminal is screened from public view once he has slipped through the gate. There is little to be lost and much to be gained by lowering the wall to waist-height and converting the back garden into a front garden on a road frontage: private surveillance of the road from the windows, public surveillance from the road, an opportunity to project a self-image in a garden that is on view, and a means of developing public acquaintanceship, as well as scope for dispensing with noisy and dangerous internal corridors.

Blocks with external corridors on the Mozart Estate are unusual in already having rudimentary front gardens, and these cast an interesting light upon one of our unexpected findings in Southwark and Tower Hamlets, viz. that communal entrances are less abused if they are the only entrances than if there are also individual external front doors to ground-floor flats. We conjectured that designs with individual front doors might be improved if they were fronted with semi-private buffer zones, and in the Mozart Estate this is the case. Even with imperfect front gardens the blocks with individual doors overtake those with communal entrances only (Table 19). They could be further improved by raising the front fences to waist-height, providing gates and inserting extra walls to divide each front garden from its neighbours.

Garden walls should be continued across the front of communal entrances and provided with gates so that the boundary between public space and private property is distinct and unbroken, and hence easier for children to learn to respect. Proper boundary walls would complete the conversion of the upper floors into separate blocks, more of which would be within the threshold for block size. The disadvantagement score would fall to 5.6.

Secondary thresholds

The aim of design improvement is to bring as many variables as possible down to their thresholds, but sometimes building regulations or other impediments may cause the change to fall short of that target, so that the disadvantagement score is not reduced. The improvement may be substantial but does not show up in the score, which detracts from the stimulus that the scoring system is intended to embody.

To overcome this problem a system of weighting is introduced. It is not used for the initial score, which merely points out which designs need attention, but is applied to modification plans in order to assess the improvement they will bring. It is effected by defining a secondary threshold for certain variables which, if achieved, is acknowledged by the subtraction of half a point.

The secondary thresholds are applied only in strict conditions. The overall score must have been reduced below the average of eight. The second exit is permissible only if it is not visible from the street and leads into an enclosed semi-public area. Two vertical routes are permissible only if one staircase is intervisibly adjacent to one lift. Two access points are permissible only if they are in the same side of the site perimeter so that they do not afford short cuts. Six dwellings per corridor applies only if their doors are intervisible and not concealed round corners.

If both sets of thresholds are applied to the Mozart Estate proposals, the final score is reduced to 4.8. Instead of being among the 4 per cent worst of all sites studied, it becomes among the 25 per cent best. This would bring a marked drop in the abuse score and, apart from the six worst blocks, there would be rarely be anything worse than clean and casual litter. A reduction in staffing costs might well become possible, and there would also be a substantial benefit from some 40 infill houses occupying what is now useless confused space.

Design variable	Primary threshold	Secondary threshold
Interconnecting exits	1	2
Vertical circulation channels	1	2
Gates or gaps in the site perimeter	1	2
Number of storeys	3	4
Dwellings per corridor	4	6
Dwellings per entrance	6	10
Dwellings per block	12	20
Maisonettes	0	single maisonette above quasi-house

From theory into practice

As funding becomes available, the Mozart Report is being put into action. A small Stage 1 removed four overhead walkways in March 1986 and the beat policemen logged an immediate 55 per cent drop in the burglary rate, sustained without further expenditure for some three years. Stage II, due for completion in April 1991, is applying as many improvements as possible to all blocks in the southwest quadrant of the estate.

The first step was an extensive series of tenant consultations, which elicited overwhelming support. This was followed by a steering group of tenants, housing officers and myself, to ensure that the scheme was not distorted by the architect's Modernist training. This did, in fact, happen at detailed design stage, after the steering group was disbanded, and indicates the need for supervision right through the completion of site works. Fortunately, the worst distortions were caught, and tenants on the rest of the estate are eager for Stage III.

To date, people involved in design improvement on some 40 estates have reported benefits that have exceeded our predictions. The individual fencing of front gardens for ground-floor flats is just one example. Its favourable effect on children has been mentioned on page 72, and a social worker in Camden, after similar fencing had been carried out on the Denton Estate, commented on the resulting dramatic reduction in racial harassment. Gloucester Grove tenants, in Southwark, found that gardens distancing children from the doorsteps reduced noise, stress and window breakage.

The Nationwide and Anglia Building Society found that garden enclosure was a powerful remedial measure in the Cherrymead Estate of starter-homes in Toxteth. These were originally designed with open-plan lawns which the children from nearby flats treated as public space and trespassed on intolerably. The value of the property plummeted. The starter-home investment was turning sour and many owners decided to cut their losses and surrender their properties, whereupon the empty houses were stripped, from floorboards to roof tanks. I was asked to visit Cherrymead to see whether design disadvantagement could possibly be a factor, and I recommended front-garden walls and gates to provide defensible space. This was done, and the estate has regained its popularity and full occupancy.

On the negative side, it is sad to report that the advice given, in the first edition of *Utopia on Trial*, for the Ferdinand Estate in Camden, was not adopted and its problems have continued.

Modification complexities

Although the aim of any modification programme would always be to reduce every design variable to at least its primary threshold levels, there is no possibility of doing so by means of rule-of-thumb measures. Problem estates are so varied that each needs an individual approach. Some are so perversely designed that the improvement of one variable is precluded by the existence of another, and sometimes additional defeating factors have been introduced by improvement schemes.

The Design Improvement Controlled Experiment (DICE) Project, set up by the Department of the Environment as described on page ix, explores a wide range of design improvement options to select the combination that reduces the score the most. Scientifically, it is interesting to see what one design change alone can achieve, but in human terms it is desirable to remedy as many defects as possible simultaneously. The planning of the most effective design improvement turns out to be a complex skill which needs considerable demonstration before it can diffuse into normal expertise; fortunately, DICE is affording a systematic demonstration opportunity.

DICE recommendations for transforming problem estates are generally meeting with a high degree of co-operation from planners, but in some cases they are criticised as infringing planning principles. This is not surprising as it is the planning principles in question that have created problem estates, and that we are now trying to reverse. One of these, low density, is less frequently urged by planners, and privacy has become the chief argument for wanting to space houses out. There is also a strong defence of road layouts, which we believe to be mistaken, and certain problems with fire regulations.

Privacy

It is sometimes objected that the insertion of houses among flats would be impractical because they would be overlooked and lacking in privacy, so that there would be no demand for them. This criticism is another myth which seems to possess so much life and vigour that it persists even when it has been proved wrong. In fact it contains two fallacies. Firstly, the residents of flats are provided with shared grounds which they are expected to enjoy in full view of all the windows towering above them. The individual back gardens of ground-floor flats are similarly overlooked. We have never heard of any official criticism of the lack of privacy inherent in these arrangements for flat dwellers, but as soon as houses are mentioned, sensitive antennae are often whipped out with astonishing speed. The Mozart Estate belies the myth. It already contains 31 houses which are more in demand than the flats, and there is no doubt that the 40 proposed new houses would also be very much wanted.

The second fallacy is an obsession with visual privacy and a neglect of auditory privacy, which is a matter for greater tenant concern. Visual privacy is easily obtained indoors by closing doors and drawing curtains, and can be achieved in back gardens by planting trees or shrubs. In front gardens it is an unnecessary interference with surveillance and self-policing, and this is why we use the term *semi-private*. The invasion of privacy by noise is not so easily overcome. Nerve-shattering decibels cannot be screened out. Thin walls that admit private conversations from next door can be embarrassing, and the fear of having one's own private life overheard can be stressfully inhibiting. Sound-proofing would be a far more practical measure than visual screening.

Routeways

Road planners maximise estate circulation space to at least twice what is necesssary, on the principle of separating vehicle from pedestrian routes in the interests of safety. The roads are frequently culs-de-sac to ensure that traffic is slowing down near its destination, and there are numerous paths between the two types of route to enable drivers to get away from the vehicle space. Despite the plausibility of this argument, it does not seem to have worked. As culs-de-sac have multiplied, so have deaths and serious injuries to child pedestrians, for which Britain has one of the worst rates in Europe. It could be that ultra-safe culs-de-sac teach children that it is normal to play on a road surface, which makes them more at risk when they are old enough to go out on ordinary roads alone. DICE recommends traditional street plans, where kerb drill has to be learnt. They also reduce escape routes for criminals, concentrate the public presence along fewer routes, where people feel safer, and cut the cost of maintaining an unnecessarily labyrinthine network.

Attention is sometimes drawn to an apparent contradiction in recommendations on alternative routes. Oscar Newman advocated their elimination through apartment buildings and we would also eliminate them through the grounds of estates. But Jane Jacobs thought that a dense network of through streets was preferable to fewer, longer routes.

The apparent contradiction is not, in fact, a real one. Jane Jacobs stressed the need to differentiate public and private space, and her comments apply to the public space of the street pattern. But Oscar Newman's comments and our own apply to residential space which should be as private and semi-private as possible. To maximise control of the residential territory we are advocating smaller territories, smaller blocks and smaller self-contained sections, with less inter-connectedness of all kinds. The interconnectedness needs to be out on the street, where it is favoured by a dense road network. Jane Jacobs' plea for denser roads is completely compatible with the 'small is beautiful' concept; if the roads are close together there is no room for large anonymous estates between them. We support Jane Jacobs' recommendation when we urge that estate roads should be adopted as public streets to satisfy Oscar Newman's approval of street-facing entrances. There is no conflict among the three viewpoints.

Fire hazard

Fire regulations vary among authorities, and some have been cited as precluding certain design improvements. Overhead walkways and interconnecting staircases and exits are treasured by fire officers as desirable escape routes, even though the police regard them as undesirable escape routes for criminals, and our research proves them to disrupt social stability.

Two factors are combining to resolve this conflict of views. The first is evidence that the fire-escape features can actually increase fire frequency by promoting anti-social behaviour that includes arson. In 1983 Shaw Associates revealed that the London Fire Brigade had attended 38 major fires and 250 secondary fires on the North Peckham Estate during the previous year, and we calculated that this was an annual rate of one per five dwellings, as compared with one per 810 dwellings in a better-designed estate of the same age, Giles Coppice, also in Southwark. The contrast stimulated Belinda Chan of King's College to study Fire District B28 in a different part of the borough, where high-scoring flats proved to have five times as many major fires per head as houses and 25 times as many secondary fires. There seems little point in providing counter-productive types of escape route from fires that would never happen if less damaging types were substituted.

Secondly, the experience of the fire service is also helping to transform attitudes towards fire precautions. Smoke from polyurethane upholstery has become a more lethal hazard than flames, and it no longer makes sense to design vast interconnecting warrens that facilitate smoke penetration. Corridor partitions would act as smoke barriers and contain compressed air injected to drive smoke back, while the associated new entrances would bring many flats within the regulation 30 feet of a staircase. In this way design improvement could assist fire control as well as crime control.

IX | Local Differences

Design appears to be the chief factor affecting the six types of social malaise, but we do not claim it explains everything. Other contributory factors remain to be discovered. Several possibilities were explored in Chapter VI, but most of them were found wanting, and we now turn to a new line of enquiry: a comparison of different places. If we can identify areas that have unexpectedly high or low abuse scores for their disadvantagement scores, we can investigate whether there are any local characteristics that seem to be responsible.

The abuse scores of the three study areas reflect differences in their disadvantagement scores:

Area	Mean disadvantagement score (Max: 15)	Mean abuse score (Max: 8)
Western Blackbird Leys	3.9	0.7
Eastern Blackbird Leys	5.3	1.0
Blackbird Leys total	4.5	0.9
Southwark	8.0	2.5
Tower Hamlets	8.3	3.7
Total area, 4099 blocks	8.1	3.0

The 54 blocks in Blackbird Leys are dispersed in 36 small sites among a much larger area of housing (Fig. 32). The western part, which has more houses, is better in terms of both design and abuse levels than the eastern part with more flats, and both are much better than either of the London boroughs.

Southwark is a little better than Tower Hamlets in its disadvantagement and abuse scores, but there is an enormous range of differences among its 645 sites (Fig. 33). The south part of the borough has relatively small and scattered sites, and only two of them have disadvantagement scores above 10. The north is a profound contrast, with larger and more closely packed sites, no fewer than 72 of which are above 10. Some

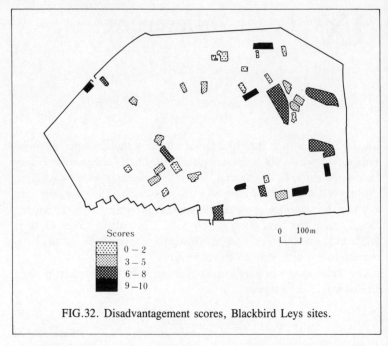

Scores

0 — 2
3 — 5
6 — 8
9 —10

0   100m

FIG.32. Disadvantagement scores, Blackbird Leys sites.

site averages are as high as 14, and there are seven individual blocks with the maximum score of 15.

The core of northern Southwark is a much vaunted experiment in comprehensive redevelopment on a grandiose scale, which has become the most notorious ultra-Utopia in London and, according to some, in the whole of Europe. It was built in the early 1970s when the vogue for 'streets in the sky' was at its peak, and the original plan was for a complete network of raised pedestrian walkways, stretching for three kilometres from the Heygate Estate to the Camden Estate, interrupted only by a descent to ground level across a new central space, Burgess Park. The layout includes 10 sites with disadvantagement scores of 10 to 14, where many residents say they live in a permanent state of fear and stress.

Tower Hamlets is the worst area on average, but Fig. 34 shows that it has fewer gargantuan black spots than Southwark and also fewer small, low-scoring sites.

A comparison of so few areas is not enough to be conclusive. If any disturbing factor is to be taken seriously, its effect must be shown to be consistent through many more cases, and this can be tried by break-

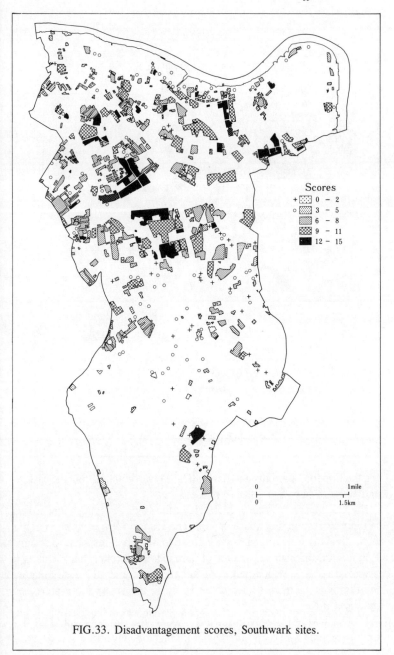

Scores

+ [::] 0 – 2
∘ [∷] 3 – 5
[▓] 6 – 8
[▨] 9 – 11
[■] 12 – 15

0   1mile
0   1.5km

FIG.33. Disadvantagement scores, Southwark sites.

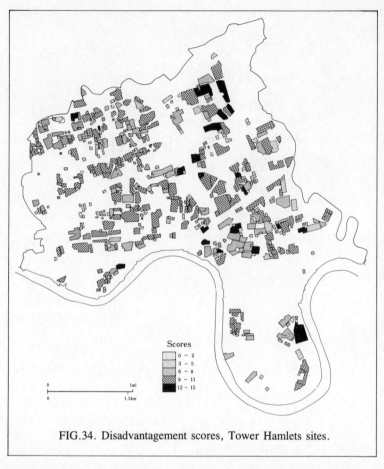

FIG.34. Disadvantagement scores, Tower Hamlets sites.

ing the London boroughs down into their 44 wards and adding the eastern and western halves of Blackbird Leys.

Fig. 35 is a scattergram, which relates the 46 disadvantagement scores to their corresponding abuse scores. The scatter of symbols rises to the right, showing a clear tendency for abuse to worsen in response to design. Running up through the scatter of symbols is a broken line. This is a 'regression line', which picks out the average trend and shows that as the disadvantagement score increases by 1, the abuse score increases by about 0.4.

If design were the only influence at work, the symbols would all fall exactly on the regression line. Disturbing factors have the effect of mov-

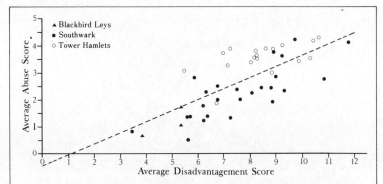

FIG.35. Relationship between disadvantagement scores and abuse scores. Each symbol represents one ward. The broken line is a regression line showing the average rate at which abuse increases in relation to design $(y = -0.461 + 0.413x)$. The ward figures average out any anomalous individual blocks, giving a Kendall's tau C correlation coefficient of $+0.599$, as compared with $+0.284$ for blocks. The ward scores are also suitable data for the more powerful Pearson's method of correlation which yields a still higher coefficient of $+0.720$.

ing them upward or downward away from the line, and the stronger the disturbance, the more distant the symbol. The measure of a symbol's distance from the regression line is called its 'regression residual', and this can be used to identify which wards are most out of line, either for better or for worse.

The ward-average scores in Fig. 36 are a simplification of the more detailed site maps, but the regression residuals in Fig. 37 present a quite different pattern. They sieve out the accident of where comprehensive redevelopment has located the worst designs, and show which wards have better or worse abuse than their designs would predict, regardless of whether the designs are good or bad.

All except one of the worse-than-predicted wards are in Tower Hamlets suggesting that some adverse factor is at work there, especially in the north-west, the east and the Isle of Dogs. The only worse-than-predicted ward in Southwark is Newington which has relatively well-designed blocks.

Better-than-predicted abuse scores occur in north, central and south Southwark and the eastern part of Blackbird Leys, and whatever benign disturbing factor is at work there is affecting areas of high, medium and low disadvantagement scores alike.

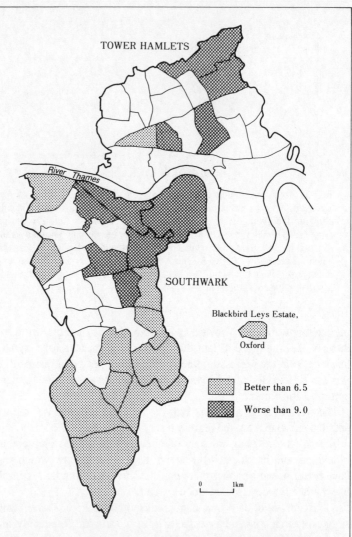

FIG.36. Wards with the best and the worst average disadvantagement scores. The worst designed areas are in north-east Southwark and Tower Hamlets. The better areas are mainly in southern Southwark and Blackbird Leys, but also include some inner-city areas with old blocks.

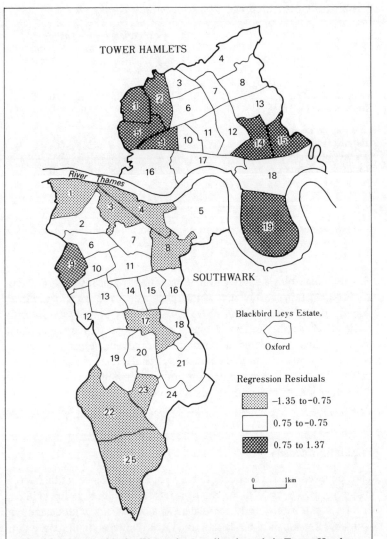

FIG.37. Abuse residuals. Worse-than-predicted wards in Tower Hamlets are: 1–Weavers, 2–St Peter's, 5–Spitalfields, 9–St Mary's, 14–Lansbury, 15–East India, and 19–Millwall in the Isle of Dogs. The only worse-than-predicted ward in Southwark is Newington. Better-than-predicted wards are all in Southwark: 1–Cathedral, 3–Abbey, 4–Riverside, 8–Rotherhithe, 17–The Lane, 22–Ruskin, 23–Alleyn, 25–College.

TABLE 20 *Possible disturbing factors — Pearson's coefficients*

	No. of areas	Correlation coefficient for					
		Abuse score		Disadvantage-ment score		Abuse residual	
Redevelopment standards							
Population density	44	0.17	•	0.05	•	0.17	•
Concentration of flats	46	0.77	***	0.78	***	0.34	**
Environmental factors *(Percentages of ward area)*							
Derelict or wasteland	46	0.42	***	0.28	*	0.34	**
Residential open space	46	0.46	***	0.45	***	0.23	•
Public open space	46	−0.16	•	0.02	•	−0.18	•
Child density	44	0.56	***	0.51	***	0.27	*

46 areas measured from maps; 44 London wards obtained from Population Census
• Not significant   ** Highly significant
* Significant   *** Very highly significant

Possible disturbing factors can now be tested by means of three Pearson's correlation coefficients, which relate them to *abuse scores, disadvantagement scores* and *abuse residuals*. If they are not significantly related to abuse, they can be dismissed at once, but if they are significant, they are then considered in relation to disadvantagement. A strong correlation here alerts us to the possibility that the relationship with abuse might be due to design rather than to the disturbing factor itself. The third coefficient, by contrast, shows how far the factor is acting independently and producing the disturbances measured by the residuals.

Population density

The supposedly malign effect of dense population is a belief that keeps cropping up. Table 20 shows that it is false. The number of people per hectare is not significantly correlated with abuse, nor with design nor with abuse residuals. Jane Jacobs and Oscar Newman both reached the same conclusion.

Nevertheless, evidence of this kind is repeatedly ignored. A recent report on one of the worst estates in our study area, North Peckham, by Shaw Associates, categorically states that one of the estate's major problems is its dense population. North Peckham was redeveloped in the early 1970s to lower density standards than existed before, and the result has been a great increase in the various kinds of malaise tested

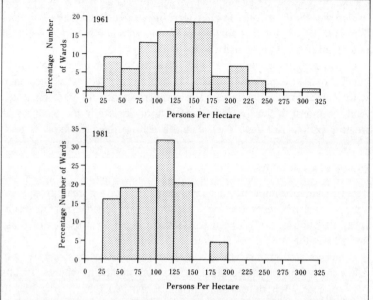

FIG.38. Reduction of population density in Southwark and Tower Hamlets. In 1961 35 per cent of the wards had densities exceeding 150 persons per hectare, but in 1981 only 4.5 per cent still exceeded this figure. The mean density of Southwark fell from 109 to 74 p.p.ha, and that of Tower Hamlets from 104 to 72, with much larger decreases over a longer period.

during our research, as well as soaring crime rates and the appalling incidence of fires at the rate of one per five dwellings per annum. Fig. 38 shows that there has been a marked trend towards lower densities throughout Southwark and Tower Hamlets over the 20-year period of most intensive redevelopment, and there is no evidence for the benefits so persistently claimed for it.

Why, then, has low density become a myth in planning theory? A frequently cited 'justification' is a classic psychological experiment with rats, by J. B. Calhoun. In a paper entitled *A Behavioral Sink* (1962) he described how, when a rat colony became too large, its orderly social structure broke down, and normal behaviour gave place to aggressiveness, homosexuality, and other deviations. Modern psychologists, notably J. L. Freedman, have shown that others have interpreted this experiment wrongly. The breakdown did not occur when the rats became too dense, but when they became too numerous. Normality cannot be restored by giving them larger areas and lower densities, but by fencing them off into smaller territories even at the same density. This shows that proper spatial organisation, with less sharing, is a more potent influence than density reduction.

Unfortunately for Southwark and Tower Hamlets, the erroneous myth has led to vast expenditure on ineffective density reduction combined with counter-productive increases in numbers sharing the same territory. And the moral of that is that if local authorities are in the business of treating people like rats, they should brush up their rat knowledge.

Concentration of flats

The rat evidence indicates that separate territories for small groups are superior to shared territories for larger groups. In human terms this would mean that houses with fenced gardens are better than estates of flats, and this is the next local difference to be tested.

If houses predominate, their benign effect upon social structure may dilute the effect of isolated blocks of flats among them, whereas if flats predominate, their detrimental influence may spill over from one to another. We can measure the extent to which flats are concentrated as the percentage of the residential area which they occupy in each ward.

Table 20 showed that the concentration of flats is strongly related to abuse scores. It is also strongly related to disadvantagement scores; the worst-designed flats are in the areas where most houses have been demolished. However, concentration has also been to some extent independent of the disadvantaging design variables, and then it has a highly significant effect in producing abuse not related to design (shown in the abuse residual column of the table). This is not a case of design being offset by a non-design factor, as concentration is itself an aspect of design, with an important lesson to impart. It is not enough to avoid only the worst design values and still go on building flats, as an increasing concentration of even the more innocuous blocks can produce problems that are worse than would be predicted from their design features alone.

The role of the concentration factor makes it easier to understand why it took so long to recognise the ill-effects of flats. In the early stages of the modern trend, the blocks were not only small and relatively harmless in design, but also few and relatively harmless in their concentration. It was only as they became progressively more numerous, more monstrous and more concentrated that the wrong turning in housing policy became obvious, and even then the direction of the detour was not identified sufficiently well to permit successful reorientation. Hence the need for the design-disadvantagement research project.

Environmental factors

It is often assumed that the quality of the urban landscape is an important influence: that derelict land, for example, is prejudicial while tended open space is salutary. These ideas can now be put to the test.

Derelict land and other kinds of dead space, such as overgrown waste areas or unofficial rubbish dumps, are eyesores which may set children bad examples of environmental care, and undermine residents' pride in keeping their territory well groomed. The field maps of Southwark show that many individual blocks with extreme worse-than-predicted abuse scores are located next to some kind of unused and untended site, and in order to see how general this kind of disturbance is, dead space has been measured as a percentage of each ward.

Derelict and wasteland are highly significantly related to abuse scores; they clearly live up to their bad reputation (Table 20). This is partly because they occur in areas of bad design, but also, and rather more strongly, because they affect abuse levels directly, as shown by the highly significant coefficient for abuse residuals. Dead space is definitely pernicious, just as commonly believed.

The lesson here is that urban areas which have been kept out of use, mostly in council ownership, should be recycled into active service. It is strongly recommended that new houses of non-disadvantaging design should be built on them, as this would not only remove the negative effect of the dereliction, but would also reduce the concentration of flats with its socially corrupting consequences.

The alleged favourable effect of tended open space is another belief which has became a sacred cow in planning theory. If it were true, it would result in a very highly significant *negative* correlation with abuse scores but, as Table 20 demonstrated, this is simply not the case.

Two measures of tended open space have been probed: green space included in residential estates and public open space outside the estates.

The amount of residential open space is very highly significantly related to abuse; the larger the green areas, the more widespread is the occurrence of litter, graffiti, damage and excrement. This is completely contrary to planning theory but fully compatible with the finding that large areas shared in common are harmful. It is also compatible with the conclusion that low density is a fallacy, as large green areas are the chief means of producing low densities. Both are sacred cows in a false creed, and should now be sacrificed on the altar of reality.

Residential open space is itself a design feature – a quantification of the confused space concept. As a design, it has a direct relationship with abuse and not a disturbing effect, so it is not significantly related to abuse residuals.

It was shown earlier that facilities such as shops, services, play areas and places of entertainment are best located outside residential sites. Is this also true for tended open space? If so, the parks, recreation grounds and other public spaces of each ward should be less harmfully related to abuse than that within the estates. Table 20 confirmed that this is the case. Public open space is negatively, i.e. benignly, related to abuse score and abuse residuals, although not to the extent of being significant. Its influence seems to be overrated, although not actively counter-productive as shared residential space is.

Child density

It has already been proved, in Chapter VI, that the reduced child densities of the 1980s no longer affect abuse levels more strongly than design, as they did in the 70s. Table 20 corroborated this result. The coefficient of 0.56 relating child density to abuse levels is definitely lower than the corresponding coefficients for the design, 0.72, or the concentration of flats, 0.77.

Nevertheless, the reduced child densities remain very highly significant. They are more consistently related to abuse than either derelict land or tended open space. However, they appear to operate mainly as a function of design; the worst designs bring out the worst behaviour in children. The independent effect of child density as a disturbing factor is only barely significant.

Ownership factors

It is a common belief that owner-occupancy generates pride in one's property, leading to more responsible care of home territory, and by implication, of the surrounding environment also. This idea is tested in Table 21 by reference to owner-occupied percentages and council-owned percentages of all dwellings in each ward. There are also other types of ownership: housing trusts, housing associations, private rental, community homes, etc., but this group is small, and so mixed that it has produced no significant correlations and has been omitted.

TABLE 21 *Ownership as a possible disturbing factor*

	Abuse score		Disadvantagement score		Abuse residuals	
Owner-occupied dwellings	−0.75	***	−0.68	***	−0.40	**
Council-owned dwellings	0.76	***	0.79	***	0.32	**

Figures used are Pearson's coefficients

** Highly significant   *** Very highly significant

The coefficients for owner-occupancy are strong and negative; as the percentage increases, the incidence of litter, etc., goes down, not only in the houses themselves but also in neighbouring blocks of flats. Conversely, the coefficients for council-ownership are strong and positive. The more publicly-owned housing there is, the more litter, etc., goes up.

Owner-occupancy is also strongly and negatively correlated with disadvantagement scores, which leads us to suspect it may be exerting much or most of its effect through the medium of design. The coefficients for abuse residuals show that it can act as a disturbing factor when it is independent of design, but to a markedly lesser extent.

Council housing is definitely worse designed than private, while housing trust property is intermediate between the two. This difference holds good for all 15 of the design variables independently and is also illustrated for disadvantagement score in Fig. 39, drawn for Southwark only, as Tower Hamlets has insufficient private blocks to compare. It is immediately clear that the great majority of private blocks are concentrated in the better part of the scale, while housing trust blocks are more commonly near the middle and council blocks are predominantly in the worse part. Their respective average scores are 4.0, 6.6, and 9.1. This suggests that a great deal of human misery could have been prevented if councils had adopted commercial designs.

Market forces appear to be a positive power for good in housing design. Private builders cannot survive unless they can profitably meet both the tastes and the price range of purchasers. Designs which sell quickly tend to be repeated, while those that hang fire are discontinued, and this has led to a preponderance of small, low-rise buildings, subdivided into self-contained sections with few dwellings per entrance. Purchasers tend to be single people, young childless couples or older people whose children

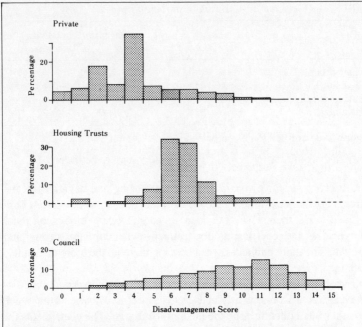

FIG.39. Disadvantagement score related to type of ownership. Private blocks are mainly concentrated toward the lower end of the scale of scores, housing trust blocks are concentrated towards the middle, and council blocks towards the upper end.

have left home. Families with children choose houses rather than flats, and consequently private flat-builders avoid maisonette designs and play areas. They also avoid unnecessary expense in the form of overhead walkways, long corridors, large numbers of interconnecting exits, lifts and staircases, and concrete stilts under the block. And they do not tie up capital in large land assemblies, but build on what they have, which makes for fewer blocks per site, with better spatial organisation, fewer gates and gaps, and street-oriented entrances.

Public builders, by contrast, have been free from both the financial discipline and the impact of consumer choice. They have received lavish housing subsidies which have been used to pursue doctrinaire gimmicks, and they have been encouraged to disregard residents' preferences as automatically inferior to the grand design principles of Utopia. Only now, when the flow of spendthrift money has dwindled, are councils adopting some of the more conservative features of private blocks.

Housing trust designs are usually better than council designs because they cannot afford to waste money, but worse than private designs because they do not consult the preferences of prospective occupiers.

These contrasts are all relative, however. Market discipline can only go so far in a system governed by planning. The planned multiplication of flats at the expense of houses constrains many people to settle for flats as the best they can afford, and then their apparent choice is described as a demand for flats and a justification for withholding planning permission for houses. This is an example of how interventionist policies lead to their own perpetuation, right or wrong.

Distribution of disturbing factors

The concentration of flats, derelict land, residential open space, two types of ownership and child density are six significant disturbing factors, but it remains to be proved that they exert their influence in the precise areas where abuse levels deviate most strongly from the prediction derived from design. This is now attempted by considering which of them affect the eight wards that are shown as significantly better than predicted in Fig. 37 and also the eight wards that are worse than predicted.

Of the eight better-than-predicted wards, four are in the Dulwich housing district of south Southwark. These all score well for at least three of the six significant disturbing factors, and Ruskin ward, with the best regression residual of all, scores well on all six. These factors could well be a sufficient explanation.

The other four better-than-predicted wards are clustered in the Bermondsey and Rotherhithe housing districts which form the northern edge of the borough. Three of them, Abbey, Riverside and Rotherhithe wards, are not characterised by even one of the six redeeming factors, and it may be that the two districts concerned are perhaps more efficient in their housing administration than the normal run.

One of the eight worse-than-predicted wards, Newington, is in Southwark; the other seven are in Tower Hamlets. All are among the worst scores for at least one of the six disturbing factors. Two score very badly for residential open space only and two for child density only. The latter is a factor which in the past has actually outweighed design, and although it no longer does so, it is not surprising to find it still exercising a strong disturbing effect locally.

Management

The concept of housing improvement through better management originated with Anne Power, who developed her ideas while employed in the North Islington Housing Rights Project in London, and was subsequently appointed as a consultant to the Department of the Environment's Priority Estates Project. This project is concerned with housing improvement schemes, which are interpreted in practice as modernisation, repairs, replacement of defective parts, landscaping, security devices and management reorganisation.

Anne Power's first heroic breakthrough was made in the notorious Tulse Hill Estate in the London borough of Lambeth, which was described as depressing, with old blocks close together and a lack of green space. It had suffered from being neglected, and had become 'hard to let', with 90 vacant dwellings representing an annual rent of £45,000. Anne Power demonstrated that the management costs needed to improve the estate could easily be financed out of the increased rent income that results from attracting a full complement of tenants.

She set to work to introduce any conceivable improvement, beginning with the clearing of revolting accumulations of garbage in the refuse storage areas, and as a result was able to inspire the residents with renewed hope and willingness to cooperate. She found that their foremost complaint was the Council's failure to attend to repairs, which seemed to be due to the remoteness of the huge, centralised GLC housing department, and by dint of force of personality, she negotiated a decentralised, full-time housing office in the estate itself. This took over responsibility for lettings, rent arrears, repairs and all tenancy matters, and within a month there were more applicants than vacant flats. The 'hard-to-let' label was no longer justified, and seemed to have been a result of inefficient management rather than an intrinsic revulsion against the estate. In fact, as design mapping has subsequently proved, the Tulse Hill Estate has an average disadvantagement score of 8.9, which is only a little worse than the average for our 4,099 blocks.

It was stipulated that new tenants must have chosen to apply to the Tulse Hill Estate itself; this avoided the hostility that is often associated with forced allocations. Despite this restriction there were enough applicants to fill all the vacant flats, and also a steady demand for new vacancies as they arose.

Later, when the Tulse Hill Estate had been transferred from the GLC to Lambeth, the local estate office was also allocated its own locally based repair staff, and repairs were accelerated. In Tower Hamlets, for example, repair workers tend to call without an appointment, which means tenants may be out. After failing to gain admittance three times, they write off the repair as no longer needed — a regrettable compounding of tenant frustration and wages paid to achieve nothing. In Tulse Hill, the estate officers and repair workers became locally known and trusted, with the result that tenants became willing to leave their keys at the office for work to go ahead in their absence.

The tenants' second priority was rubbish, and the extra rent revenue helped to finance extra collections, extra bins, free plastic bags and more resident caretakers to keep the problem under control.

The third priority was security. Better beat policing was introduced, including a daily patrol of the estate, and a weekly advice session. There was an 80 per cent drop in break-ins, although it did not immediately affect the mugging rate. An entryphone programme was initiated, but a design-disadvantagement survey in 1984 has revealed the same problem as elsewhere; some of the supposedly secure doors are, in practice, wedged open.

A further complaint was vandalism, predominantly affecting empty flats. Once the flats were let, they were automatically guarded by their occupants, avoiding thousands of pounds of damage. Other vandalism was reduced by target hardening, for example, brighter vandal-proof balcony lights and laminated glass in the stairwells. The latter was 50 per cent more expensive than normal glass, but paid for itself and brought a net saving within three months.

The success of the Tulse Hill experiment brought high hopes for the role of better management in salvaging problem estates. 'Almost any estate with 20 or more empty units and a vandalism problem cannot but benefit from localised management and *pay for itself*' (Anne Power's italics). It is unfortunate that in the light of this rosy prognosis, the Department of the Environment leaped to the conclusion that design and management were mutually exclusive explanations of problem estates, and told the Design Disadvantagement Team that as improved management had proved efficacious, design improvement would be dismissed as having nothing to offer.

Neither Anne Power nor members of our team accept this simplistic dichotomy. Both perceive that the basic principles are the same for management and design improvement alike: reducing the scale of operations and returning autonomy to residents. Anne Power advocated bringing control down from the mammoth central housing authority to the individual estate. We advocate splitting large estates into single-block sites and partitioning large blocks into small self-contained sections, coming as close as possible to the ultimate optimum of the single-family house in its own garden. We both agree that improved management and improved design would reinforce each other, and we presented a joint submission on the topic at the Royal Geographical Society under the title *Trouble in Utopia* in 1983.

Anne Power has found that management changes are harder to sustain in badly-designed estates; even efficient local authorities can be defeated by the worst concrete jungles especially where there is poor housing demand. Although she did not map design in detail, she adopted a broad, three-fold classification for a nationwide sample of 20 estates: cottage estates (houses); walk-up blocks with external corridors; and modern concrete complexes with overhead walkways, underground garages and large expanses of shared space. All of these have been improved as a result of estate-based management, but the last type benefits in fewer ways and proves much the hardest to manage.

Anne Power issued two warnings in her 1984 report. The first is that at present there is simply not the expertise available for a widespread replication of the complex activities demanded for management improvement. The second is that progress will not survive any dilution of effort. Decentralisation is not a once-and-for-all project to set an estate on its feet, but a continuing dedicated routine. Any relaxation of the new standards may lead to back-sliding, which has now been observed on all three kinds of estate, but is particularly disappointing where design disadvantagement is most severe. Even Tulse Hill soon reverted to problem status when Lambeth decided not to pay for extra management permanently.

Design modification, if properly carried out, seems to hold more promise of permanence, and if management reform had been accompanied by reductions in disadvantagement scores, the gains might well have been easier to hold.

Mozart, six years after completion, was such a serious problem that it was selected for intensive management improvement of the type pioneered by the Priority Estates Project. This achieved a great deal but neither tenants nor housing officers were satisfied, and because there were few vacant dwellings, there was little scope for extra rent to pay the six extra maintenance staff. Moreover, there were strong grounds for suspecting that the incidence of abuse was not actually reduced, but only cleared, cleaned and repaired more quickly. The hope that attitudes would change was disappointed, and there has since been a gradual slipping back.

Adjoining Mozart is the Queen's Park Estate, managed from the same local office but without any special management scheme. If management were the main factor, Queen's Park would be more plagued with problems, but the reverse is true. Its 1984 abuse score was only 0.3, whereas Mozart's was 3.9, or 13 times as bad. Clearly some other factor was outweighing management.

If we look to design as that factor, we find that the difference in abuse levels was very close to what could be predicted from the character of the two estates. Queen's Park consists of Victorian artisan cottages with small front and back gardens, and its abuse score of 0.3 was closely in line with that of 700 pre-1914 houses observed elsewhere. Although Mozart was improved by its management scheme, it was still 80 per cent in line with the abuse score predicted by its design. Queen's Park may also have benefited from its age and stability; it was certainly not suffering from being twice as large as Mozart, as its traditional streets of autonomous dwellings can accommodate large size in a way that large blocks in large expanses of confused space cannot. Its popularity with its residents was shown by the fact that by 1984 one third of them had exercised the right to buy their homes, while only three Mozart tenants had done so.

Badly-designed estates demand unusually high standards of excellence and devotion from their managers. Officers who would be perfectly competent to run well-designed areas may find themselves out of their depth in the flood-tide of social decay which is swamping the Utopian townscape, and it would be unfair to hold them to blame for failing to resolve it.

Cost considerations

Anne Power has shown that improved management brings social benefits at no extra cost. Expenditure has to be increased to cover additional staff, but the cost can be met, partly by increased rent revenues and partly from savings on repairs to vandalised property.

Can design modification also pay for itself? We believe that it can, and furthermore that it can go beyond merely breaking even. It seems to offer scope for achieving genuine savings in the high cost of housing administration.

TABLE 22 *Comparison of certain housing costs*

	Queen's Park Estate	Mozart Estate
Predominant dwelling type	Terrace houses	Blocks of flats
Mean disadvantagement score	0.0	12.8
Number of dwellings	1700	737
Number of housing officers	2	3
Cost	£12.40	£40.70
Number of cleaners, caretakers	0	7
Cost	£0.0	£67.80
Cost of graffiti removal	£0.30	£10.70
Cost of vandal-damage repairs	£3.20	£100.10
Total of the costs cited	£15.90	£219.30

Cost figures are expressed per dwelling for 1984

Setting aside the ordinary maintenance costs of the dwellings themselves, which are incurred irrespectively of design and layout features, it has been possible to itemise some of the cost differentials involved in the upkeep of the Mozart and Queen's Park Estates (Table 22). In 1984 the annual cost per dwelling was 14 times as great on the Mozart Estate as on Queen's Park, yet the abuse level was 13 times as bad. This was the differential that remained after Mozart's management had been improved, and it is an ongoing cost that will have to be met year after year. In these circumstances it is logical to enquire whether design modification can ease the financial burden.

Until design modification has been tried in a cost-monitored situation, it is not possible to produce hard figures, but there are several reasons for thinking there would be substantial savings.

Firstly, design modification removes the causes of the various abuses instead of merely containing them, so that the estate becomes more self-tending and self-policing. This means that fewer management staff are needed and repair costs diminish.

Secondly, design modification can obviate the need for expensive security installations such as entryphones, which are rarely effective. If the money which some authorities are currently setting aside for entryphone systems were to be spent on building walls to create single-block sites, there would be more real benefit at no extra cost.

Thirdly, design changes are permanent: they do not revert if vigilance is relaxed. This takes a great deal of strain off housing staff, as well as avoiding recurrent costs such as repeated repairs or initiatives to re-involve tenants at intervals. The initial outlay has more certainty of being recouped by successive annual savings.

Fourthly, there would be financial gains in areas outside the housing budget. As children are reared in a more stable community, the scale of school vandalism should decline. The reduction in crime should permit police-force economies. Victims' calls upon the health service should lessen. The fire service would have fewer cases of arson to deal with. And so on.

X | Summing-up

Social breakdown, like charity, begins at home. Psychologists have long stressed the importance of the home, as a family, during the child's formative years, and we now stress its importance as a *place*. Shared nests, however lovingly designed by experts, can interfere with the quality of parenting and colour the attitudes of the generations reared in them.

Disturbance of child-rearing practice is a fourth mechanism of design disadvantagement that can now be added to Newman's anonymity, escape routes and lack of surveillance. While these three show that certain designs are vulnerable to any criminals who happen to be around, the fourth explains how problem estates can breed their own anti- social elements, leading to increased delinquency and crime. The design disadvantagement research gives a more general understanding of how human behaviour tends to deteriorate under the stress of inappropriate habitats. The worse the design, the greater the probability that more families will fail, in more ways, to develop their children's capacity for adjusting to civilised life, and the probability becomes a smoother progression when it is related to the combination of all the designs together.

The mildest form of social deviance is litter. It is rare in traditional houses with all the design safeguards that have evolved over time, but the more these safeguards have been abandoned, the more likely is a copious and obnoxious accumulation of garbage. As design worsens, litter is joined by graffiti, and then successively by vandal damage, by family breakdown necessitating the placing of children in care, and by excrement. Each of these increases in a classic S-shaped growth curve (Fig. 8), which begins slowly, then accelerates and finally slows down towards saturation point. The later any form of abuse appears, the more slowly it grows. Litter and graffiti have already reached saturation point in the worst existing blocks, but the other measures have not. They would do so, however, if even worse blocks were to be built in the future.

The amount of public money spent on cleaning, repairing and administering design-disadvantaged buildings has yet to be costed. One thing is certain, however. It is a total waste, since all these functions would be carried out by the inhabitants themselves if post-war housing had been styled to facilitate self-tending by occupiers.

There are also probably many other concealed costs traceable to faulty housing design, arising from other kinds of social breakdown that have been growing during the Utopian period. Oscar Newman demonstrated that crime is associated with design, and during 1984 the Land Use Research Unit collaborated with research workers from the Neighbourhood Policing Project Team within the Metropolitan Police in a similar investigation in London. Nine categories of crime were identified for each of 729 blocks of flats in the Carter Street Division of Southwark, and Fig. 40 shows crime trend lines in relation to disadvantagement scores for seven types. (The other two were vehicle offences with closely similar trends.) It is immediately clear that crime is related to design in much the same way as vandalism, children in care and excrement, and, consequently, that design-disadvantaged areas cause higher public expenditure for policing, courts and prisons, higher private and insurance losses, and higher social costs in the suffering of crime victims.

The crime data refute, once more, the simplistic criticism that worse social breakdown in badly-designed blocks is merely a pro rata effect of their more numerous dwellings. Figures show that juveniles in blocks that score 13 or more are nearly eight times as likely, per dwelling, to acquire a criminal record than those in blocks scoring 0–2.

As well as the broad agreement between our six social malaise measures and the several categories of crime, we also have preliminary evidence that arson rates and some kinds of psychiatric illness are related to the malign effect of Utopian designs. There is no reason to think that the list of design-induced ills has been fully explored. They certainly appear to be wide-ranging, which emphasises the wide range of benefits that design modification could bring.

Design has not been investigated in isolation. Alternative explanations of the various forms of social malaise have been explored, and while some appear to be definite contributory factors, none has emerged as being stronger than design.

Some rather cherished ideas have been found to be totally irrelevant, such as population density and the amount of nearby public

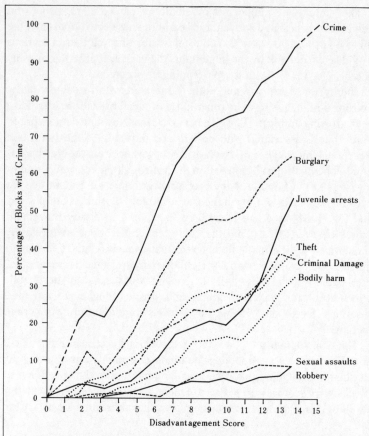

FIG.40. Trend lines for seven classes of crime in 729 blocks of flats in the Carter Street Police Division of Southwark. Crime increases as design disadvantagement worsens. No crimes were reported from the blocks with zero disadvantagement score, but the average rate for blocks with scores of 13, 14 and 15 exceeded one crime per five dwellings (1980 figures).

open space. Other equally cherished ideas prove to have an effect that is completely opposite to that claimed. Various measures of poverty are associated with less, rather than more, social breakdown. Unemployment is not associated with increased vandalism. More residential green space brings more intensive abuse, and so does the presence of shops, services or community halls located inside the estate.

Some of the main additional features that help to explain litter, graffiti, damage, etc., are themselves design variables: the presence of non-residential facilities, and the concentration of flats to the exclusion of houses. These have both been implemented as mistaken measures in the same way as the disadvantaging designs of the buildings and the grounds.

Other explanatory factors involve the existence of unused areas, whether in the form of derelict or wasteland sites, abandoned buildings or empty boarded-up flats. These are partly due to misconceived policies, but also partly due to inefficiency in recycling idle land or reletting empty dwellings.

Child density definitely contributes to high levels of abuse in badly designed dwellings. It used to be a stronger factor than design but since the Home Office recommended decreasing the number of children in the worst blocks, it has become a weaker influence. We have been able to identify a target figure for density reduction. There should not be more than one child under 15 per six adults aged 20 or more in a block of flats.

Ownership is also an important factor, but this is largely because most owner-occupied dwellings are either houses or the best-designed flats, while council dwellings tend to be in blocks with higher disadvantagement scores. Where ownership is independent of design it does not exert such a strong influence as the design variables do.

All these discoveries add up to the fact that it is the Utopian design imposed upon post-war Britain that appears to be the chief factor in many aspects of social decline in new or redeveloped areas.

The evidence

Our conclusions are supported by an enormous amount of detailed evidence. The basic study covered 4,099 blocks of flats and 4,172 houses and converted houses, and subsequent data from a variety of British and overseas areas have increased the totals to some 7,000 and 14,000 respectively. The new information confirms the old, and the vast scale of the research is an antidote to criticisms based on small samples or even single blocks. These may well be the exceptions that give a misleading impression. Where the behaviour of people is concerned there are bound to be exceptions, and what we have found is a set of trends, or probabilities, which make up an overall pattern and allow for the exceptions.

We have now identified 16 design variables in blocks of flats or maisonettes which affect the behaviour of at least some residents, especially children, and also of other people using the building. Litter-dropping behaviour, for example, becomes more frequent as buildings and grounds increase in size and interconnectedness, and also where residents cannot see or control the approach to their dwellings. The results are strengthened by the fact that all of the six of the test measures used – litter, graffiti, vandal damage, children in care, urine pollution and faecal pollution – become more common as the design values worsen within each variable. The same is true of nine types of crime. A very consistent picture emerges, the main exceptions to which are quite minor. They occur with design values found in too few blocks to be truly representative, or they affect only the least influential designs, or they appear to reflect the policy of reducing child densities.

Houses show less sign of social breakdown than purpose-built flats, while houses converted into flats are intermediate between the two. House litter is less common, graffiti extremely rare, and excrement virtually unheard of. Vandal damage may occur where houses are adjacent to flats, but children are taken into care much less often. Litter is therefore the main test measure for houses. It varies in frequency according to 12 design features now established. Houses of different dates show that the less stabilising designs have become more common over time. This means that some new estates of houses may be more problem-ridden than some of the better purpose-built blocks.

The global context

Some people have queried whether design is really at fault in producing anti-social behaviour, when the Scots and the Europeans manage to live successfully in flats. They suggest that the whole problem is due to the fact that the English are not used to living in shared buildings. If they are right, then problem estates are just a temporary British aberration, pending our acclimatisation to tenement habitats. On the other hand, design disadvantagement could be a widespread human response, and this alternative is more in accord with our observations.

Traditional Scottish and continental flats are quite low-scoring, and one would not expect most of them to foster serious social breakdown. By contrast, high-scoring Modernist designs are just as destructive in Scotland as they are in England, despite the supposed advantage of habituation. European conferences reveal the same concerns in many countries. Newman's work shows that design disadvantagement is an American problem also, and its spread to Canada has led to two invitations to me to cross the Atlantic in an advisory capacity. In Australia, visits to four State Housing Commissions showed that Queensland, with only a few small publicly owned blocks, has the least problem, while Victoria, with many large ones, has the most.

Nor is the Orient immune. Singapore has 30 badly-designed estates where crime rates exceed one offence per ten dwellings per year. In the Chinese city of Jinan, where traditional two-roomed hovels are being replaced by well-plumbed four-roomed flats, a nursery school head said she had observed that flat-bred three-year-olds were noticeably slower, clumsier, less self-confident and more lacking in initiative than their house-bred contemporaries.

Our survey of 600 blocks in Hokkaido, where flat-building began in about 1970, showed that most are two-storeyed, with six to eight dwellings and located along street frontages. They have few defects and correspondingly few problems. Just as British officialdom once argued that design disadvantagement was an American problem that could not happen in Britian, so the Japanese now see it as a Western problem that cannot affect them. And yet larger estates of larger blocks are already beset by litter, graffiti and broken lights and door panes, while a high-rise estate in the new town of Tomakomai found it necessary to appoint a crime prevention officer.

Hong Kong, however, is an anomalous case where extreme concentrations of high-rise blocks have less crime and social breakdown than would be expected and six possible restraining factors have been discussed with the Deputy Director of Housing there.

First, there is the exceptionally high density, with most blocks arranged along the streets instead of being dispersed in landscaped grounds. This increases the public presence, enhances surveillance and reduces escape routes. Secondly, the flats are built as shells, leaving internal walls to be provided by tenants. Because of this investment there is also a low turnover rate and more chance to overcome anonymity. Thirdly, money saved on construction is channelled into maintenance offices open 24 hours a day, so that repairs are carried out immediately, and frustration does not build up. There are also uniformed caretaker patrols with walkie-talkies to relay tenants' requests to the maintenance staff.

Fifthly, Hong Kong is at a cultural peak of the type defined by D.C. McClelland (1962) as an *achieving society*, where the child-rearing priority is goodness rather than happiness. Children are allowed little time to get into trouble. And finally, if youngsters should commit offences, the parents are fined, which is a further incentive to home enforcement of good behaviour. These facts reinforce our theme that child-rearing is an important fourth mechanism mediating between design and social breakdown.

There is much to be learned from the ways in which Hong Kong mitigates the effects of design disadvantagement, but little prospect of transferring them to Britain or elsewhere. This is especially true of the vital cultural peak, and one dreads to think of the design legacy Hong Kong is creating for the time when that peak is past. It seems better to avoid disruptive designs in the first place, rather than to create a problem and then devote energy to overcoming it.

In summary, therefore, the global context suggests that design disadvantagement is a widespread human response. The Modern Movement's brand of Utopia is a virtually universal disaster.

RECOMMENDATIONS

Design disadvantagement research supports the use of design improve-ment as a practical measure, based on more hard evidence than any other approach in vogue today. Its *corrective* aspect is being tackled by the DICE Project to provide technical models and costings for what is a highly complex procedure. DICE is already revealing that although houses are generally less harmful than flats, they can cost more to put right, as individual changes are needed for each dwelling instead of group changes that can affect all the dwellings in a block simultaneously. This highlights the need for the *preventive* aspect of design improvement: the immediate cessation of flat-building, and the reform of contemporary house design to revive features that aid the proper socialisation of children.

Guide to the prevention of design disadvantagement in houses

Twelve disadvantaging features should be avoided and twelve socially
stabilising features encouraged in their place.

1. Three facade features (surveillance)
There should be scope for surveillance from a front ground-floor
window in a living room or kitchen. It should be large enough and set
at the right height to afford easy, casual *visibility* to residents sitting,
standing or moving about in the course of normal activities. Tiny
windows, slits above eye level and beaded, frosted or patterned glass
are to be avoided. The best *window form* is a walk-in bay that
maximises the view of the street approaches. Oriels and flush windows
are acceptable but those set in a recessed part of the facade are
inadequate. There should be *no projecting features*, such as porches,
garages, pram sheds, meter compartments, etc., that obstruct the
sight lines from the windows, and nor should the doors give cover to
house-breakers by being too deeply recessed, or tucked away round
the side of the building.

2. Four frontage features (control)
Front garden *depth* should be three to five metres and preferably
nearer to five metres, but not greater, as homes set too far back have
less surveillance up and down the road. There should be waist-high
side fences to help avoid neighbour disputes, and waist-high *front
walls* and *gates* to help train pre-school children to respect other
people's territory. A continuous frontage of walls and gates also acts
as a conversation bar, where passers-by can stop to chat to people
working in their front gardens; this helps to establish the web of
acquaintanceships needed for proper community formation. Low
step-over fences that do not deter dogs, flimsy fencing materials that
are easily vandalised, wires or rails that let litter in, and high faceless
hedges and walls, that impede surveillance by both the residents and
the passing public, are all undesirable.

3. Five features of the spatial setting (defensible space)
Houses should be arranged as island sites surrounded by traditional
roads. The interior of the island should consist of directly abutting
back gardens, with *no back gates* and *no rear fences exposed* to
criminal access from paths, alleys, roads, car parks, garage groups,

play areas or green spaces. Only the front side of the territory should be exposed and this should face *a through road with pavements* on both sides, in order to give young children the kerb drill that culs-de-sac do not. The houses should also *face other house fronts* across the road, so that suspicious behaviour in gardens opposite can be more easily observed, and hence deterred by natural neighbourhood watch. Side roads should also have facing houses on both sides. The present practice of designing end houses with exposed gables and exposed side fences to back gardens should be abandoned. Instead there should be *corner houses* with side as well as front windows to overlook L-shaped front gardens that wrap round along both intersecting roads.

These features of spatial setting necessitate both pedestrian and vehicle access from the front. Garages should be included in the house grounds and so should any paths from front to rear.

The island-site layout is a more economical use of land, which eliminates confused space and stimulates environmental improvement by maximising semi-private space.

Guide to the modification of design disadvantagement in blocks

In carrying out a disadvantagement survey we map the layout of the estate and log the values of the 16 relevant variables for each block. Those values that breach their respective thresholds are the targets for design improvement, and each one that can be improved to its threshold level deducts one point from the disadvantagement score (−1). Provided that the score can be reduced below the average of eight, secondary thresholds and the deduction of half-points are also brought into play (−0.5).

1. Overhead walkways
All walkways radiating from the block above ground level should be demolished (−1). The insertion of barriers is not sufficient. Some blocks may need new staircases and exits in lieu of walkway access.

2. Blocks per site
Each block should have its grounds enclosed by a wall or fence to secure an autonomous territory, not shared by any other block (−1). Where necessary, the name of the block should be changed to distinguish it from all other blocks.

3. Spatial organisation

Walls between blocks should be located to absorb the entire grounds of the estate inside the single-block territories (–1). There should be no left-over pieces of confused space. Confused space open to the estate as a whole is replaced by semi-public space fully under the control of the block's own residents, or, in the case of the larger spaces, by infill with semi-private designs (houses with gardens), to dilute the concentration of flats.

4. Access into the site

Each single-block site should have only one access point in its perimeter wall (–1). The rear grounds should be enclosed by high walls adjoining other housing or other land uses, and lined with prickly shrubs to increase their security. The front grounds should be enclosed by waist-high walls along the street frontage and between neighbours, to permit surveillance of the approaches. The front gardens of the flats should be three to five metres in depth. The point of access should have a gate and formal gateposts, which are potent signals of private territory. If it is desirable to leave double gates open for cars, they still fulfil a useful signalling role. If traffic flow demands both an entrance and an exit gate, these should be located on the same side of the site (–0.5) to avoid opening up a short cut across the grounds.

5. Play areas

Play areas can be modified in one of the following three ways (–1):
(a) Complete removal.
(b) Inclusion in single-block sites, if the residents wish it, so that they are restricted to fewer children who will then be less anonymous.
(c) Enclosure in separate sites with independent entrances from the street, so that they no longer form part of the residential territory.

6. Number of storeys in the block

After making each block autonomous in its own grounds, attention should be paid to reducing its size. Lopping storeys off the top is not normally practicable, but is recommended as a possibility in the following circumstances:
(a) Where flats are in low demand, as in the north of England, storey lopping is being used to convert maisonettes into two-storeyed houses.

(b) When roofs have to be replaced, it may be possible to reduce the height of the building at the same time.

(c) If a lift needs expensive replacement, there may be a case for reducing the block to walk-up height.

(d) If a building is condemned to demolition, it may be feasible to save the bottom two storeys to convert to houses.

The disadvantagement score is reduced by one point if the building is lowered to a height of two or three storeys (–1), or by half a point if it is lowered to four storeys (–0.5). Some blocks do not have the right sort of structure to stand partial demolition.

7. Number of dwellings in the block

Block size can also be decreased by vertical partitioning of both buildings and grounds, so that each part functions as a separate block with no intercommunication except via the street. This creates attached blocks similar to terraced houses, each with its own spatial autonomy. Ideally, they should not exceed the threshold of 12 dwellings (–1) with a secondary threshold at 20 (–0.5). Extra staircases and exits may be needed for the newly self-contained sections.

8. Dwellings served by each entrance

The restriction of the number of dwellings accessible from each entrance is at least partly achieved by walkway removal and vertical partitioning, but it does not reduce the score unless the number of dwellings served is reduced to its threshold value of six (–1), or its secondary threshold of 10 (–0.5). Another way of restricting the sharing of entrances is horizontal partitioning. At the very least, ground-floor flats can be given their own entrances and semi-private gardens, walled off from the communal entrances, and in some cases the next layer may also be served by a separate staircase, leaving the higher levels to be reached by means of the main vertical routes.

9. Corridors

The number of dwellings accessible on each floor should be as few as possible. This is an additional reason for vertical partitioning as advocated above in 7. If dwellings per corridor are reduced to the threshold of four, the score is improved by one point (–1), or if the secondary threshold of six is the best attainable, by half a point (–0.5).

10. Vertical routes

Each block or self-contained section created by vertical or horizontal partitioning should be served by only one staircase (–1). If fire regulations require an alternative, or if building height requires a lift as well as stairs, the secondary threshold of two vertical routes may be the best attainable (–0.5), but they must be intervisible side by side.

11. Interconnecting exits

Each block of flats is best served by a single exit (–1) but fire regulations may require two. If the block has its own semi-public grounds, the two exits may be made analogous to the front and back doors of houses. Only one of them faces the street, which enhances defensibility by signalling an appearance of no through way. The second exit is also more defensible as it opens into securely walled rear grounds (–0.5).

12. Stilts and garages

If the block is raised up above ground level over stilts or garages, there is a case for inserting a few ground-floor flats located where the inhabitants can see the communal entrances. This helps to make the entrance less faceless (–1). If the block is raised up above shops, services, clinics, nursery schools, estate offices, places of entertainment, etc., they should be walled out of the residential territory and given independent street entrances in the same way as option (c) for play areas in 5.

13. Position of the entrance

The entrance should face the street (–1). In some cases this may be achieved by redesigning an estate road or path to incorporate the visual and functional characteristics of a public street. The block should preferably be set back four or five metres from the frontage which should consist of a waist-high wall, with gateways serving each individual or communal entrance. (See also *Streetscape*, below.)

14. Type of entrance and 15. Door

Separate front doors for ground-floor flats should be fronted by individual gardens three to five metres deep, and provided with waist-high front and side walls with a street gate for each one (–1). Communal entrances should be equipped with a door instead of being merely a crude aperture, and the door should be glazed to make stairs and lifts visible from outside. As far as possible the communal entrances should be visible from at least some of the ground-floor flats in the same blocks, i.e. not too far recessed nor too far projecting from the line of the facade.

16. Storeys per dwelling
Maisonettes with two storeys are worse than single-storeyed flats, and so too are designs which mix flats and maisonettes in the same block. Maisonettes are larger, and intended to house larger families, so child densities have been least reduced there and may still be a powerful factor. The solution is managerial rather than architectural – to reduce child densities to the recommended threshold of 17 per cent of the adults in the block.

Streetscape
Some of the guidelines above require attention to the nature of streetscape. The traditional British streetscape that has evolved over the centuries proves to have a more stabilising social influence than the layouts of estates of flats, and the visual and functional essentials are as follows: a vehicular carriageway flanked on both sides by a gutter, kerb and pedestrian path with street lamps; continuous frontages of waist-high walls with gates serving each individual and communal entrance separately; a front-garden buffer zone of three to five metres depth, divided by party walls into semi-private individual gardens and semi-public space in front of communal entrances. Streetscape can be made more urbane by inserting houses into the gaps between blocks to give a better sense of closure along both the building facade and the garden frontage. (See also the guide for houses.)

Why?

Why should Utopia have been such an all-pervading failure, when it was envisaged as a form of national salvation? It was conceived in compassion but has been born and bred in authoritarianism, profligacy and frustration. It aimed to liberate people from the slums but has come to represent an even worse form of bondage. It aspired to beautify the urban environment, but has been transmogrified into the epitome of ugliness. Its redemption, after 40 years, is not only a matter of improving the buildings, but also of winning the hearts and minds of those who create and control them.

It is the natural condition of human beings to make progress by trial and error, and it is the misfortune of our age that the trial and error have been both large-scale and prolonged, with only minimal attention to the question of progress. Planners, architects, developers and housing managers have all been drawn into the same huge plausible vortex – so plausible, indeed, that none of them can be blamed for lacking the foresight to see where it would lead. It is not our intention to ascribe blame unless to do so we can achieve a constructive purpose.

When this book was first written, the Department of the Environment was the villain of the piece; its powerful bureaucracy had subsidised and dragooned public housing into a monolithic Utopian conformity which it refused to recognise as a disaster. Secretary of State Nicholas Ridley changed that when he set up the DICE Project specifically to undo some of the damage perpetrated by the DoE's design misguides. Another positive step was the 1986 issue of British Standard 2880, which called for ten of the twelve recommendations on house design contained in this chapter.

However, it is a distressing fact that, just as the DoE is moving away from counterproductive design dictatorship, the Home Office has stepped in to reinforce it, with an advisory video and a seal-of-approval system urging all the design defects that encourage anti-social behaviour in houses (such as unfenced front gardens). These crime-inducing features are then to be offset by locks, bolts and other security devices that have no effect upon criminal attitudes and merely displace the locale of offences elsewhere. The crime rate continues to rise.

The other great brake on housing improvement is local planning. Even though it has largely abandoned the folly of compulsory eviction to leave large numbers of homes empty for many years, it still presides over the creation of housing shortages by insistence on pointless density standards, by planning delays, and by necessitating the diversion of resources away from new-build to deal with large-scale building defects that would not have occurred if people had been free to follow the unplanned tradition of homes in individual houses.

The whole burden of our research shows that autonomy in housing is better than regimentation. John F.C. Turner's book *Housing by People* (1976) has demonstrated that the much-reviled shanty towns of the Third World are actually a constructive housing solution, because people are free to build their own homes and then progressively improve them, according to their means. The inhabitants' control of the design, construction and management of their own dwellings is a process which stimulates individual and social well-being. If they are denied control and responsibility, the dwelling environment becomes a barrier to personal fulfilment and a burden on the economy – a judgement which applies just as aptly to the concrete jungles of Britain.

In his preface to Turner's book, Colin Ward, author of *The Child in the City* (1978), summarises its philosophy as follows: The important thing about housing is not what it *is*, but what it *does* in people's lives. Dweller satisfaction is not necessarily related to the imposition of standards, and people find deficiencies in housing infinitely more tolerable if they are their own responsibility than if they are someone else's. Colin Ward also distils a profound piece of wisdom when he says, 'The moment that housing, a universal human activity, becomes defined as a problem, a housing problems industry is born, with an army of experts, bureaucrats and researchers, whose existence is a guarantee that the problem won't go away'.

Britain's great housing/planning problems industries have been manufacturing the problems they are supposed to be solving. To appreciate this point we have only to ask whether any post-war government would have been happy with the following state of affairs:

- Sufficient housing for all;
- House prices and rents within people's means;
- A varied choice of accommodation;
- A steady improvement in housing quality through a reduction in slum property and an expansion of new property responsive to people's preferences;
- A growing sense of housing satisfaction and progress.

Probably they would have regarded such a blueprint as an unrealistic dream, but in fact it is just the opposite: a factual description of the real advances that were actually being made in the 1930s. They would probably have resumed after the war (and at a sufficient speed to take war damage in their stride) if they had been allowed to.

What can be done to recreate these constructive conditions today? There seem to be three essential steps:

First, the Home Office should abandon its advocacy of crime-inducing house designs and promote more positive features instead.

Secondly, planning should stop creating housing shortages and house-price inflation. This could be done if simplified planning were carried to its logical conclusion. Each planning authority should aim to maintain a published map indicating a five-year supply of unencumbered house-building land, where any public objections have already been dealt with. They should also publish clear regulations on what may or may not be built – for example, a ban on flats and on the design defects identified in this book. The rules should be so explicit that they leave builders free to go ahead without planning delays and negotiations, apart from consulting immediate neighbours. In this way, supply could catch up with demand, for the first time since 1939, and house design would no longer encourage anti-social behaviour.

And thirdly, it is not reasonable to expect the private sector to redeem all existing problem estates. They were created by central and local government initiatives, and public expenditure is needed to cure them. However, it must not be of the type that perpetuates the problem. There are many estates which failed panaceas have left still in need of help, and several where lavish improvement projects have been followed by a decision to demolish. If we are to avoid throwing good money after bad, a far more rigorous assessment is needed as to how far the various nostrums are genuinely good value for money.

If we can prise open the triple stranglehold of Home Office misdirection, the planning straitjacket, and the festering influence of existing estates, housing initiatives can be genuinely returned to the free market, with unfettered responsiveness to people's needs. The role of this book has been to show that there is a tested alternative vision of design, which can abandon the present dinosaur branch of housing evolution and rejoin the mainstream. Housing choice and responsibility for one's home should be decisions made not by the bureaucrats but by the occupants. The future should be in their own hands.

Appendix I
Frequencies, Percentages
and Thresholds

Frequencies

This appendix records the frequency distributions of 4,099 blocks of flats in 15 tables for the design variables. The values of the variables are used as row headings and the classes of the test measures are used as column headings; the frequencies in the cells of each table are numbers of blocks (Table 27).

Individual design values are given for non-interval variables, and also interval variables up to a value of nine. Larger interval values are grouped in tens from 10 to 99, hundreds from 100-999, and thousands above that. This pattern of grouping is necessitated by the positively skewed distribution of many variables; their high values are too few and too scattered to yield meaningful results unless they are amalgamated. Exceptions to the grouping system appear in the relevant tables.

The figure following the design value is the total number of blocks having that value. These totals apply to litter, graffiti, damage and faeces. Separate totals are given for children in care and urine for which data were mapped in one borough only.

Percentages and trend lines

The percentages following the frequencies show what proportion of blocks at each design value are affected by each kind of social malaise.

For the interval variables a second set of percentages has been calculated to smooth out irregularities due to small numbers of blocks and give a better idea of trends and probabilities. The smoothing is based on running means derived from three successive frequencies, weighted for the three different numbers of cases involved.

In drawing the trend lines the first and last positions are plotted as unsmoothed percentages. Between them the smoothed percentages are plotted at positions determined by weighting the values according to their frequencies. An example is worked out below for a value of 2 (Table 23).

Southwark's social malaise percentages are significantly lower than Tower Hamlets', while those for the whole study area lie between the two. It was therefore assumed that the children-in-care data (Southwark only) would be too low to be comparable with the whole area, while the urine pollution data (Tower Hamlets only) would be too high. Both needed adjustment if they were to be placed in proper context and this was done as follows.

Southwark's percentages for the four universally surveyed measures (Table

186

TABLE 23 *Calculation of smoothed percentage and plotting position*

Design value	Total cases	No. with litter	Unsmoothed percentage	Smoothed percentage	Weighted total	Plotting position
1	300	60	20	113 ÷ 455	300 × 1	745 ÷ 455
2	20	8	40	= 24.8	20 × 2	= 1.6
3	135	45	33	———	135 × 3	———
	455	113			745	

TABLE 24 *Observed and estimated test-measure percentages*

Test measure	Tower Hamlets	Total area (4,099 blocks)	Southwark	Southwark sample (C.C.R. Redknap)
Litter	96.8	86.1	78.3	77.6
Graffiti	87.0	76.2	69.1	68.6
Damage	49.5	38.8	30.7	—
Faeces	7.8	7.5	7.3	6.7
Mean of four	60.4	52.2	46.6	—
Children in care		(30.4) est.	24.6	—
Urine	43.9	(22.9) est.	(17.1) est.	16.5

24) average 5.8 points below the corresponding figures for the total area. It was assumed that the children-in-care figure might also be 5.8 points too low, and consequently its trend line was raised by this amount, retaining its shape but adjusting its level to an overall value of 30.4 instead of 24.6.

It was not possible to adjust the Tower Hamlets figure downward in the same simple way, as the incidence of urine pollution there is believed to be exceptionally high, owing to the concentration of alcoholics who—social workers have told us—migrate there. Fortunately, we were able to obtain a substitute figure for Southwark (Table 24). Celia Redknap mapped litter, graffiti and faeces in a sample of 624 entrances to Southwark blocks of flats, and obtained figures which were remarkably close to those found for the total population of Southwark blocks, differing on average by only 0.6 percentage points. It seemed likely that her figure of 16.5 per cent for urine pollution would similarly be 0.6 per cent too low, and this permitted us to arrive at an assumption of 17.1 per cent for Southwark as a whole. To this we added 5.8 per cent as before, producing a figure for the whole area of 22.9 per cent. This would suggest an expected value of 31.1 per cent for Tower Hamlets, whereas the observed figure there is 12.8 per cent higher. This could be the order of the difference attributable to the presence of alcoholics.

When the children-in-care and urine curves are adjusted thus, they prove to be a better fit for the theoretical model of growth curves explained in Chapter

TABLE 25 *The effect of speed of deterioration*

Slow deterioration			Intermediate deterioration			Rapid deterioration		
0	1	2	0	1	2	0	1	2
*	*	*	*	*	*	*	•	*
*	*	*	*	•	*	*	•	*
•	•	*	•	•	*	•	*	•
•	•	*	•	•	*	•	*	•
•	•	*	•	•	*	•	*	•
•	•	*	•	*	•	•	*	•
•	•	*	•	*	•	•	*	•
•	•	*	•	*	•	•	*	•
100	100	0	100	50	50	100	0	100

The percentage figures at the bottom of each column indicate how many values below the threshold line are worse than chance (black spots).

V. The number of crossed trend lines is minimised and the shape of the six curves, from highest to lowest, progresses from convex to concave. This suggests that the degree of adjustment is about right.

Thresholds

Chapter VIII gives a simplified explanation of threshold levels, substituting percentages for the equivalent frequencies used in practice with the chi-squared method. This method calculates an expected frequency to match each observed frequency by multiplying the latter's row total by its column total and dividing by the grand total.

The expected value is here considered equal to the observed if it differs by no more than one block, or two blocks where the row total exceeds 100. Abuse-free frequencies are classified as better-than-expected if they definitely exceed the expected values while frequencies of the various classes of abuse are classified as better if they definitely fall short of the expected. These cases are marked with asterisks while those that are equal to, or worse than, the expected are marked with black spots. Zero cases that equal the expected are left unmarked.

The disadvantagement threshold is drawn before the first row where the abuse-free frequency and at least one other become worse than expected. The threshold is given the name of the last better-than-expected row, which is the limiting value for design recommendations.

In the most straightforward cases all the values before the threshold would be better than expected and all those after it would be worse but this happens in only 18 of the 90 sub-tables in Table 27. Usually there are some asterisks after the threshold and often some black spots before it, and their distribution seems to depend mainly on the speed at which the test measure deteriorates once it has set in. The role of speed of deterioration may be illustrated by means of three idealised cases, shown in Table 25 as skeleton tables.

All these cases have worse-than-expected frequencies in every cell below the threshold line in the first, no-abuse, column. In the slow-deterioration table the weight of the abuse distribution remains in the middle, or moderate-abuse, column, whereas in the rapid-deterioration table the weight of the distribution passes straight into the heavy abuse class as soon as the threshold is breached. This leaves the moderate-abuse cells better than expected, which means that occurrences of moderate abuse tend to occur before the threshold rather than after it, thus accounting for the presence of black spots above the line.

The case representing an intermediate deterioration rate is the midpoint between these two extremes. The weight of the distribution passes diagonally from the moderate abuse to the heavy-abuse column, and moderate-abuse may begin to be worse than expected just before the threshold.

In practice the 90 sub-tables of Table 27 do not show such clear cut patterns as these three idealised cases. There is a certain amount of random disturbance caused by the co-presence of designs other than the one being considered. The main reason, however, is the fact that most of the distributions fit neither of the two extremes nor the exactly balanced midpoint. The litter and graffiti tables mostly fall somewhere between the midpoint and the rapid extreme, while the other four test measures fall on the opposite side of the midpoint, towards the slow extreme.

The thresholds obtained for a given design variable are not always identical for all test measures, but only one value can be recommended in practice. The choice has been made after examining the separate thresholds for Tower Hamlets and Southwark, as well as those for the total area. Separate thresholds cannot be satisfactorily calculated for Blackbird Leys, as 54 blocks are too few, but this area is included in the total figures. In a few cases the low values in Tower Hamlets also have too few blocks to give a clear better- or worse-than-expected verdict, and are marked with a dash in Table 26.

The first three variables in Table 26 are those whose absence is better than their presence. The second group consists of variables which cannot be absent, but which have the minimum value, one, as their threshold. This is most clear-cut for interconnecting exits and vertical routes. It is also chosen for access points, as one is a safer recommendation than the alternative value of two. In the case of blocks per site, the individual thresholds range from one to 5, and one is chosen as the threshold for three reasons. The first is that it is the safest. The second is that the spatial-organisation variable also stresses the desirability of single-block sites. And the third is that those multi-block sites that fall below the threshold have special redeeming features that might well be overlooked if a higher number is taken to be a blanket threshold.

The variables of the third group have higher thresholds. Three clearly predominates as the permissible number of storeys, with the excrement taboos becoming more frequently broken in blocks with over four. Four is the threshold number of dwellings per corridor, which includes landings and balconies. Both are necessary design options, as improvements upon longer internal and external corridors respectively. Litter and children in care exclude balconies from the threshold range, but only by the narrowest of margins. Dwellings per entrance

TABLE 26   COMPARISON OF THRESHOLD LEVELS

DESIGN VARIABLE	LITTER			GRAFFITI			DAMAGE			CHILDREN IN CARE	URINE	FAECES			OVERALL
	TH	S	ALL	TH	S	ALL	TH	S	ALL	S	TH	TH	S	ALL	
Overhead walkways	0	0	0	0	0	0	0	0	0	0	0	0	0	0	0
Play areas	0	0	0	0	0	0	0	0	0	0	0	1	0	0	0
Stilts and garages	-	0	-	0	0	0	0	0	0	0	0	0	0	0	
Vertical circulation	1	1	1	1	1	1	1	1	1	1	1	2	1	1	1
Interconnected exits	1	1	1	2	3	1	1	1	1	1	1	1	1	1	1
Access points	1	2	2	2	2	2	1	1	1	2	1	1	2	1	1
Blocks per site	2	3	4	2	4	5	2	4	2	1	4	1	1	1	1
Number of storeys	3	3	3	3	3	3	4	3	3	3	4	5	4	4	3
Dwellings per corridor	4	4	4	4	4	4	4	4	4	4	4	1	4	4	4
Dwellings per entrance	-	7	6	12	7	7	7	9	9	9	-	5	1	6	6
Dwellings per block	12	12	12	24	24	17	24	12	12	17	24	-	12	7	12
Flats (F) or maisonettes	F	F	F	F	F	F	F	F	F	F	F	F	F	F	F
Entrance type	C	C	C	C	C	C	SF	C	C	C	C	C	C	C	C
Entrance position	S	C	SF	S	S	S	SPS	SF	SF	SF	SPS	SPS	C	S	S
Spatial organisation	SPS	S	*	SPS SPM	S	S	SPM SCS	*	*	SPS SPM SCS	SPM	*	*	SPS SCS CS	*

Borough

TH - Tower Hamlets
S - Southwark

Entrance Type and Position

C   Communal Entrances Only
F   Flush with the street
S   Set back, facing the street
SF Both F and S

Spatial Organisation

SPS   Semi-public single-block estate
SPM   Semi-public multiple-block estate
SCS   Semi-confused single-block estate
CS   Confused single-block estate
*   All four of the above

has a great variety of threshold levels. Half of them are in the 5-7 range, and six has been selected as the threshold. Twelve is the predominant figure for dwellings per block which suggests that the block should be divided in two self-contained units of six each.

The last group are variables having non-interval data and non-quantitative thresholds. Flats (F) prove consistently better than maisonettes, though probably as a result of child density rather than design. Communal entrances only (C) are better than separate entrances to individual ground-floor flats, but this, too, appears to be due to a disturbing factor: the absence of a buffer zone in front of the individual doors. Communal entrances are taken as the threshold value, however, to serve as a reminder to look into the question of providing semi-private territories in front of ground-floor doors.

Entrance position has the set-back (S) design below the threshold in 11 cases and the flush-with-the-street (F) design in seven cases. Set back is therefore chosen as the threshold value, but as flush is the runner-up, the set-back should be only a few metres deep.

Finally, there is the complex spatial-organisation variable. Semi-public single blocks (SPS) qualify in 14 cases, semi-public multiple blocks (SPM) in 11, semi-confused single blocks (SCS) in 10 and confused single blocks (CS) in eight. Of the 593 blocks which fall within the threshold for at least one test measure, 88 per cent are in single-block sites, which lends strength to the decision to designate the blocks-per-site threshold as one.

TABLE 27   FREQUENCY TABLES, DESIGN VALUES BY ABUSE CLASSES

LITTER

DESIGN VALUE	TOTAL NO. OF BLOCKS	LITTER FREE	CLEAN AND CASUAL	DIRTY AND DECAYED	PERCENTAGE WITH LITTER	SMOOTHED PERCENTAGE
	4099	572	2316	1211	86.1	

NUMBER OF DWELLINGS IN THE BLOCK

(Low values are irregularly spread and have been grouped in fives)

1-4	134	50*	74•	10*	62.7	62.7
5-9	788	147*	437*	204*	81.3	81.5
10-14	660	95*	380•	185*	85.6	84.4
15-19	557	70•	312•	175•	87.4	87.3
20-29	833	96*	519•	218•	88.5	88.0
30-39	415	50•	235•	130•	88.0	88.4
40-49	275	30•	135*	110•	89.1	88.1
50-59	117	16•	53•	48•	86.3	89.8
60-69	97	4•	63•	30•	95.9	91.4
70-79	67	6•	26•	35•	91.0	94.4
80-89	50	2•	16*	32•	96.0	94.2
90-99	37	1•	20•	16•	97.3	94.6
100-199	61	5•	39•	17•	91.8	95.2
200-317	8	-•	7•	1*	100.0	100.0

DWELLINGS SERVED PER ENTRANCE

1	58	39*	17*	2*	32.8	32.8
2	28	9*	15•	4*	67.9	58.0
3	83	23*	52•	8*	72.3	70.6
4	216	64*	117*	35*	70.4	73.2
5	96	19*	59•	18*	80.2	75.4
6	431	100*	234•	97*	76.8	78.8
7	91	12•	49*	30•	86.8	84.7
8	464	39•	307•	118•	91.6	90.1
9	143	18•	94•	31*	87.4	87.7
10-19	948	135*	529•	284•	85.8	88.0
20-29	482	42•	288•	152•	91.3	87.9
30-39	211	22•	107*	82•	89.6	90.6
40-49	139	14•	64*	61•	89.9	90.2
50-59	78	6•	30*	42•	92.1	92.4
60-69	71	2•	37•	32•	97.2	95.9
70-79	48	-•	24*	24•	100.0	97.7
80-89	52	2•	13*	37•	96.2	95.7
90-99	63	5•	31•	27•	92.1	94.8
100-199	156	7•	99•	50•	95.5	93.4
200-299	53	7•	45•	1*	86.8	91.2
300-399	29	7*	3•	19•	75.9	85.1
400-499	12	-•	12•	-*	100.0	86.0
500-599	9	-•	-*	9•	100.0	100.0
800-899	22	-•	2*	20•	100.0	100.0
1000-1999	75	-•	47•	28•	100.0	100.0
2000-2268	41	-•	41•	-*	100.0	100.0

NUMBER OF STOREYS IN THE BLOCK

2	230	88*	108*	34*	61.7	61.7
3	803	197*	475•	131*	75.5	83.3
4	1610	156•	965•	489•	90.3	87.2
5	813	60•	453*,	300•	92.6	90.9
6	277	29•	134*	114•	89.5	91.8
7	89	8•	51•	30•	91.0	88.2
8	50	12*	18*	20•	76.0	84.9
9	20	4*	5•	11•	80.0	85.3
10-19	156	17•	85*	54•	89.1	90.3
20-27	51	1•	22*	28•	98.0	98.0

NUMBER OF OVERHEAD WALKWAYS

0	3375	545*	1922•	908*	83.9	83.9
1	328	11•	192•	125•	96.7	85.7
2	265	10•	143*	112•	96.2	95.9
3	60	6•	37•	17•	90.0	95.6
4	40	-•	17•	23•	100.0	94.5
5	9	-•	3*	6•	100.0	100.0
6/9	22	-•	2*	20•	100.0	100.0

GRAFFITI

GRAFFITI FREE	INSIDE OR OUTSIDE	INSIDE AND OUTSIDE	PERCENTAGE WITH GRAFFITI	SMOOTHED PERCENTAGE
975	1252	1872	76.2	
61*	49•	24*	54.5	54.4
240*	274•	274*	69.5	70.2
170*	221•	269*	74.2	72.4
144*	162*	251*	74.2	76.3
172•	271•	390•	79.4	77.9
83•	113*	219•	80.0	80.0
50•	67*	158•	81.8	81.3
18•	38•	61•	84.6	83.6
12•	19*	66•	87.6	87.8
6•	13*	48•	91.0	89.3
5•	4*	41•	90.0	92.2
1•	11•	25•	97.3	87.2
13•	10*	38•	78.7	86.8
-•	-*	8•	100.0	100.0
47*	9*	2*	19.0	19.0
10*	10•	8*	64.3	46.2
34*	39•	30*	59.0	53.8
107*	58*	51*	50.5	58.0
25*	46•	25*	74.0	59.0
173*	167•	91*	60.0	64.2
23*	33•	35*	74.7	70.9
91•	154•	219•	80.4	77.8
41*	54•	48*	71.3	76.7
231*	260*	457•	75.6	77.2
87•	133*	262•	82.0	78.2
39•	48•	124•	81.5	82.9
16•	40*	83•	88.5	86.2
4•	16*	58•	94.9	91.7
4•	16*	51•	94.4	94.9
2•	7*	39•	95.8	94.7
3•	5*	44•	94.2	94.5
4•	14•	45•	93.7	88.6
24•	43*	89•	84.6	87.1
7•	30•	16*	86.8	87.0
-•	9•	20•	100.0	92.6
-•	8•	4*	100.0	100.0
-•	-*	9•	100.0	100.0
-•	2*	20•	100.0	99.1
1•	42•	32*	98.7	97.8
2•	9*	30•	95.1	95.1
129*	45*	56*	43.9	43.9
357*	316•	130*	55.5	71.3
273•	513•	824•	83.0	76.7
121•	228*	464•	85.1	84.2
34•	65•	178•	87.7	84.9
22•	24*	43•	75.3	84.4
9•	12*	29•	82.0	77.4
5•	3*	12•	75.0	84.5
21•	39•	96•	86.5	86.8
4•	7*	40•	92.2	92.2
919*	1036•	1420*	72.8	72.8
37•	109•	182•	88.7	75.5
15•	81•	169•	94.3	91.6
3•	22•	35•	95.0	94.8
1•	4*	35•	97.5	96.3
-•	-*	9•	100.0	98.6
-•	-*	22•	100.0	100.0

TABLE 27   FREQUENCY TABLES, DESIGN VALUES BY ABUSE CLASSES - continued

		DAMAGE					
DESIGN VALUE	TOTAL NO. OF BLOCKS	NUMBER OF TYPES OF TARGET PER BLOCK 0	1	2	3-5	PERCENTAGE WITH DAMAGE	SMOOTHED PERCENTAGE
	4099	2510	1182	239	168	38.8	

NUMBER OF DWELLINGS IN THE BLOCK

(Low values are irregularly spread and have been grouped in fives)

1-4	134	119*	14*	1*	-*	11.2	11.2
5-9	788	610*	147*	19*	12*	22.6	26.9
10-14	660	427*	186*	23*	24*	35.3	31.6
15-19	557	334●	161●	42●	20*	40.0	37.6
20-29	833	519*	249●	39*	26*	37.7	40.7
30-39	415	218●	145●	30●	22●	47.5	43.0
40-49	275	131●	96●	32●	16●	52.4	50.2
50-59	117	53●	41●	13●	10●	54.7	55.0
60-69	97	36●	41●	15●	5●	62.9	62.7
70-79	67	17●	26●	11●	13●	74.6	70.6
80-89	50	10●	28●	4●	8●	80.0	77.3
90-99	37	8●	22●	5●	2●	78.4	69.6
100-199	61	27●	23●	4●	7●	55.7	66.0
200-317	8	1●	3●	1●	3●	87.5	87.5

DWELLINGS SERVED PER ENTRANCE

1	58	55*	3*	-*	-*	5.2	5.2
2	28	21*	6*	-*	1●	25.0	11.2
3	83	74*	9*	-*	-*	10.8	18.0
4	216	173*	33*	8*	2*	19.9	20.3
5	96	68*	27*	1*	-*	9.2	23.5
6	431	327*	88*	8*	8*	24.1	25.6
7	91	65*	17*	5●	4●	28.6	26.1
8	464	337*	99*	23●	5*	27.4	28.8
9	143	95*	40●	6*	2*	33.6	36.7
10-19	948	551●	303●	70●	24●	41.9	41.6
20-29	482	273●	169●	22*	18●	43.4	43.4
30-39	211	105●	69●	22●	15●	50.2	47.1
40-49	139	62●	50●	19●	8●	55.4	54.9
50-59	78	26●	38●	5●	9●	66.7	61.1
60-69	71	24●	27●	11●	9●	66.2	69.0
70-79	48	11●	27●	4●	6●	77.1	72.3
80-89	52	12●	25●	8●	7●	76.9	65.6
90-99	63	33●	24●	6●	-*	47.6	52.0
100-199	156	85●	54●	6*	11●	45.5	39.7
200-299	53	46●	3●	2*	2●	13.2	38.2
300-399	29	16●	11●	1	1●	44.8	24.5
400-499	12	9*	3●	-	-	25.0	50.0
500-599	9	-●	8●	1●	-	100.0	74.4
800-899	22	2●	8●	5●	7●	90.9	69.8
1000-1999	75	30●	21●	2*	22●	60.0	69.6
2000-2268	41	10●	20●	4●	7●	75.6	75.6

NUMBER OF STOREYS IN THE BLOCK

2	230	195*	28*	4*	3*	15.2	15.2
3	803	654*	123*	18*	8*	18.6	30.6
4	1610	986●	471●	99●	54●	38.8	37.0
5	813	393●	313●	55●	52●	51.7	43.4
6	277	149●	92●	20●	16●	46.2	50.2
7	89	45●	33●	7●	4●	49.4	47.6
8	50	24●	16●	5●	5●	52.0	51.6
9	20	8●	8●	3●	1●	60.0	65.5
10-19	156	46●	71●	23●	16●	70.5	71.8
20-27	51	10●	27●	5●	9●	80.4	80.4

NUMBER OF OVERHEAD WALKWAYS

0	3375	2158*	912*	194*	111*	36.1	36.1
1	328	179●	118●	18●	13●	45.4	38.1
2	265	119●	99●	16●	31●	55.1	49.5
3	60	32●	23●	2*	3●	46.7	54.8
4	40	14●	19●	6●	1●	65.0	56.0
5	9	2●	3●	-	4●	77.8	69.0
6/9	22	6●	8●	3●	5●	72.7	72.7

FAECES				URINE (Tower Hamlets only)				
FAECES FREE	FAECES PRESENT	PERCENTAGE WITH FAECES	SMOOTHED PERCENTAGE	TOTAL NO. OF BLOCKS	URINE FREE	URINE PRESENT	PERCENTAGE WITH URINE	SMOOTHED PERCENTAGE
3793	306	7.5		1782	999	783	43.9	
126*	8*	6.0	6.0	26	17*	9*	34.6	34.6
754*	29*	4.3	6.3	298	235*	63*	21.4	32.0
602•	58•	8.8	6.1	280	159*	121*	43.2	34.4
526*	31*	5.6	7.2	277	167*	110*	39.7	43.6
775*	58*	7.0	7.4	380	202•	178•	46.8	47.6
370•	45•	10.8	8.5	170	64•	106•	62.4	52.3
249•	26•	9.5	9.9	137	62•	75•	54.7	58.5
108•	9•	7.7	7.8	54	24•	30•	55.6	51.9
94*	3*	3.1	7.2	52	31*	21•	40.4	51.4
59•	8•	11.9	10.8	36	14•	22•	61.1	52.3
38•	12•	24.0	16.2	21	7•	14•	66.7	66.2
32•	5•	13.5	17.6	20	5•	15•	75.0	65.3
52•	9•	14.8	13.2	31	13•	18•	58.1	58.1
8•	-	0.0	0.0	-	-	-	-	-
58*	-*	0.0	0.0	2	2*	-*	0.0	0.0
27*	1*	3.6	3.0	6	5*	1*	16.7	19.4
79*	4*	4.8	3.7	23	18*	5*	21.7	18.0
209*	7*	3.2	4.1	88	73*	15*	17.1	24.8
91*	5*	5.2	3.6	46	27•	19•	41.3	30.6
416*	15*	3.5	4.4	170	111*	59*	34.7	38.4
84•	7•	7.7	3.7	52	27•	25•	48.1	31.4
450*	14*	3.0	4.0	221	166*	55*	24.9	30.2
136*	7*	4.9	4.6	61	40*	21*	34.3	38.7
897*	51*	5.4	6.9	415	221•	194•	46.8	48.3
432•	50•	10.4	7.4	244	111•	133•	54.5	51.0
190•	21•	10.0	9.7	114	47•	67•	58.8	55.0
128•	11•	7.9	8.2	89	43•	46•	51.2	57.5
72•	6•	7.7	9.4	51	18•	33•	64.7	53.5
59•	12•	16.9	11.7	34	20•	14•	41.8	56.9
41•	7•	14.6	25.7	33	13•	20•	60.6	58.2
27•	25•	48.1	25.8	24	5•	19•	79.2	58.8
53•	10•	15.9	18.8	28	17*	11*	39.3	61.1
140•	16•	10.3	11.0	56	20•	36•	64.3	50.0
49•	4•	7.6	9.7	-	-	-	-	(56.2)
26•	3•	10.3	7.5	17	12*	5*	29.4	56.1
12•	-	0.0	6.0	-	-	-	-	-
9•	-	0.0	41.9	9	4•	5•	55.6	55.6
4•	18•	81.8	28.3	-	-	-	-	-
63•	12•	16.0	21.7	-	-	-	-	-
41*	-*	0.0	0.0	-	-	-	-	-
220*	10*	4.4	4.4	65	39*	26*	40.0	40.0
774*	29*	3.6	6.0	279	206*	73*	26.2	38.1
490•	120•	7.5	6.6	724	416*	308*	42.5	41.3
750•	63•	7.7	8.3	396	199•	197•	49.8	46.5
235•	42•	15.2	9.2	144	61•	83•	57.6	51.6
86•	3*	3.4	13.7	39	20•	19•	48.7	57.2
38•	12•	24.0	10.7	18	5•	13•	72.2	56.5
18•	2•	10.0	12.0	12	5•	7•	58.3	53.8
143•	13•	8.3	11.9	76	39•	37•	48.7	54.7
39•	12•	23.5	23.5	29	9•	20•	69.0	69.0
3174*	201*	6.0	6.0	1462	837*	625*	42.7	42.7
289•	39•	11.9	7.1	165	90•	75•	45.5	43.6
225•	40•	15.1	13.5	110	53•	57•	51.8	48.1
51•	9•	15.0	14.8	10	5•	5•	50.0	53.9
35•	5•	12.5	13.8	23	8•	15•	65.2	56.8
8•	1•	11.1	23.9	4	3•	1•	25.0	60.0
11•	11•	50.0	50.0	8	3•	5•	62.5	62.5

TABLE 27   FREQUENCY TABLES, DESIGN VALUES BY ABUSE CLASSES - continued

CHILDREN IN CARE (Southwark only)

DESIGN VALUE	TOTAL NO. OF BLOCKS	NO OF HOUSEHOLDS PER BLOCK WITH CHILDREN IN CARE							PERCENTAGE OF BLOCKS	SMOOTHED PERCENTAGE
		0	1	2	3	4	5	6-11		
	1955	1474	282	112	50	21	8	8		

NUMBER OF DWELLINGS IN THE BLOCK

(Low values are irregularly spread and have been grouped in fives)

1-4	95	95*	–*	–*	–*	–	–	–	0.0	0.0
5-9	441	415*	20*	5*	–*	1*	–	–	5.9	8.3
10-14	274	233*	33*	7*	1*	–*	–	–	15.0	12.2
15-19	229	181*	35●	7*	5●	1●	–	–	21.0	23.2
20-29	377	262●	72●	25●	10●	6●	–	2●	30.5	31.0
30-39	221	128●	53●	27●	9●	3●	1●	–	42.1	36.0
40-49	122	71●	27●	9●	7●	5●	2●	1●	41.8	41.9
50-59	56	33●	8●	10●	5●	–	–	–	41.1	44.7
60-69	39	16●	10●	4●	3●	1●	4●	1●	59.0	50.0
70-79	29	13●	7●	7●	1●	–	–	1●	55.2	59.1
80-89	25	9●	6●	3●	1●	3●	1●	2●	64.0	63.2
90-99	14	3●	2●	4●	4●	–	–	1●	78.6	60.9
100-199	25	13●	5●	3●	4●	–	–	–	48.0	61.7
200-317	8	2●	4●	1●	–	1●	–	–	75.0	75.0

DWELLINGS SERVED PER ENTRANCE

1	56	55*	1*	–*	–*	–	–	–	1.8	1.8
2	22	22*	–*	–*	–	–	–	–	0.0	1.5
3	60	59*	1*	–*	–*	–	–	–	1.7	2.1
4	107	104*	2*	–*	–*	1●	–	–	2.8	2.3
5	49	48*	1*	–*	–*	–	–	–	2.0	9.9
6	237	202*	27*	6*	1*	1*	–	–	14.8	12.8
7	35	30*	3*	1*	1●	–	–	–	14.3	13.9
8	225	196*	20*	7*	1*	1●	–	–	12.9	13.7
9	55	46*	5*	1*	2●	1●	–	–	16.4	24.7
10-19	454	311●	76●	38●	18●	4●	1●	6●	31.5	31.9
20-29	210	132●	46●	21●	8●	2●	–	1●	37.1	33.9
30-39	86	53●	15●	8●	6●	1●	3●	–	38.4	36.6
40-49	48	33●	9●	2●	2●	2●	–	–	31.2	36.3
50-59	25	15●	7●	3●	–	–	–	–	40.0	32.4
60-69	29	21●	7●	1●	–	–	–	–	27.6	40.6
70-79	15	5●	5●	3●	1●	–	–	1●	66.7	40.0
80-89	11	7●	3●	1●	–	–	–	–	36.4	48.7
90-99	13	8●	1●	2●	2●	–	–	–	38.5	38.3
100-199	36	22●	10●	1●	1●	2●	–	–	38.9	30.4
200-299	20	16●	2●	2●	–	–	–	–	20.0	35.2
300-399	12	6●	5●	1●	–	–	–	–	50.0	34.1
400-499	12	7●	5●	–	–	–	–	–	41.7	56.5
500-599	–	–	–	–	–	–	–	–	–	–
800-899	22	7●	4●	3●	3●	1●	–	–	68.2	45.9
1000-1999	75	45●	19●	8●	2●	1●	–	–	40.0	44.9
2000-2268	41	24●	8●	2●	2●	2●	3●	–	41.5	41.5

NUMBER OF STOREYS IN THE BLOCK

2	146	145*	1*	–*	–*	–*	–*	–*	0.7	0.7
3	471	435*	28*	5*	2*	1*	–*	–*	7.6	16.2
4	677	505●	102●	39●	20●	9●	1*	1*	25.4	24.5
5	380	213●	88●	42●	19●	6●	6●	6●	43.9	32.5
6	121	77●	20●	15●	6●	2●	1●	–	36.4	40.6
7	34	28*	5●	1●	–	–	–	–	17.6	35.7
8	30	14●	11●	3●	–	1●	–	1●	53.3	35.2
9	7	4●	2●	1●	–	–	–	–	42.9	47.7
10-19	70	38●	18●	6●	2●	2●	–	–	45.7	40.6
20-27	19	15●	4●	–	–	–	–	–	21.1	21.1

NUMBER OF OVERHEAD WALKWAYS

0	1692	1303*	225*	95*	43*	14*	4*	8●	23.0	23.0
1	104	77●	24●	3*	–*	–	–	–	26.0	23.8
2	106	69●	22●	9●	3●	3●	–	–	34.9	31.4
3	26	16●	7●	1●	2●	–	–	–	38.5	37.1
4	11	5●	2●	–	–	1●	3●	–	54.5	46.3
5	4	1●	1●	–	–	1●	1●	–	75.0	66.7
6/9	12	3●	1●	4●	2●	2●	–	–	75.0	75.0

		LITTER				
DESIGN VALUE	TOTAL NO. OF BLOCKS	LITTER FREE	CLEAN AND CASUAL	DIRTY AND DECAYED	PERCENTAGE WITH LITTER	SMOOTHED PERCENTAGE
NUMBER OF INTERCONNECTED EXITS						
1	2562	427*	1475•	660*	83.3	83.3
2	738	94•	407•	237•	87.4	84.5
3	173	17•	86•	70•	90.2	88.7
4	132	7•	62•	63•	94.7	92.3
5	47	3•	14•	30•	93.6	95.5
6	45	−•	20•	25•	100.0	94.7
7	40	4•	19•	17•	90.0	96.0
8	15	−•	11•	4•	100.0	94.3
9	15	−•	5*	10•	100.0	90.0
10-19	120	15•	59*	46•	87.5	91.4
20-29	86	4•	62•	20•	95.3	90.7
30-39	10	1•	8•	1*	90.0	97.1
50-59	75	−•	47•	28•	100.0	99.2
80-89	41	−•	41•	−*	100.0	100.0
VERTICAL CIRCULATION CHANNELS (lifts and staircases)						
1	2282	417*	1319•	546*	81.7	81.7
2	879	98•	501•	280•	88.9	84.4
3	244	18•	135•	91•	92.6	90.0
4	126	9•	57*	60•	92.9	92.7
5	57	4•	11•	42•	93.0	94.1
6	72	2•	28*	42•	97.2	93.0
7	42	6•	19•	17•	85.7	94.2
8	25	−•	13*	12•	100.0	93.3
9	23	−•	19•	4*	100.0	92.8
10-19	133	13•	61•	59•	90.2	92.3
20-29	78	5•	63•	10*	93.6	92.3
40-49	22	−•	2*	20•	100.0	97.1
60-69	75	−•	47•	28•	100.0	100.0
103	41	−•	41•	−*	100.0	100.0
ACCESS POINTS (number of sides)						
1	692	165*	357*	170*	76.2	76.2
2	654	115*	380•	159*	82.4	82.8
3	915	109•	537•	269*	88.1	86.9
4	1417	168•	825•	424•	88.1	88.8
5	174	5•	79*	90•	97.1	90.0
6-7	247	10•	138•	99•	96.0	96.0
NUMBER OF BLOCKS IN THE SITE						
1	524	129*	269*	126*	75.4	75.6
2	420	81*	223*	116*	80.7	78.2
3	420	88*	216*	116*	79.1	81.5
4	404	61*	243*	100*	84.9	83.9
5	305	33•	184•	88*	89.2	87.5
6	234	24•	150•	60*	89.7	89.8
7	154	14•	92•	48•	90.9	91.5
8	224	14•	125•	85•	93.8	93.1
9	243	15•	132*	96•	93.8	90.5
10-19	768	89•	471•	208*	88.4	90.3
20-29	232	17•	83*	132•	92.7	90.4
38/54/81	171	7•	128•	36*	95.9	95.9

TABLE 27   FREQUENCY TABLES, DESIGN VALUES BY ABUSE CLASSES - continued

GRAFFITI

DESIGN VALUE	TOTAL NO. OF BLOCKS	GRAFFITI FREE	INSIDE OR OUTSIDE	INSIDE AND OUTSIDE	PERCENTAGE WITH GRAFFITI	SMOOTHED PERCENTAGE
NUMBER OF INTERCONNECTED EXITS						
1	2562	725*	832●	1005*	71.7	71.7
2	738	174●	194*	370●	76.4	73.3
3	173	29●	37*	107●	83.2	79.5
4	132	11●	32*	89●	91.7	88.1
5	47	2●	10*	35●	95.7	93.3
6	45	2●	8*	35●	95.6	92.4
7	40	6●	1*	33●	85.0	89.0
8	15	3●	5●	7●	80.0	87.1
9	15	-●	-*	15●	100.0	90.7
10-19	120	11●	22*	87●	90.8	92.3
20-29	86	6●	56●	24●	93.0	90.7
30-39	10	3●	4●	3*	70.0	94.2
50-59	75	1●	42●	32*	98.7	95.2
80-89	41	2●	9*	30●	95.1	95.1
VERTICAL CIRCULATION CHANNELS (lifts and staircases)						
1	2282	710*	741●	831*	68.9	68.9
2	879	177●	242●	460●	79.9	72.8
3	244	39●	61*	144●	84.0	81.8
4	126	11●	36*	79●	91.3	87.8
5	57	2●	14*	41●	96.5	93.3
6	72	4●	11*	57●	94.4	90.1
7	42	11*	6*	25●	73.8	89.2
8	25	-●	5*	20●	100.0	82.2
9	23	5●	1*	17●	78.3	95.0
10-19	133	4●	26●	103●	97.0	92.3
20-29	78	9●	56●	13*	88.5	94.4
40-49	22	-●	2*	20●	100.0	94.3
60-69	75	1●	42●	32*	98.7	97.8
103	41	2●	9*	30●	95.1	95.1
ACCESS POINTS (number of sides)						
1	692	253*	211●	228*	63.4	63.4
2	654	219*	182*	253*	66.5	70.8
3	915	188●	258*	469●	79.5	77.4
4	1417	268●	456●	693●	81.1	81.1
5	174	17●	50*	107●	90.2	82.9
6-7	247	30●	95●	122●	87.9	87.9
NUMBER OF BLOCKS IN THE SITE						
1	524	221*	142*	161*	57.8	57.8
2	420	134*	104*	182*	68.1	64.8
3	420	125*	108*	187●	70.2	70.7
4	404	105*	119*	180*	74.0	72.6
5	305	80*	83*	142●	73.8	76.0
6	234	41●	76●	117●	82.5	77.5
7	154	35●	45●	74●	77.3	77.5
8	224	62*	61*	101*	72.3	78.1
9	243	39●	51*	153●	84.0	83.6
10-19	768	102●	310●	356●	86.7	87.2
20-29	232	18●	58*	156●	92.2	88.6
38/54/81	171	13●	95●	63*	92.4	92.4

DAMAGE						FAECES			
NUMBER OF TYPES OF TARGET PER BLOCK				PERCENTAGE WITH DAMAGE	SMOOTHED PERCENTAGE	FAECES FREE	FAECES PRESENT	PERCENTAGE WITH FAECES	SMOOTHED PERCENTAGE
0	1	2	3-5						
1721*	662*	120*	59*	32.8	32.8	2450*	112*	4.4	4.4
404•	245•	61•	28*	45.3	36.2	658•	80•	10.8	5.9
90•	62•	14•	7•	48.0	48.0	159•	14•	8.1	10.6
48•	59•	11•	14•	63.6	55.1	115•	17•	12.9	11.9
20•	12*	5•	10•	57.4	61.2	36•	11•	23.4	15.8
19•	21•	1*	4•	57.8	56.1	39•	6•	13.3	22.7
19•	8*	9•	4•	52.5	51.0	27•	13•	32.5	19.0
11*	3*	–	1•	26.7	48.6	15*	–*	0.0	25.7
6•	6•	3•	–	60.0	47.3	10•	5•	33.3	14.7
62•	49•	4*	5•	48.3	41.6	103•	17•	14.2	18.6
61*	13*	5•	7•	29.1	38.9	67•	19•	22.1	16.7
9*	1*	–	–	10.0	41.5	10*	–*	0.0	18.1
30•	21•	2*	22•	60.0	61.1	63•	12•	16.0	9.5
10•	20•	4•	7•	75.6	75.6	41*	–*	0.0	0.0
1611*	542*	83*	46*	29.4	29.4	2186*	96*	4.2	4.2
471•	297•	79•	32*	46.4	35.8	796•	83•	9.4	6.0
104•	93•	27•	20•	57.4	50.0	219•	25•	10.2	9.4
49•	63•	11•	3*	61.1	58.6	117•	9•	7.1	10.1
24•	23•	6•	4•	57.9	61.2	48•	9•	15.8	12.6
26•	28•	5•	13•	63.9	55.0	58•	14•	19.4	18.1
27*	9*	6•	–*	35.7	53.2	34•	8•	19.0	18.7
12•	8•	2•	3•	52.0	43.3	21•	4•	16.0	13.3
12•	5*	4•	2•	47.8	49.7	23*	–*	0.0	17.1
67•	53•	4*	9•	49.6	38.5	106•	27•	20.3	12.0
65*	12*	1*	–*	16.7	42.5	77*	1*	1.3	19.7
2•	8•	5•	7•	90.9	44.6	4•	18•	81.8	17.7
30•	21•	2*	22•	60.0	69.6	63•	12•	16.0	21.7
10•	20•	4•	7•	75.6	75.6	41*	–*	0.0	0.0
552*	116*	11*	13*	20.2	20.2	668*	24*	3.5	3.5
398•	194•	43•	19*	39.1	31.9	605•	49•	7.5	6.1
539•	280•	63•	33*	41.1	41.6	851•	64•	7.0	7.2
807•	456•	94•	60•	43.0	43.3	1316*	101*	7.1	7.5
76•	68•	19•	11•	56.3	44.5	152•	22•	12.6	9.2
138•	68*	9•	32•	44.1	44.1	201•	46•	18.6	18.6
355*	132*	21*	16*	32.3	32.3	502*	22*	4.2	4.2
267*	113*	25•	15*	36.4	35.9	382•	38•	9.1	6.3
253•	133•	27•	7*	39.8	38.0	394•	26*	6.2	7.6
251•	113•	30•	10*	37.9	39.6	373•	31•	7.7	7.1
178•	97•	17•	13•	41.6	39.6	282•	23•	7.5	7.6
141•	63•	22•	8*	39.7	41.3	216•	18•	7.7	6.9
88•	39•	13•	14•	42.9	37.6	147*	7•	4.6	7.4
153•	57•	6•	8*	31.7	40.7	204•	20•	8.9	6.9
127•	82•	17•	17•	47.7	38.2	227•	16*	6.6	6.6
483*	211*	47•	27*	37.1	42.0	722*	46*	6.0	8.0
110•	99•	12•	11•	52.6	40.5	195•	37•	16.0	9.0
104•	43*	2*	22•	39.2	39.2	149•	22•	12.9	12.9

TABLE 27   FREQUENCY TABLES, DESIGN VALUES BY ABUSE CLASSES - continued

URINE   (Tower Hamlets only)

DESIGN VALUE	TOTAL NO. OF BLOCKS	URINE FREE	URINE PRESENT	PERCENTAGE WITH URINE	SMOOTHED PERCENTAGE
NUMBER OF INTERCONNECTED EXITS					
1	1219	749*	470*	38.6	38.6
2	298	135●	163●	54.7	43.2
3	102	35●	67●	65.7	58.2
4	57	21●	36●	63.2	62.1
5	23	13●	10●	43.5	55.6
6	19	10●	9●	47.4	39.0
7	17	13*	4*	23.5	38.5
8	3	1●	2●	66.7	34.8
9	3	1●	2●	66.7	51.1
10-19	41	21●	20●	48.8	48.8
20-29	-	-	-	-	-
30-39	-	-	-	-	-
50-59	-	-	-	-	-
80-89	-	-	-	-	-
VERTICAL CIRCULATION CHANNELS (lifts and staircases)					
1	989	654*	335*	33.9	33.9
2	428	187●	241●	56.3	41.9
3	112	48●	63●	56.3	56.7
4	76	32●	44●	57.9	56.7
5	48	22●	26●	54.2	58.5
6	40	14●	26●	65.0	56.1
7	19	11●	8●	42.1	62.3
8	18	4●	14●	77.8	60.5
9	1	-●	1●	100.0	55.7
10-19	42	23●	19●	45.2	48.1
20-29	9	4●	5●	55.6	55.6
40-49	-	-	-	-	-
60-69	-	-	-	-	-
103	-	-	-	-	-
ACCESS POINTS (number of sides)					
1	243	201*	42*	17.3	17.3
2	269	149●	120●	44.6	40.7
3	447	219●	228●	51.0	47.3
4	592	322●	270●	45.6	48.7
5	145	67●	78●	53.8	47.8
6-7	86	41●	45●	52.3	52.3
NUMBER OF BLOCKS IN THE SITE					
1	210	113●	97●	46.2	46.2
2	182	98●	84●	46.2	48.0
3	189	91●	98●	51.9	49.5
4	148	73●	75●	50.7	49.5
5	130	72●	58●	44.6	46.9
6	114	63●	51●	44.7	45.8
7	77	39●	38●	49.4	43.9
8	96	59*	37*	38.5	44.5
9	126	68●	58●	46.0	41.7
10-19	356	210*	146*	41.0	38.5
20-29	154	113*	41*	26.6	26.6
38/54/81	-	-	-	-	-

CHILDREN IN CARE (Southwark only)

TOTAL NO. OF BLOCKS	NO OF HOUSEHOLDS PER BLOCK WITH CHILDREN IN CARE							PERCENTAGE OF BLOCKS	SMOOTHED PERCENTAGE
	0	1	2	3	4	5	6-11		
1212	972*	142*	56*	26*	9*	1*	6●	19.8	19.8
374	263●	66●	27●	12●	2*	3●	1●	29.7	22.2
57	44*	6●	5●	1●	1●	-	-	22.8	28.9
57	40●	7*	4●	4●	1●	-	1●	29.8	24.8
19	16●	2●	1●	-	-	-	-	15.8	28.9
21	13●	7●	-	-	1●	-	-	38.1	30.9
15	9●	4●	2●	-	-	-	-	40.0	36.4
8	6●	1●	1●	-	-	-	-	25.0	33.3
7	5●	2●	-	-	-	-	-	28.6	33.3
29	19●	7●	2●	-*	1●	-	-	34.5	46.4
33	13●	9●	4●	3●	3●	1●	-	60.6	46.4
7	5●	2●	-	-	-	-	-	28.6	45.2
75	45●	19●	8●	2●	1●	-	-	40.0	39.8
41	24●	8●	2●	2●	2●	3●	-	41.5	41.5
1153	947*	117*	48*	24*	9*	2*	6●	17.9	17.9
390	265●	75●	32●	12●	2*	2●	2●	32.1	22.3
113	74●	23●	9●	5●	2●	-	-	34.5	32.7
39	26●	8●	3●	2●	-	-	-	33.3	34.4
8	5●	2●	1●	-	-	-	-	37.5	27.8
32	26*	5●	-	-	1●	-	-	18.8	19.0
18	16*	1●	1●	-	-	-	-	11.1	20.4
4	1●	2●	-	-	1●	-	-	75.0	30.3
11	6●	4●	1●	-	-	-	-	45.5	39.2
36	24●	9●	3●	-	-	-	-	33.3	36.7
13	8●	5●	-	-	-	-	-	41.0	45.1
22	7●	4●	4●	3●	3●	1●	-	68.2	45.5
75	45●	19●	8●	2●	1●	-	-	40.0	44.9
41	24●	8●	2●	2●	2●	3●	-	41.5	41.5
420	383*	19*	12*	5*	-*	-	1●	8.8	8.8
335	256*	43*	21●	7●	4●	1●	3●	23.6	20.7
348	236●	65●	24●	16●	5●	-	2●	32.2	27.8
680	492●	115●	4●	17●	8●	6●	2●	27.6	39.4
26	16●	8●	2●	-	-	-	-	38.5	29.7
146	91●	32●	13●	5●	4●	1●	-	37.7	37.7
255	211*	25*	12*	6*	-*	-	1●	17.3	17.3
204	146●	32●	13●	6●	5●	-	2●	28.4	23.5
201	148●	29●	15●	6●	1●	1●	1●	26.4	25.4
224	175*	34●	7*	5●	3●	-	-	21.9	26.4
155	104●	25●	17●	6●	2●	-	1●	32.9	27.7
108	73●	20●	3*	4●	4●	2●	2●	32.4	31.3
56	42●	10●	3●	1●	-	-	-	25.0	26.5
96	76*	11*	2*	5●	-*	2●	-	20.8	26.7
99	66●	18●	12●	2●	1●	-	-	33.3	20.6
402	332●	46*	16*	4*	1*	2●	1●	17.4	22.1
74	50●	13●	4●	3●	3●	1●	-	32.4	22.3
81	51●	19●	8●	2●	1●	-	-	37.0	37.0

TABLE 27　FREQUENCY TABLES, DESIGN VALUES BY ABUSE CLASSES － continued

DESIGN VALUE	TOTAL NO. OF BLOCKS	LITTER				GRAFFITI				DAMAGE				PERCENTAGE WITH DAMAGE
		LITTER FREE	CLEAN AND CASUAL	DIRTY AND DECAYED	PERCENTAGE WITH LITTER	GRAFFITI FREE	INSIDE OR OUTSIDE	INSIDE AND OUTSIDE	PERCENTAGE WITH GRAFFITI	NUMBER OF TYPES OF TARGET PER BLOCK				
										0	1	2	3-5	
FLATS OR MAISONETTES														
Flats	2532	443*	1409*	680*	82.5	741*	792●	999*	70.7	1661*	658	131*	82*	34.4
Mixed	522	56●	395●	71●	89.3	105●	191●	226*	79.9	313	150●	27●	32●	40.0
Maisonettes	1045	73●	512●	460●	93.0	129●	269*	647●	87.7	536●	374●	81●	54●	48.7
HORIZONTAL CIRCULATION CHANNELS (corridor type)														
Landing	1393	323*	760●	310*	76.8	494*	449*	450*	64.5	1018*	285*	57*	33*	26.9
Balcony	582	80●	354●	148●	86.3	145●	208●	229*	75.1	371●	170●	29●	12*	36.3
External	1859	150●	1074●	635●	91.9	291●	525*	1043●	84.4	993●	638●	137●	91●	46.6
Internal/intermediate	265	19●	128*	118●	92.8	45●	70*	150●	83.0	128●	89●	16●	32●	51.7
ENTRANCE POSITION														
Set back from street	602	91*	331*	180●	84.9	175*	174*	253*	70.9	373*	175*	33*	21*	38.0
Flush on street	871	128*	488*	255*	85.3	196●	298*	377●	77.5	588*	227*	36*	20*	32.5
Inside the estate	2626	353●	1497●	776*	86.6	604●	780*	1242●	77.0	1549●	780●	170●	127●	41.0
ENTRANCE TYPE														
Communal only	1686	328*	944*	414*	80.5	510*	537●	639●	69.8	1139*	399*	79*	69*	32.4
Communal and individual	2413	244●	1372●	797●	89.9	465●	715*	1233●	80.7	1371●	783●	160●	99●	43.2
STILTS AND GARAGES UNDER THE BLOCK														
Neither	3859	539*	2171*	1149●	86.0	929*	1194●	1736●	75.9	2387*	1102●	224●	146*	38.1
Stilts and/or garages	240	33●	145●	62*	86.3	46●	58●	136●	80.8	123●	80●	15●	22●	48.1
SPATIAL ORGANISATION														
Semi-public multiple	71	30*	28*	13*	57.7	43*	25*	3*	39.4	65*	6*	-*	-*	8.5
Semi-public single	105	31*	52*	22*	70.5	61*	32*	12*	41.9	86*	14*	-*	4●	18.1
Semi-composed single	95	25*	48*	22*	73.7	41*	26*	28*	56.8	63*	30*	2*	-*	33.7
Confused single	322	73●	164●	85●	77.3	116●	81*	125●	64.0	201●	90●	19●	12●	37.6
Semi-confused multiple	1170	147●	640●	383●	87.4	228●	377●	565●	80.5	684●	366●	61●	59●	41.5
Confused multiple	2061	245●	1226●	590●	88.1	460●	612*	989●	77.7	1198●	615●	156●	92●	41.9
Row blocks	275	21●	158o	96●	92.4	26●	99●	150●	90.5	213●	61●	-*	1*	22.5
PLAY AREAS														
Absent	3183	474*	1807●	902*	85.1	821*	987●	1375●	74.2	2028●	876●	160●	119*	36.3
Present	916	98●	509*	309●	89.3	154●	265*	497●	83.2	482●	306●	79●	49●	47.4

DESIGN VALUE	FAECES TOTAL NO. OF BLOCKS	FAECES FREE	FAECES PRESENT	PERCENTAGE WITH FAECES	URINE (Tower Hamlets only) TOTAL NO. OF BLOCKS	URINE FREE	URINE PRESENT	PERCENTAGE WITH URINE	CHILDREN IN CARE (Southwark only) TOTAL NO. OF BLOCKS	NO OF HOUSEHOLDS PER BLOCK WITH CHILDREN IN CARE 0	1	2	3	4	5	6-11	PERCENTAGE OF BLOCKS
FLATS OR MAISONETTES																	
Flats	2532	2393*	139*	5.5	1080	634*	446•	41.3	1314	1036*	166•	63*	28*	10*	4•	7•	21.2
Mixed	522	408•	42•	8.0	8	3•	5•	62.5	346	227•	59•	35•	16•	3•	3•	1•	34.4
Maisonettes	1045	920•	125•	12.0	964	362•	332•	47.8	295	211•	57•	14•	6•	6•	1•	-	28.5
HORIZONTAL CIRCULATION CHANNELS (corridor type)																	
Landing	1393	1338*	55*	3.9	505	354*	151•	29.9	811	710*	68*	22*	8*	1*	1•	2*	12.5
Balcony	582	544*	38*	6.5	242	152•	90*	37.2	237	180•	37•	8•	6•	3•	1•	4•	24.1
External	1859	1689•	170•	9.1	927	436•	491•	53.0	765	499*	146•	70•	30•	10•	6•	4•	34.8
Internal/Intermediate	265	222•	43•	16.2	108	57•	51•	47.2	142	85•	31•	12•	6•	7•	1•	-	40.1
ENTRANCE POSITION																	
Set back from street	602	572*	30*	5.0	341	190•	151•	15.0	225	188•	24•	10*	2*	-*	-•	••	16.4
Flush on street	871	806•	65•	7.5	341	226•	115•	31.3	454	397•	43•	7*	4*	2*	-*	6•	12.6
Inside the estate	2626	2415•	211•	8.0	1100	583•	517•	47.4	1276	889•	215•	95•	40•	19•	8•	6•	30.3
ENTRANCE TYPE																	
Communal only	1686	1588*	98*	5.8	610	386*	224*	36.7	982	806•	119•	33•	13•	6•	3•	2*	17.9
Communal and individual	2413	2205•	208•	8.6	1172	613•	559•	47.7	973	668•	163•	79•	37•	15•	5•	6•	31.3
STILTS AND GARAGES UNDER THE BLOCK																	
Neither	3859	3580*	279*	7.2	1713	972*	741•	43.3	1818	1374*	261•	105•	46•	19•	5*	8•	24.4
Stilts and/or garages	240	213•	27•	11.3	69	27•	42•	60.9	137	100•	21•	7•	4•	2•	3•	-	27.0
SPATIAL ORGANISATION																	
Semi-public multiple	71	66•	5•	7.0	28	27*	1*	3.6	36	31•	2*	-*	1*	-	-	-	5.6
Semi-public single	105	103*	2*	1.9	44	33*	11•	25.0	56	52•	1*	2*	1*	-	-	-	7.1
Semi-composed single	95	89*	6*	6.3	41	20•	21•	51.2	39	35•	3*	1*	-	-	-	-	10.3
Confused single	322	307*	15*	4.7	125	58•	67•	53.6	157	120•	22•	5•	5•	1•	-	1•	23.6
Semi-confused multiple	1170	1039•	131•	11.2	510	297•	213•	41.8	509	392•	77•	22*	9•	3•	3•	1*	23.0
Confused multiple	2061	1924*	139*	6.7	928	464•	464•	50.0	989	673•	176•	68•	35•	15•	5•	7•	32.0
Row blocks	275	265*	10*	3.6	106	100*	6*	5.7	169	168•	1*	-*	-	-	-	-	0.6
PLAY AREAS																	
Absent	3183	2953*	230*	7.2	1402	808*	594*	42.4	1498	1164•	197•	75•	35•	15o	6•	6•	22.3
Present	916	840•	76•	8.3	380	191•	189•	49.7	457	310•	85•	37•	15•	6•	2•	2•	32.2

Appendix II
Correlation

Kendall's tau C is the most appropriate method of correlation because it is non-parametric and can use ordinal data. It requires certain variables to be grouped in order to avoid classes containing very few cases, and this has been done for five variables as follows.

Number of storeys:	1, 2, 3, 4, 5, 6, 7, 8-9, 10-12, 13-27
Dwellings per block:	1-9, 10-19, 20-29, 30-39, 40-49, 50-59, 60-69, 70-79, 80-89, 90-99, 100-317
Dwellings per entrance:	1-9, 10-19, 20-29, 30-39, 40-49, 50-199, 200-999, 1000-2268
Interconnecting exits:	1, 2, 3, 4, 5-15, 16-80
Vertical routes:	1, 2, 3, 4, 5-15, 16-103

Blocks with voids or facilities do not fit the general pattern and have been omitted, leaving 3,654 cases for correlation; coefficients for design and malaise are set out in Table 28. The tau C method yields conservatively low coefficients as compared with Pearson's product moment method, used by Oscar Newman and the Home Office, and allowing for this, our results seem to be of at least the same order of strength as theirs.

Table 29 lists the coefficients obtained for Blackbird Leys, Southwark and Tower Hamlets separately; this reduces the interference due to contrasted local characteristics. Blackbird Leys, as the smallest and most homogenous area has some of the highest coefficients of all. Ten are higher than any for Southwark or Tower Hamlets. Most of the others are not particularly low in the general picture, but too low to be significant when there are only 54 blocks. The Blackbird Leys damage table is omitted as only five blocks had any, too few to yield meaningful results.

Of the 60 coefficients for Southwark, 49 are higher than their counterparts for the total area, but Tower Hamlets generally has lower values. It is thought that the drop reflects the generally high levels of abuse in the borough (Table 2), which leaves less scope for abuse differences between the best and worst designs, and hence less scope for strong coefficients.

Mutual interference among the design variables can be partly offset by correlating the combined disadvantagement score with the test measures. The resulting coefficients are higher than those for any individual variable in the same column except in the case of graffiti in Blackbird Leys and children in care in Southwark. In general they are about double the mean coefficients for the individual designs, suggesting that mutual interference approximately halves the

TABLE 28   CORRELATION OF DESIGN VARIABLES WITH TEST MEASURES

Kendall's tau C coefficients for 3654 blocks (excluding blocks with voids and facilities)

*** Very highly significant   ** Highly significant   * Significant   . Not significant

DESIGN VARIABLE	LITTER	GRAFFITI	DAMAGE	CHILDREN IN CARE	URINE	FAECES	ABUSE SCORE
Dwellings per block	0.1211 ***	0.1929 ***	0.1887 ***	0.2120 ***	0.2398 ***	0.0430 ***	0.1794 ***
Dwellings per entrance	0.1733 ***	0.2709 ***	0.1946 ***	0.1573 ***	0.2311 ***	0.0874 ***	0.2387 ***
Number of storeys	0.2027 ***	0.3024 ***	0.2162 ***	0.1826 ***	0.1924 ***	0.0557 ***	0.2618 ***
Flats or maisonettes	0.1337 ***	0.1808 ***	0.0976 ***	0.0690 ***	0.0688 **	0.0582 ***	0.1916 ***
Overhead walkways	0.1072 ***	0.1371 ***	0.0704 ***	0.0406 ***	0.0458 **	0.0527 ***	0.1167 ***
Interconnecting exits	0.1080 ***	0.1620 ***	0.1132 ***	0.0742 ***	0.1512 ***	0.0793 ***	0.1517 ***
Vertical routes	0.1513 ***	0.2199 ***	0.1645 ***	0.0998 ***	0.2221 ***	0.0798 ***	0.2082 ***
Corridor type	0.1781 ***	0.2263 ***	0.1326 ***	0.1483 ***	0.1910 ***	0.0633 ***	0.2286 ***
Entrance position	0.0076 .	0.0409 ***	0.0336 **	0.0943 ***	0.0588 **	0.0199 **	0.0389 **
Entrance type	0.1504 ***	0.1727 ***	0.0833 ***	0.1101 ***	0.0994 ***	0.0278 **	0.1822 ***
Stilts or garages	0.0038 .	0.0349 ***	0.0314 ***	0.0133 .	0.0282 **	0.0100 .	0.0313 ***
Spatial organisation	0.0926 ***	0.1640 ***	0.0671 ***	0.0760 ***	0.0902 ***	0.0075 .	0.0725 ***
Blocks per site	0.1255 ***	0.1731 ***	0.0520 ***	0.0139 .	0.0854 **	0.0308 **	0.1297 ***
Access points	0.1492 ***	0.1855 ***	0.1239 ***	0.0894 ***	0.1518 ***	0.0505 ***	0.1707 ***
Play areas	0.0570 ***	0.1104 ***	0.0924 ***	0.0771 ***	0.0479 *	0.0099 .	0.1163 ***
Mean coefficient	0.1173	0.1716	0.1108	0.0972	0.1155	0.0451	0.1546
Disadvantagement score	0.2248 ***	0.3453 ***	0.2096 ***	0.1729 ***	0.2775 ***	0.0887 ***	0.2836 ***

TABLE 29 KENDALL'S TAU C CORRELATION COEFFICIENTS

DESIGN VARIABLE	BLACKBIRD LEYS (52 blocks)		SOUTHWARK (2017 blocks)				TOWER HAMLETS (1585 blocks)			
	LITTER	GRAFFITI	LITTER	GRAFFITI	DAMAGE	FAECES	LITTER	GRAFFITI	DAMAGE	FAECES
Dwellings per block	0.1010 .	0.1272 .	0.1254 ***	0.2031 ***	0.1975 ***	0.0347 **	0.0492 *	0.1263 ***	0.1480 ***	0.0493 ***
Dwellings per entrance	0.4860 ***	0.4068 **	0.2200 ***	0.3151 ***	0.2130 ***	0.1099 ***	0.1488 ***	0.2260 ***	0.1646 ***	0.0519 ***
Number of storeys	0.4172 ***	0.1095 .	0.2094 ***	0.3134 ***	0.2184 ***	0.0737 ***	0.1171 ***	0.2230 ***	0.1684 ***	0.0246 .
Flats or maisonettes	0.0921 .	0.1257 *	0.1324 ***	0.2124 ***	0.1339 ***	0.0820 ***	0.0977 ***	0.1237 ***	0.0268 .	0.0290 *
Overhead walkways	0.3240 ***	-	0.1351 ***	0.1686 ***	0.0910 ***	0.0883 ***	0.0968 ***	0.1073 ***	0.0399 .	0.0072 .
Interconnecting exits	0.0821 .	0.5355 ***	0.1988 ***	0.2261 ***	0.1558 ***	0.1175 ***	0.1377 ***	0.1682 ***	0.0948 ***	0.0344 .
Vertical routes	0.2485 **	0.1065 .	0.2093 ***	0.2611 ***	0.1813 ***	0.1121 ***	0.1434 ***	0.2017 ***	0.1446 ***	0.0556 **
Corridor type	-	-0.0414 .	0.2015 ***	0.2729 ***	0.1686 ***	0.0825 ***	0.0761 ***	0.1132 ***	0.0427 .	0.0332 .
Entrance position	-0.0766 .	-0.4660 ***	0.0532 ***	0.0813 ***	0.0543 ***	0.0360 ***	0.0034 .	0.0328 .	0.0312 .	0.0035 .
Entrance type	0.1110 .	0.0976 .	0.1207 ***	0.1518 ***	0.0620 ***	0.0392 ***	0.0428 *	0.0778 ***	0.0378 .	0.0056 .
Stilts or garages	-	-	0.0125 .	0.0547 ***	0.0502 ***	0.0058 .	0.0229 .	0.0345 *	0.0211 .	0.0164 .
Spatial organisation	0.4249 ***	0.1982 .	0.0836 ***	0.1250 ***	0.0374 *	-0.0170 .	0.0397 *	0.0439 *	0.0382 *	-0.0382 *
Blocks per site	0.3051 **	0.0710 .	0.1748 ***	0.2376 ***	0.0878 ***	0.0573 ***	0.0744 ***	0.0749 ***	-0.0131 .	-0.0115 .
Access points	0.4360 *	0.4408 ***	0.1633 ***	0.2048 ***	0.1427 ***	0.0495 ***	0.0768 **	0.1059 ***	0.0659 *	0.0465 .
Play areas	0.2249 .	-0.1183 .	0.0778 ***	0.1602 ***	0.1178 ***	0.0165 *	0.0609 **	0.0662 ***	0.0708 **	0.0021 .
Disadvantagement score	0.5170 ***	0.2500 *	0.2681 ***	0.3893 ***	0.2312 ***	0.1155 ***	0.1549 ***	0.2537 ***	0.1535 ***	0.0483 ***

*** Very highly significant   ** Highly significant   * Significant   . Not significant

TABLE 30   DESIGN AND SOCIO-ECONOMIC COEFFICIENTS COMPARED

Data for 90 blocks in Southwark. Kendall's tau C coefficients

	LITTER	GRAFFITI	DAMAGE	FAECES
DESIGN VARIABLES				
Disadvantagement score	0.2693 ***	0.3952 ***	0.1719 *	0.0741 .
Strongest individual variable	0.2089 ** (Inter-connecting exits)	0.3533 *** (No. of storeys)	0.2407 ** (Dwellings per entrance)	0.2405 *** (Dwellings per entrance)
SOCIO-ECONOMIC VARIABLES				
Unemployed as a percentage of all economically active	0.2408 **	0.2052 *	-0.0283 .	-0.0193 .
Pensioners as a percentage of population	-0.2407 **	-0.3619 ***	-0.1202 .	-0.0133 .
Percentage No. of households with pensioners	-0.1189 .	-0.3311 ***	-0.0747 .	-0.0721 .
Percentage of under-fifteens in single parent families with female heads	0.1737 *	0.2796 **	0.2193 **	-0.0598 .
Under-fifteens as a percentage of adults over 19	0.1593 .	0.3578 ***	0.0487 .	-0.1269 .
Teenagers (10-19) as a percentage of adults over 19	0.1007 .	0.3578 ***	0.0583 .	-0.1314 .
Percentage of households having over 1.5 persons per room	0.0682 .	0.0893 .	-0.0392 .	-0.0464 .
Council dwellings as a percentage of all dwellings	0.1019 .	0.1148 .	0.0556 .	-0.1348 .

strength of the individual coefficients.

Stronger coefficients also emerge when the designs are correlated with the combined abuse score instead of the separate abuse measures, but the improvement is less marked than with the disadvantagement scores. Only five are stronger than all the separate coefficients, but five more are stronger than all except graffiti. The remaining five are more average.

The coefficient for disadvantagement score by abuse score is stronger than that for any individual design by abuse, and also stronger than any individual abuse measure by disadvantagement except graffiti.

Graffiti emerges as the strongest test measure, although it has a weaker mean range than damage and children in care. We deduce that design affects vandalistic behaviour and care orders more powerfully, but graffiti more consistently.

In Table 30 coefficients for disadvantagement score and the strongest individual design variable in 90 blocks of flats (i.e. all those where design is consistent with enumeration districts) are compared with coefficients for socio-economic data derived from the Census. In every column one or other of the two design coefficients is stronger than all the socio-economic variables. Of the seven socio-economic coefficients that exceed those for one of the design factors, four are negative. They are good influences, offsetting the effect of design, which would be even stronger in their absence, as also, of course, would these good influences in the absence of bad design. Of the genuinely rival bad influences, three affect graffiti. These are firstly the ratio of under-fifteens to adults over 19, secondly the ratio of teenagers to adults and thirdly the percentage of under-fifteens in single-parent families with female heads. The third one also affects vandal damage. These child-density factors are not negligible, but in no case are they as strong as at least one design factor.

The ward means used in Chapter IX reduce the idiosyncrasies of individual blocks, and they produce a high tau C coefficient of +0.599 for disadvantagement score by abuse score. This is higher than any disadvantagement coefficient for separate test measures, except litter in Blackbird Leys.

However, the ward means are interval data with a distribution that approximates to normal, and it is therefore appropriate to use the more powerful Pearson's method of correlation. This yields a coefficient of +0.720, which indicates the conservatism of the tau C value. The two are not directly comparable and therefore the Pearson's coefficients used in Chapter IX should not be quantitatively compared with the tau C coefficients used elsewhere in the book. A Pearson's coefficient of +0.799 is obtained for Southwark and Blackbird Leys when Tower Hamlets is omitted. The Tower Hamlets coefficient of +0.478 may be lower because the disadvantagement scores of this borough are less dispersed.

References

Adam, R. and others. 'Revive Into Style: The Search for a New Context'. (1983) *Architects' Journal,* Vol 178 No 46.

Calhoun, J.B. 'A Behavioral Sink'. *Roots of Behavior.* (1962) Harper, New York.

Chyba, A. P. *The Significance of Common Floor Space Provision to Housing Developments* (1983) Unpublished dissertation, Geography Department, King's College London.

Coleman, A. 'Urban Housing and Social Malaise' (1984) *Land Use Policy* Vol 1 No 1.

Coleman, A. 'Vandalism on Council Estates' (1984) *Architectural Annual Review 1983.*

Coleman, A. 'Trouble in Utopia: Design Influences in Blocks of Flats' (1984) *Geographical Journal,* Vol 150 Part 3.

Cottle, L. and Sex, R. 'The New Residential Environment of the Inner City' (1982) *International Journal of Environmental Studies,* Vol 19 No 2.

Department of the Environment, Scottish Development Department and Welsh Office. *Housing and Construction Statistics 1972-82.*

Department of the Environment. Design Bulletins, HMSO, London:

22 *New Housing in a Cleared Area: A study of St. Mary's Oldham* (1971).

23 *Housing for Single People 1: How They Live at Present* (1971).

29 *Housing for Single People 2: A Design Guide with a Description of a Scheme at Leicester* (1974).

33 *Housing for Single People 3: An Appraisal of a Purpose-Built Scheme* (1978).

25 *The Estate Outside the Dwelling: Reactions of Residents to Aspects of Housing Layout* (1972).

26 *New Housing and Road Traffic Noise* (1972).

27 *Children at Play* (1973).

32 *Residential Roads and Footpaths: Layout Considerations* (1977).

Department of the Environment. *Children's Play Space* (1972) Circular 79/72 HMSO.

Edwards, A. M. *The Design of Suburbia* (1981) Pembridge Press, London.

Freedman, J. L. *Crowding and Behavior* (1976) W. H. Freeman, San Francisco.

Green, I. V. *Housing Allocation Research Report* (1983) Prepared for Oxford City Council.

Hillier,W. and others. 'Space Syntax'. (1984) *Architects' Journal,* Vol 178 No 48.

Howard, E. *Tomorrow: A Peaceful Path to Real Reform (1898)* Re-issued as *Garden Cities of Tomorrow* (1902) Faber (1965).

Hughes, R. 'Architecture and the Utopian Dream' (1980) *The Listener* 16th October.

209

Institute of Housing and Royal Institute of British Architects. *Homes for the Future: Standards for New Housing Development* (1983).

Jacobs, J. *The Death and Life of Great American Cities* (1961) Random House, New York. (1962) Jonathan Cape.

Jephcott, P. and Robinson, H. *Homes in High Flats* (1971) Oliver and Boyd, Edinburgh.

Johnson, P. 'What Makes Me Tick' (1979) *Philip Johnson: Writings* Oxford University Press, New York.

Jones, E. 'Aspects of Urbanisation in Venezuela'. (1964) *Ekistics,* Vol 18 No. 109.

Le Corbusier (Charles Édouard Jeanneret) *Vers une Architecture* (1923) Translated into English by F. Etchells (1974) Architectural Press.

Mayhew, P. 'Defensible Space: The Current Status of a Crime Prevention Theory' (1979) *The Howard Journal* Vol 18.

Macmillan H. *Hansard* 5th series 493HC DEB/5s.

Ministry of Health. *Report on the Design of Dwellings Sub-committee.* Chairman: The Earl of Dudley (1944) Central Housing and Advisory Committee.

Ministry of Housing and Local Government. Design Bulletins, HMSO, London:
1 *Some Aspects of Designing for Old People* (1968)
2 *Landscaping for Flats* (1963)
6 *Space in the Home* (1968)
7 *Housing Cost Yardstick* (1963)
10 and 12. *Cars in Housing* (1966)
14 *House Planning* (1968)
15 *Family Houses at West Ham* (1969)
18 *Designing a Low Rise Housing System* (1970)
19 *Living in a Slum: A Study of St. Mary's Oldham* (1970)
20 *Moving Out of a Slum: A Study of People Moving Out of St. Mary's Oldham* (1970)
21 *Families Living at High Density. A Study of Estates in Leeds, Liverpool and London* (1970)

Ministry of Housing and Local Government. Planning Bulletins, HMSO, London:
1 *Town Centres, Approach to Renewal* (1962)
2 *Residential Areas. Higher Densities* (1962)

Ministry of Housing and Local Government. *Homes for Today and Tomorrow* (Parker Morris Report). (1961)

Newman, O. *Defensible Space* (1972) Macmillan, New York. (1973) Architectural Press, London.

Newman, O. *Design Guidelines for Creating Defensible Space* (1976) United States Department of Justice, Washington D.C.

Newman, O. *Community of Interest* (1980) Anchor Press, New York.

Newman, O. and Franck, K. A. *Factors Influencing Crime and Instability in Urban Housing Developments* (1981) National Institute of Justice, Washington D.C.

Newman, O. *New York State Program to Reduce Crime in Communities of the Elderly* (1980) Institute of Community Design Analysis, for the New York State Division of Housing and Community Renewal, New York.

Newman, O. and Franck, K. A. *Housing Design and Children's Antisocial Behavior* (1981) Institute for Community Design Analysis, New York.

Newman, O. *Review and Analysis of the Chicago Housing Authority and Implementation of Recommended Changes* (1982) First Report of Phase 1: Recommended Changes and Resulting Savings. Institute for Community Design Analysis, New York.

Oliver, P., Davis, I. and Bentley, I. *Dunroamin: The Suburban Semi and Its Enemies* (1981) Barrie and Jenkins, London.

Power, A. *Priority Estates Project* (1982) Department of the Environment, London.

Power, A. 'Housing Case Study: Difficult to Let'. (1982) *Architects' Journal,* Vol 176 No 48.

Power, A. *Local Housing Management: A Priority Estates Project* (1984) Department of the Environment, London.

Power, A. 'Reversing Problems on Unpopular Estates through Local Management'. (1984) *Geographical Journal,* Vol 150 Part 3.

Ravetz, A. *Remaking Cities: Contradictions of the Recent Urban Environment* (1980) Croom Helm, London.

Redknap, C. *An Evaluation of the Inner Urban Environment, with Specific Reference to the London Borough of Southwark* (1981) Unpublished undergraduate dissertation, School of Human Environmental Studies, King's College, London.

Redknap, C. *The Effect of Entrance Designs in Blocks of Flats* (1983) Unpublished report to the Nuffield Foundation, Land Use Research Unit, King's College, London.

Reynolds, F., Duffy, F. and Harding, P. *All Mod Cons: A Study of a 'Problem' Housing Estate* (1983) Unpublished report to the Joseph Rowntree Memorial Trust.

Sagan, C. *The Dragons of Eden* (1977) Hodder and Stoughton, London.

Shaw Associates. *North Peckham Estate: Project and Cost Report* (1983). London Borough of Southwark.

Stamp, L.D. *The Land of Britain: its Use and Misuse* (Second Edition, 1962) Longman, London.

Sturman, A. and Wilson, S. 'Vandalism Research Aimed at Specific Remedies.' (1976) *Municipal Engineering* 7th May.

Turner, J.F.C. *Housing by People: Towards Autonomy in Building Environments* (1976) Marion Boyars, London.

Turner, J.F.C. and Fichter, R. (Eds). *Freedom to Build* (1972) Collier Macmillan, New York.

Ward, C. *The Child in the City* (1978) Architectural Press, London.

Ward, C. Preface to John F.C. Turner's *Housing by People* (1976).

Wilson, S. 'Vandalism and 'Defensible Space' on London Housing Estates'. (1980) *Designing Out Crime,* Chapter 4. R.G.V. Clarke and P. Mayhew (Eds.). Home Office Research Unit, HMSO, London.

Wilson, S. 'Crime and Public Housing: Evidence from An Investigation of Unpopular Housing Estates'. (1980) *Crime and Public Housing.* M. Hough and P. Mayhew (Eds.). Home Office Research and Planning Unit, London.

Additional reading

Chan, B. *Dwelling Type as a Factor in the Incidence of Fires* (1985) Unpublished undergraduate dissertation, Geography Department, King's College, London.

Coleman, A. 'Inner City Design: Precautions and Outcome' (1988) *Seminar Paper Reprints*, International Fire and Security Exhibition and Conference, Communication House, London N12.

Coleman, A. 'More Sensitive House Design Criteria, Please' (1987) *The House Builder*, October 1987, pp 23–26.

Coleman, A. and Brown, S.F. *Crime and Disadvantagement in Blocks of Flats* (1985) Report to A2(3) Branch, Metropolitan Police.

McClelland, D.C. *The Achieving Society* (1961) D. van Nostrand, New York.

South-East Region Senior Crime Prevention Officers Conference *Secured by Design* (1989).

Index

WHY DON'T TEACHERS TEACH LIKE THEY USED TO?
Rachel Pinder
'Survival guide for perplexed parents.'

The Sunday Times

TELEVISION IS GOOD FOR YOUR KIDS
Máire Messenger Davies
'At last a book from somebody properly qualified to discuss the subject . . . one of the most calm, sane and sensible ever written.'

Financial Times

NEWS OUT OF AFRICA
Biafra to Band Aid
Paul Harrison and Robin Palmer
'Will shock those who are ignorant of the machinations of our mass media . . . the information, ideas and revelations with which this book is packed are depressing as well as fascinating.'

Times Educational Supplement

WOMEN IN THE JAPANESE WORKPLACE
Mary Saso
'Destined to become a standard reference work on working women.'

Japan Times

IN SEARCH OF CHINA
David Kellogg
'There is no better travel book about China today.'

Observer

Hilary Shipman is at 19 Framfield Road, Highbury, London N5 1UU   Telephone 071-226 0246